Minor British Poetry, 1680-1800

An Anthology

Selected, with an Introduction
by
J. ERNEST BARLOUGH

The Scarecrow Press, Inc.
Metuchen, N.J.   1973

Library of Congress Cataloging in Publication Data

Barlough, J Ernest, 1953–   comp.
  Minor British poetry: 1680–1800.

    1. English poetry—18th century. I. Title.
PR1215.B3   821'.008   73–4878
ISBN 0–8108–0619–3

TABLE OF CONTENTS

iv

xi

xii

INTRODUCTION

Anyone who observes a large throng of people will verify that the most noticeable persons are those of superior height, who rise above the others around them. Those of average size, the great majority of people, tend to be diminished and disappear into the background, our view being captured by their taller brethren.

Similarly, in the study of history and literature, those of established superiority and renown often tend to dominate the periods in which they lived and overshadow those of lesser stature, who are frequently of equal significance. Such a case of "figura obscura" can be extremely misleading when studying true historical perspective. There may be five great figures in a particular period of a hypothetical nation's history; but these five figures in no way can be said to represent the thoughts, ideals, and expectations of the totality of that nation. Even if there were a hundred of these figures, they would only represent a part of the universal whole. But it must also be concluded that a hundred opinions or ideas, regardless of stature, must give a broader and deeper perspective than five. That is precisely why it is of the utmost importance that many figures be studied, especially in a period of great social, economic, and political transformation, such as the England of the eighteenth century.

Many events contributed to the great metamorphosis that took place: the interactions of foreign policy with established religion; the Scottish wars and the problem of the Jacobites; the Whig and Tory controversies; the Hanoverian succession; the Seven Years' War; the industrial revolution; the American revolution; the turmoil in Parliament; the revolution of the French and their subsequent conflicts with the English.

Important as these political events were, there was perhaps an even deeper revolution occurring all over: the revolution in science. Discoveries about the world and its mysteries, the heavens, and human beings themselves, were causing people to begin to question the authority of their previous beliefs, ideas, and religions. How could they reconcile the Biblical story of Creation with new studies of the earth? How could it be that the earth is not the center of the universe? Where is God if the heavens above are so terribly vast and frightening? What, now, indeed, is good, and what is evil?

The seventeenth century, and much of the eighteenth, had emphasized and exulted in man's use of his rational intellect, apart from emotion, to judge the realities around him, to make conclusions from what he saw, and to explain the reasons for existence. But a new breed of men were beginning to arise as the 1750's approached: those who questioned this type of thought, and who wished to return to the study of true humanity and human feelings--those who would, half a century later, become known as the foundations of romanticism.

Previously, literature had been considered as belonging to the elite and the courtly alone, for the very reason that they constituted most of the small minority of the population which was literate. By the eighteenth century another great change was occurring: the rise of the small businessman, the merchant class. A middle-class literature was being born, and the courtliness and patronage were in their death throes. No longer would writing be meant only for the rich, the noble, the gently-bred: and, of course, with this, would come an inevitable change in the literature itself.

The first half of the eighteenth century was dominated primarily by the shadows of that era which had begun a century before and which many refer to as "neoclassicism." Like most definitions, this one is most inadequate; it generally pertains to a period in which literature was primarily "in imitation" of "classic" works. Because of the great rise of democracy and individual freedom during this time, literature naturally looked back to the days of Greece and Rome, the very birthplaces of democracy. And there they also found models on which to base their writing: Horace, whose odes inspired countless imitations; Catullus; and Virgil, the gentle poet, perhaps ultimately the model for all the western poetry for almost two thousand years.

But the "Augustans," referring to the great Caesar, as Nicholas Rowe termed them, were doomed to destruction, for their children and their children's children turned from this view back to "the human heart." The great revolution

that was to culminate in Lord Byron began with those few
writers who began to question the emphasis on reason and
rationality. Nature began to be admired not for her com-
plexity but for the pleasure and contentment that she brought
to the human observer. By the middle of the century, "neo-
classicism" had vanished.

Certainly the eighteenth century was a time of growing
social conscience, of humanism, of solitude and reflection.
But more than this, it marked a turning point in the history
of literature.

Ever since the eighteenth century ended, historians
have been trying to locate a suitable catch-all word or phrase
to sum up this era. They have met with very limited suc-
cess. Indeed, phrases such as "The Enlightenment," "The
Age of Prose," "Neoclassicism," etc., have served to illumi-
nate only a fraction of what the age was about. Perhaps no
such neat, all-encompassing phrase exists? What then do
we do with this melting pot of a century that saw so many
different and varied new ideas?

There we have come upon the exact definition itself:
A time of formation. A great cauldron, wherein countless
influences and ideas sifted together to form a new substance
that would mature a century later. What we have is a time
of experimentation and discovery out of which the whole
course of subsequent literature has been molded. New ideas
that have endured and will endure were born; old ideas, in-
correct and obsolete, were discarded. In short, the eight-
eenth century can rightly be called the birthplace of modern
man.

In this volume I have attempted to fill out the picture
of English literature in the eighteenth century by including
as many of the lesser authors and types of their poetry as
feasible. Much of the writing is excellent; much is good;
and much is mediocre. But these lesser writers were the
driving force behind those who reached the pinnacle of poetic
success, and their importance to an adequate understanding
of this complicated age is indisputable. It was with this
idea in mind that the book was formulated and executed, and
it is hoped that it will provide enjoyment, as well as serve
as an historical reference work on the backgrounds of poetic
thought during the eighteenth century.

J. E. B.

Los Angeles, California
September 20th, 1972

RICHARD DUKE (1658-1711)

A SONG

See what a conquest Love has made!
Beneath the myrtle's amorous shade
The charming fair Corinna lies
    All melting in desire,
Quenching in tears those flowing eyes
    That set the world on fire!

What cannot tears and beauty do?
The youth by chance stood by, and knew
For whom those crystal streams did flow;
    And though he ne'er before
To her eyes brightest rays did bow,
    Weeps too, and does adore.

So when the Heavens serene and clear,
Gilded with gaudy light appear,
Each craggy rock, and every stone,
    Their native rigour keep;
But when in rain the clouds fall down,
    The hardest marble weeps.

TO A ROMAN CATHOLIC UPON MARRIAGE

Censure and penances, excommunication,
Are bug-bear words to fright a bigot nation;
But 'tis the Church's more substantial curse,
To damn us all for better or for worse.
Falsely your church seven sacraments does frame,
Penance and matrimony are the same.

1

THOMAS SOUTHERNE (1660-1746)

A SONG

from "Sir Antony Love, or the Rambling Lady"

Pursuing Beauty, Men descry
   The distant Shore, and long to prove
(Still richer in Variety)
   The Treasures of the Land of Love.

We Women, like weak Indians, stand
   Inviting, from our Golden Coast,
The wandring Rovers to our Land:
   But she, who Trades with 'em, is lost.

With humble Vows they first begin,
   Stealing, unseen, into the Heart;
But by Possession setled in,
   They quickly act another part.

For Beads and Baubles, we resign,
   In Ignorance, our shining Store,
Discover Nature's richest Mine,
   And yet the Tyrants will have more.

Be wise, be wise, and do not try,
   How he can Court, or you be Won:
For Love is but Discovery,
   When that is made, the Pleasure's done.

ANNE FINCH, COUNTESS OF WINCHILSEA (1661-1720)

A NOCTURNAL REVERIE

In such a Night, when every louder Wind
Is to its distant Cavern safe confin'd;
And only gentle Zephyr fans his Wings,
And lonely Philomel, still waking, sings;
Or from some Tree, fam'd for the Owl's delight,
She, hollowing clear, directs the Wand'rer right:
In such a Night, when passing Clouds give place,
Or thinly vail the Heav'ns mysterious Face;
When in some River, overhung with Green,
The waving Moon and trembling Leaves are seen;
When freshen'd Grass now bears it self upright,
And makes cool Banks to pleasing Rest invite,
Whence springs the Woodbind, and the Bramble-Rose,
And where the sleepy Cowslip shelter'd grows;
Whilst now a paler Hue the Foxglove takes,
Yet checquers still with Red the dusky brakes:
When scatter'd Glow-worms, but in Twilight fine,
Show trivial Beauties watch their Hour to shine;
Whilst Salisb'ry stands the Test of every Light,
In perfect Charms, and perfect Virtue bright:
When Odours, which declin'd repelling Day,
Thro' temp'rate Air uninterrupted stray;
When darken'd Groves their softest Shadows wear,
And falling Waters we distinctly hear;
When thro' the Gloom more venerable shows
Some ancient Fabrick, awful in Repose,
While Sunburnt Hills their swarthy Looks conceal,
And swelling Haycocks thicken up the Vale:
When the loos'd Horse now, as his Pasture leads,
Comes slowly grazing thro' th' adjoining Meads,
Whose stealing Pace, and lengthen'd Shade we fear,
Till torn up Forage in his Teeth we hear:
When nibbling Sheep at large pursue their Food,
And unmolested Kine rechew the Cud;
When Curlews cry beneath the Village-walls,
And to her straggling Brood the Partridge calls;
Their shortliv'd Jubilee the Creatures keep,
Which but endures, whilst Tyrant-Man do's sleep;
When a sedate Content the Spirit feels,
And no fierce Light disturbs, whilst it reveals;
But silent Musings urge the Mind to seek
Something, too high for Syllables to speak;
Till the free Soul to a compos'dness charm'd,

Finding the Elements of Rage disarm'd,
O'er all below a solemn Quiet grown,
Joys in th' inferiour World, and thinks it like her Own:
In such a Night let Me abroad remain,
Till Morning breaks, and All's confus'd again;
Our Cares, our Toils, our Clamours are renew'd,
Or Pleasures, seldom reach'd, again pursu'd.

TO THE NIGHTINGALE

Exert thy Voice, sweet Harbinger of Spring!
   This Moment is thy Time to Sing,
   This Moment I attend to Praise,
And set my Numbers to thy Layes.
   Free as thine shall be my Song;
   As thy Musick, short, or long.

Poets, wild as thee, were born,
   Pleasing best when unconfin'd,
   When to Please is least design'd,
Soothing but their Cares to rest;
   Cares do still their Thoughts molest,
   And still th' unhappy Poet's Breast,
Like thine, when best he sings, is plac'd against a Thorn.

She begins, Let all be still!
   Muse, thy Promise now fulfill!
Sweet, oh! sweet, still sweeter yet
Can thy Words such Accents fit,
Canst thou syllables refine,
Melt a Sense that shall retain
Still some Spirit of the Brain,
Till with Sounds like these it join.
   'Twill not be! then change thy Note;

   Let Division shake thy Throat.
Hark! Division now she tries;
Yet as far the Muse outflies.
   Cease then, prithee, cease thy Tune;
   Trifler, wilt thou sing till June?
Till thy Bus'ness all lies waste,
And the Time of Building's past!
   Thus we Poets that have Speech,
Unlike what thy Forests teach,
   If a fluent Vein be shown
   That's transcendent to our own,

4

Criticize, reform, or preach,
Or censure what we cannot reach.

WILLIAM KING (1663-1712)

THE OLD CHEESE

Young Slouch the farmer had a jolly wife,
That knew all the conveniences of life,
Whose diligence and cleanliness supplied
The wit which Nature had to him denied:
But then she had a tongue that would be heard,
And make a better man than Slouch afeard.
This made censorious persons of the town
Say, Slouch could hardly call his soul his own:
For, if he went abroad too much, she'd use
To give him slippers, and lock up his shoes.
Talking he lov'd, and ne'er was more afflicted
Than when he was disturb'd or contradicted:
Yet still into his story she would break
With, " 'Tis not so——pray give me leave to speak."
His friends thought this was a tyrannic rule,
Not differing much from calling of him fool;
Told him, he must exert himself, and be
In fact the master of his family.
　　He said, "That the next Tuesday noon would show
Whether he were the lord at home, or no;
When their good company he would entreat
To well-brew'd ale, and clean, if homely, meat."
With aching heart home to his wife he goes,
And on his knees does his rash act disclose,
And prays dear Sukey, that, one day at least,
He might appear as master of the feast.
"I'll grant your wish," cries she, "that you may see
'Twere wisdom to be govern'd still by me."
　　The guests upon the day appointed came,
Each bowsy farmer with his simpering dame.
"Ho! Sue!" cries Slouch, "why dost not thou appear!
Are these thy manners when aunt Snap is here?"
"I pardon ask," says Sue; "I'd not offend
Any my dear invites, much less his friend."
　　Slouch by his kinsman Gruffy had been taught
To entertain his friends with finding fault,
And make the main ingredient of his treat
His saying, "There was nothing fit to eat:
The boil'd pork stinks, the roast beef's not enough,
The bacon's rusty, and the hens are tough;
The veal's all rags, the butter's turn'd to oil;
And thus I buy good meat for sluts to spoil.

'Tis we are the first Slouches ever sate
Down to a pudding without plumbs or fat.
What teeth or stomach's strong enough to feed
Upon a goose my grannum kept to breed?
Why must old pigeons, and they stale, be drest,
When there's so many squab ones in the nest?
This beer is sour; this musty, thick, and stale,
And worse than any thing, except the ale."
   Sue all this while many excuses made:
Some things she own'd; at other times she laid
The fault on chance, but oftener on the maid.
   Then cheese was brought. Says Slouch, "This e'en shall
      roll:
I'm sure 'tis hard enough to make a bowl:
This is skim-milk, and therefore it shall go;
And this, because 'tis Suffolk, follow too."
But now Sue's patience did begin to waste;
Nor longer could dissimulation last.
"Pray let me rise," says Sue, "my dear; I'll find
A cheese perhaps may be to lovy's mind."
Then in an entry, standing close, where he
Alone, and none of all his friends, might see;
And brandishing a cudgel he had felt,
And far enough on this occasion smelt;
"I'll try, my joy!" she cried, "if I can please
My dearest with a taste of this old cheese!"
   Slouch turn'd his head, saw his wife's vigorous hand
Wielding her oaken sapling of command,
Knew well the twang: "Is't the old cheese, my dear?
No need, no need of cheese," cries Slouch: "I'll swear,
I think I've din'd as well as my lord mayor!"

UPON A GIANT'S ANGLING

His angle-rod made of a sturdy oak,
His line a cable, which in storms ne'er broke,
His hook he baited with a dragon's tail,
And sate upon a rock, and bobb'd for whale.

I WAKED, SPEAKING THESE OUT OF
A DREAM IN THE MORNING

Nature a thousand ways complains,
A thousand words express her pains:

7

But for her laughter has but three,
And very small ones, Ha, ha, he!

THE CONSTABLE

One night a fellow wandering without fear,
As void of money as he was of care,
Considering both were wash'd away with beer,
With Strap the constable by fortune meets,
Whose lanterns glare in the most silent streets.
Resty, impatient any one should be
So bold as to be drunk that night but he:
"Stand; who goes there," cried Strap, "at hours so late?
Answer. Your name; or else have at your pate."——
    "I wo'nt stand, 'cause I can't. Why must you know
From whence it is I come, or where I go?"
    "See here my staff," cries Strap; trembling behold
Its radiant paint, and ornamental gold:
Wooden authority when thus I wield,
Persons of all degrees obedience yield.
Then, be you the best man in all the city,
Mark me! I to the Counter will commit ye."
    "You! kiss, and so forth. For that never spare:
No person yet, either through fear or shame,
Durst commit me, that once had heard my name."——
"Pray then, what is't?"——"My name's Adultery;
And, faith, your future life would pleasant be,
Did your wife know you once committed <u>me</u>."

8

WILLIAM WALSH (1663-1708)

A SONG

Of all the Torments, all the Cares,
    With which our Lives are curst;
Of all the Plagues a Lover bears,
    Sure Rivals are the worst!
By Partners, in each other kind,
    Afflictions easier grow;
In Love alone we hate to find
    Companions of our Woe.

Sylvia, for all the Pangs you see,
    Are lab'ring in my Breast;
I beg not you would favour me,
    Would you but slight the rest!
How great so e'er your Rigours are,
    With them alone I'll cope;
I can endure my own Despair,
    But not another's Hope.

SIR JOHN VANBRUGH (1664-1726)

A SONG

from "The Provok'd Wife"

When yielding first to Damon's flame
    I sunk into his Arms,
He swore he'd ever be the same,
    Then rifl'd all my Charms.
But fond of what h'ad long desir'd,
    Too greedy of his Prey,
My Shepherds flame, alas, expir'd
    Before the Virge of Day.

My Innocence in Lovers Wars,
    Reproach'd his quick defeat.
Confus'd, Asham'd, and Bath'd in Tears,
    I mourn'd his Cold Retreat.
At length, Ah Shepherdess, cry'd he,
    Wou'd you my Fire renew,
Alas you must retreat like me,
    I'm lost if you pursue.

MATTHEW PRIOR (1664-1721)

THE REMEDY WORSE THAN THE DISEASE

I sent for Radcliffe; was so ill,
    That other doctors gave me over:
He felt my pulse, prescrib'd his pill,
    And I was likely to recover.

But, when the wit began to wheeze,
    And wine had warm'd the politician,
Cur'd yesterday of my disease,
I dy'd last night of my physician.

WIVES BY THE DOZEN

"O death! how thou spoil'st the best project of life!"
Said Gabriel, who still, as he bury'd one wife,
    For the sake of her family, marry'd her cousin;
And thus, in an honest collateral line,
He still marry'd on till his number was nine,
    Full sorry to die till he made up his dozen.

MERRY ANDREW

Sly Merry Andrew, the last Southwark fair
(At Barthol'mew he did not much appear,
So peevish was the edict of the mayor);
At Southwark, therefore, as his tricks he show'd,
To please our masters, and his friends the crowd;
A huge neat's-tongue he in his right-hand held,
His left was with a good black-pudding fill'd.
With a grave look, in this odd equipage,
The clownish mimic traverses the stage.
"Why how now, Andrew!" cries his brother droll:
"To-day's conceit, methinks, is something dull:
Come on, sir, to our worthy friends explain,
What does your emblematic worship mean?"
Quoth Andrew, "Honest English let us speak:
Your emble-(what d' ye call 't) is heathen Greek.
To tongue or pudding thou hast no pretence:
Learning thy talent is, but mine is sense.

11

That busy fool I was, which thou art now;
Desirous to correct, not knowing how;
With very good design, but little wit,
Blaming or praising things, as I thought fit.
I for this conduct had what I deserv'd;
And, dealing honestly, was almost starv'd.
But thanks to my indulgent stars, I eat;
Since I have found the secret to be great."
"O, dearest Andrew," says the humble droll,
"Henceforth may I obey, and thou control;
Provided thou impart thy useful skill."
"Bow then," says Andrew; "and, for once, I will——
Be of your patron's mind, whate'er he says;
Sleep very much; think little; and talk less:
Mind neither good nor bad, nor right nor wrong;
But eat your pudding, slave, and hold your tongue."
    A reverend prelate stopt his coach and six,
To laugh a little at our Andrew's tricks.
But when he heard him give this golden rule,
"Drive on," he cried; "this fellow is no fool."

THE FLIES

"Say, sire of insects, mighty Sol,"
A fly upon the chariot-pole
Cries out, "what blue-bottle alive
Did ever with such fury drive?"
"Tell, Beelzebub, great father, tell,"
(Says t'other, perch'd upon the wheel)
"Did ever any mortal fly
Raise such a cloud of dust as I?
    "My judgment turn'd the whole debate:
My valour sav'd the sinking state."
So talk two idle buzzing things;
Toss up their heads, and stretch their wings.
But, let the truth to light be brought,
This neither spoke, nor t'other thought:
No merit in their own behaviour:
Both rais'd, but by their party's favour.

A SIMILE

Dear Thomas, didst thou never pop
Thy head into a tinman's shop?

12

There, Thomas, didst thou never see
('Tis but by way of simile)
A squirrel spend his little rage,
In jumping round a rolling cage;
The cage, as either side turn'd up,
Striking a ring of bells at top?——
    Mov'd in the orb, pleas'd with the chimes,
The foolish creature thinks he climbs:
But here or there, turn wood or wire,
He never gets two inches higher.
    So fares it with those merry blades,
That frisk it under Pindus' shades.
In noble song, and lofty odes,
They tread on stars, and talk with gods;
Still dancing in an airy round,
Still pleas'd with their own verses' sound;
Brought back, how fast soe'er they go,
Always aspiring, always low.

TRUTH TOLD AT LAST

Says Pontius in rage, contradicting his wife,
"You never yet told me one truth in your life."
Vext Pontia no way could this thesis allow,
"You're a cuckold," says she, "do I tell you truth now?"

13

LADY GRIZEL BAILLIE (1665-1746)

WERE NA MY HEART LICHT

There was ance a May, and she lo'ed na men;
She biggit her bonny bower down i' yon glen,
But now she cries dool and well-a-day!
Come down the green gait, and come here away.

When bonny young Johnny cam owre the sea,
He said he saw naething sae lovely as me;
He hecht me baith rings and mony braw things;
And werena my heart licht I wad dee.

He had a wee titty that lo'ed na me,
Because I was twice as bonny as she;
She raised such a pother 'twixt him and his mother,
That werena my heart licht I wad dee.

The day it was set, and the bridal to be:
The wife took a dwam, and lay down to dee;
She maned and she graned out o' dolour and pain,
Till he vowed he never wad see me again.

His kin was for ane of a higher degree,
Said, what had he to do wi' the like of me?
Albeit I was bonny, I wasna for Johnny:
And werena my heart licht I wad dee.

They said I had neither cow nor calf,
Nor dribbles o' drink rins through the draff,
Nor pickles o' meal rins through the mill-ee;
And werena my heart licht I wad dee.

His titty she was baith wily and slee,
She spied me as I cam owre the lea;
And then she cam in and made a loud din;
Believe your ain een an he trow na me.

His bonnet stood aye fu' round on his brow;
His auld ane looked aye as weel as some's new;
But now he lets 't wear ony gait it will hing,
And casts himself dowie upon the corn-bing.

And now he gaes daunerin about the dykes,
And a' he dow dae is to hound the tykes;

The live-lang nicht he ne'er steeks his ee,
And werena my heart licht I wad dee.

Were I young for thee as I hae been
We should hae been gallopin' down on yon green,
And linkin' it on yon lily-white lea;
And wow! gin I were but young for thee.

GEORGE GRANVILLE, LORD LANSDOWNE (1667-1735)

A SONG

Love is by Fancy led about
From hope to fear, from joy to doubt;
   Whom we now an angel call,
Divinely grac'd in every feature,
Straight's a deform'd, a perjur'd creature;
   Love and hate are Fancy all.

'Tis but as Fancy shall present
Objects of grief, or of content,
   That the lover's blest, or dies:
Visions of mighty pain, or pleasure,
Imagin'd want, imagin'd treasure,
   All in powerful Fancy lies.

CLOE PERFUMING HERSELF

Believe me, Cloe, those perfumes that cost
Such sums to sweeten thee, is treasure lost;
Not all Arabia would sufficient be,
Thou smell'st not of thy sweets, they stink of thee.

CORINNA

Corinna, in the bloom of youth
   Was coy to every lover,
Regardless of the tenderest truth,
   No soft complaint could move her.

Mankind was hers, all at her feet
   Lay prostrate and adoring,
The witty, handsome, rich, and great,
   In vain alike imploring.

But now grown old, she would repair
   Her loss of time, and pleasure;
With willing eyes, and wanton air,
   Inviting every gazer.

But love's a summer flower, that dies
    With the first weather's changing,
The lover, like the swallow, flies
    From sun to sun, still ranging.

Myra, let this example move
    Your foolish heart to reason;
Youth is the proper time for love,
    And age is virtue's season.

ON AN ILL-FAVOURED LORD

That Macro's looks are good, let no man doubt,
Which I, his friend and servant——thus make out.
In every line of his perfidious face,
The secret malice of his heart we trace;
So fair the warning, and so plainly writ,
Let none condemn the light that shows a pit.
Cocles, whose face finds credit for his heart,
Who can escape so smooth a villain's art?
Adorn'd with every grace that can persuade,
Seeing we trust, though sure to be betrayed;
His looks are snares: but Macro's cry "Beware,
Believe not, though ten thousand oaths he swear;"
If thou'rt deceived, observing well this rule,
Not Macro is the knave, but thou the fool.
In this one point, he and his looks agree,
As they betray their master——so did he.

BELINDA

Belinda's pride's an arrant cheat
    A foolish artifice to blind;
Some honest glance, that scorns deceit,
    Does still reveal her native mind.

With look demure, and forc'd disdain,
    She idly acts the saint;
We see through this disguise as plain,
    As we distinguish paint.

So have I seen grave fools design,
    With formal looks to pass for wise;
But Nature is a light will shine,
    And break through all disguise.

17

Great god of sleep, since it must be,
That we must give some hours to thee,
Invade me not while the free bowl
Glows in my cheeks, and warms my soul;
That be my only time to snore,
When I can laugh, and drink no more;
Short, very short be then thy reign,
For I'm in haste to laugh and drink again.
   But O! if, melting in my arms,
In some soft dream, with all her charms,
The nymph belov'd should then surprise,
And grant what waking she denies;
Then, gentle Slumber, pr'ythee stay,
Slowly, ah! slowly bring the day,
Let no rude noise my bliss destroy,
Such sweet delusion 's real joy.

DR. THOMAS YALDEN (1670-1736)

THE BOAR AND FOREST

A Fable

A Lion, generous and brave,
For wars renown'd, belov'd in peace;
His lands in royal bounties gave,
And treasures much impair'd by acts of grace.

His ministers whole realms obtain'd;
And courtiers, much inclin'd to want,
His manors begg'd, and forfeits gain'd,
With patents to confirm the royal grant.

The Boar, to shew a subject's love,
Crav'd for the public good a boon,
His ancient forest to improve,
By felling trees, and cutting timber down.

"Alcoves and shady walks, quoth he,
Are laid aside, become a jest;
Your vistos lofty, wide, and free,
Are à la mode, and only in request."

The grant being pass'd, the ravenous Boar,
A desert of the forest made:
Up by the roots vast oaks he tore,
And low on earth the princely cedars laid.

This act of violence and wrong
Alarum'd all the savage race;
With loud complaints to court they throng,
Stripp'd of their shades, and ancient resting-place.

With generous rage the Lion shook,
And vow'd the Boar should dearly pay;
"I hate, quoth he, a down-cast look,
That robs the public in a friendly way.

"Unhappy groves, my empire's pride!
· Lov'd solitudes, ye shades divine!
The rage of tempests ye defy'd,
Condemn'd to perish by a sordid swine.

"Ye rural deities, and powers unknown,
What can so great a loss suffice!
If a hung brawner will atone,
Accept friend Chucky for a sacrifice."

THE MORAL

The British oak's our nation's strength and pride,
With which triumphant o'er the main we ride;
Insulting foes are by our navies aw'd,
A guard at home, our dreaded power abroad.
Like druids then your forests sacred keep,
Preserve with them your empire of the deep.
Subjects their prince's bounty oft abuse,
And spoil the public for their private use;
But no rapacious hand should dare deface,
The royal stores of a well-timber'd chase.

COLLEY CIBBER (1671-1757)

THE BLIND BOY

O say! what is that Thing call'd Light,
　　Which I can ne'er enjoy;
What is the Blessing of the Sight,
　　O tell your poor Blind Boy?

You talk of wond'rous things you see,
　　You say the Sun shines bright:
I feel him warm, but how can he
　　Then make it Day, or Night.

My Day, or Night my self I make,
　　Whene'er I wake, or play;
And cou'd I ever keep awake,
　　It wou'd be always Day.

With heavy sighs, I often hear,
　　You mourn my hopeless woe;
But sure with patience I may bear,
　　A loss I ne'er can know.

Then let not what I cannot have,
　　My cheer of Mind destroy,
Whilst thus I sing, I am a King,
　　Altho' a poor Blind Boy!

JOHN OLDMIXON (1673-1742)

TO CLOE

Prethee Cloe, not so fast,
Let's not run and Wed in hast;
We've a thousand things to do,
You must fly, and I persue;
You must frown, and I must sigh;
I intreat, and you deny.
Stay - If I am never crost,
Half the Pleasure will be lost;
Be, or seem to be severe,
Give me reason to Despair;
Fondness will my Wishes cloy,
Make me careless of the Joy.
Lovers may of course complain
Of their trouble and their pain;
But if Pain and Trouble cease,
Love without it will not please.

COLIN'S COMPLAINT

A Song

Despairing beside a clear Stream,
    A Shepherd forsaken was laid;
And while a false Nymph was his Theme,
    A Willow supported his Head.
The Wind that blew over the Plain,
    To his Sighs with a Sigh did reply;
And the Brook, in return to his Pain,
    Ran mournfully murmuring by.

Alas, silly Swain that I was!
    Thus sadly complaining he cry'd,
When first I beheld that fair Face,
    'Twere better by far I had dy'd.
She talk'd, and I bless'd the dear Tongue;
    When she smil'd, 'twas a Pleasure too great.
I listen'd, and cry'd, when she sung,
    Was Nightingale ever so sweet?

How foolish was I to believe
    She could doat on so lowly a Clown,
Or that her fond Heart would not grieve
    To forsake the fine Folk of the Town?
To think that a beauty so gay,
    So kind and so constant would prove;
Or go clad like our Maidens in Gray,
    Or live in a Cottage on Love?

What tho' I have Skill to complain,
    Tho' the Muses my Temples have crown'd;
What tho' when they hear my soft Strain,
    The Virgins sit weeping around.
Ah, COLIN, thy Hopes are in vain,
    Thy Pipe and thy Laurel resign;
Thy false one inclines to a Swain,
    Whose Music is sweeter than thine.

And you, my Companions so dear,
    Who sorrow to see me betray'd,
Whatever I suffer, forbear,
    Forbear to accuse the false Maid.

Tho' thro' the wide World I should range,
 'Tis in vain from my Fortune to fly,
'Twas hers to be false and to change,
 'Tis mine to be constant and die.

If while my hard Fate I sustain,
 In her Breast any Pity is found,
Let her come with the Nymphs of the Plain,
 And see me laid low in the Ground.
The last humble Boon that I crave,
 Is to shade me with Cypress and Yew;
And when she looks down on my Grave,
 Let her own that her Shepherd was true.

Then to her new Love let her go,
 And deck her in golden Array,
Be finest at ev'ry fine Show,
 And frolic it all the long Day;
While COLIN, forgotten and gone,
 No more shall be talk'd of, or seen,
Unless when beneath the pale Moon,
 His Ghost shall glide over the Green.

EPIGRAM

Whilst maudlin Whigs deplore their CATO's Fate,
Still with dry Eyes the Tory CELIA sate:
But tho' her Pride forbad her Eyes to flow,
The gushing Waters found a Vent below.
Tho' secret yet with copious Streams she mourns,
Like twenty River-Gods with all their Urns.
Let others screw an hypocritic Face,
She shews her Grief in a sincerer Place!
Here Nature reigns, and Passion void of Art;
For this Road leads directly to the Heart.

THE FAIR INCONSTANT

A Song

HE

Since I have long lov'd you in vain,
 And doted on ev'ry Feature;

Give me at length but leave to complain
    Of so ungrateful a Creature.

Tho' I beheld in your wandring Eyes
    The wanton Symptoms of Ranging;
Still I resolv'd against being wise,
    And lov'd you in spite of your changing.

SHE

Why shou'd you blame what Heav'n has made,
    Or find any Fault in Creation?
'Tis not the Crime of the faithless Maid,
    But Nature's Inclination.

'Tis not because I love you less,
    Or think you are not a True-one;
But if the Truth I must confess,
    I always lov'd a New-one.

TO LORD WARWICK ON HIS BIRTH-DAY

When fraught with all that grateful Minds can move,
With Friendship, Tenderness, Respect, and Love;
The Muse had wish'd, on this returning Day,
Something most worthy of herself to say:
To Jove she offer'd up an humble Pray'r,
To take the noble WARWICK to his Care.
Give him, she said, whate'er diviner Grace
Adorns the Soul, or beautifies the Face:
Let manly constancy confirm his Truth,
And gentlest Manners crown his blooming Youth.
Give him to Fame, to Virtue to aspire,
Worthy our Songs and thy informing Fire:
All various Praise, all Honors let him prove,
Let Men admire, and sighing Virgins love:
With honest Zeal inflame his gen'rous Mind,
To love his Country and protect Mankind.
Attentive to her Pray'r, the God reply'd,
Why dost thou ask what has not been deny'd?
Jove's bounteous Hand has lavish'd all his Pow'r,
And making what he is, can add no more.
Yet since I joy in what I did create,
I will prolong the Favorite WARWICK's Fate,
And lengthen out his Years to some uncommon Date.

25

ODE TO PEACE FOR THE YEAR 1718

I

Thou fairest sweetest Daughter of the Skies,
 Indulgent, gentle, Life-restoring Peace!
With what auspicious Beauties dost thou rise,
 And Britain's new-revolving Janus bless?

II

Hoary Winter smiles before thee,
 Dances merrily along:
Hours and Seasons all adore thee,
 And for thee are ever young:
 Ever Goddess thus appear,
 Ever lead the joyful Year.

III

In thee the Night, in thee the Day is blest;
In thee the dearest of the purple East:
'Tis thine, immortal Pleasures to impart,
Mirth to inspire, and raise the drooping Heart:
To thee the Pipe and tuneful String belong,
Thou Theme eternal for the Poet's Song.

IV

Awake the golden Lyre,
Ye Heliconian Choir,
Swell ev'ry Note still higher,
And Melody inspire
At Heav'n and Earth's Desire.

V

Hark, how the Sounds agree,
With due Complacency!
Sweet Peace 'tis all by thee,
For thou art Harmony.

VI

Who, by Nature's fairest Creatures,
Can describe her heav'nly Features?
What Comparison can fit her?

Sweet are Roses, she is sweeter;
Light is good, but Peace is better.
Wou'd you see her such as Jove,
Form'd for universal Love,
Bless'd by Men and Gods above?
Wou'd you ev'ry Feature trace,
Ev'ry sweetly smiling Grace?
Seek our CAROLINA's Face.

VII

Peace and She are Britain's Treasures,
Fruitful in eternal Pleasures:
Still their Bounty shall increase us,
Still their smiling Offspring bless us:
Happy Day, when each was given
By Caesar and indulgent Heav'n.

CHORUS

Hail, ye celestial Pair!
Still let Britannia be your Care,
And Peace and CAROLINA crown the Year.

ISAAC WATTS (1674-1748)

FRIENDSHIP

To Mr. William Nokes.   1702.

Friendship, thou charmer of the mind,
    Thou sweet deluding ill,
The brightest minute mortals find,
    And sharpest hour we feel.

Fate has divided all our shares
    Of pleasure and of pain;
In love the comforts and the cares
    Are mixt and join'd again.

But whilst in floods our sorrow rolls,
    And drops of joy are few,
This dear delight of mingling souls
    Serves but to swell our woe.

Oh! why should bliss depart in haste,
    And friendship stay to moan?
Why the fond passion cling so fast,
    When every joy is gone?

Yet never let our hearts divide,
    Nor death dissolve the chain:
For love and joy were once allied,
    And must be join'd again.

THE AFFLICTIONS OF A FRIEND

1702.

Now let my cares all buried lie,
    My griefs for ever dumb:
Your sorrows swell my heart so high,
    They leave my own no room.

Sickness and pains are quite forgot,
    The spleen itself is gone;
Plung'd in your woes I feel them not,
    Or feel them all in one.

28

Infinite grief puts sense to flight,
    And all the soul invades:
So the broad gloom of spreading night
    Devours the evening shades.

Thus am I born to be unblest!
    This sympathy of woe
Drives my own tyrants from my breast
    T' admit a foreign foe.

Sorrows in long succession reign;
    Their iron rod I feel:
Friendship has only chang'd the chain,
    But I'm the pris'ner still.

Why was this life for misery made?
    Or why drawn out so long?
Is there no room amongst the dead?
    Or is a wretch too young?

Move faster on, great Nature's wheel,
    Be kind, ye rolling powers,
Hurl my days headlong down the hill
    With undistinguish'd hours.

Be dusky, all my rising suns,
    Nor smile upon a slave:
Darkness, and Death, make haste at once
    To hide me in the grave.

THE SLUGGARD

'Tis the Voice of the Sluggard; I hear him complain,
You have wak'd me too soon, I must slumber again.
As the Door on its Hinges, so he on his Bed,
Turns his Sides, and his Shoulders, and his Heavy Head.

A little more Sleep, and a little more Slumber,
Thus he wastes half his Days, and his Hours without Number:
And when he gets up, he sits folding his Hands,
Or walks about sauntring, or trifling he stands.

I past by his Garden, and saw the wild Bryar,
The Thorn and the Thistle grow broader and higher:
The Clothes that hang on him are turning to Rags;
And his Money still wastes, till he starves, or he begs.

29

I made him a Visit, still hoping to find
He had took better Care for improving his Mind:
He told me his Dreams, talk'd of Eating and Drinking;
But he scarce reads his Bible, and never loves Thinking.

Said I then to my Heart, Here's a Lesson for me,
That Man's but a Picture of what I might be.
But Thanks to my Friends for their Care in my Breeding,
Who taught me betimes to love Working and Reading.

AMBROSE PHILIPS (1675-1749)

LOBBIN

A Pastoral

If we, O Dorset, quit the city-throng,
To meditate in shades the rural song,
By your command, be present: and, O bring
The Muse along! the Muse to you shall sing:
Her influence, Buckhurst, let me there obtain,
And I forgive the fam'd Sicilian swain.
    Begin. ——In unluxurious times of yore,
When flocks and herds were no inglorious store,
Lobbin, a shepherd-boy, one evening fair,
As western winds had cool'd the sultry air,
His number'd sheep within the fold now pent,
Thus plain'd him of his dreary discontent;
Beneath a hoary poplar's whispering boughs
He, solitary, sat to breathe his vows,
Venting the tender anguish of his heart,
As passion taught, in accents free of art:
And little did he hope, while, night by night,
His sighs were lavish'd thus on Lucy bright.
    "Ah, well-a-day! how long must I endure
This pining pain? Or who shall speed my cure?
Fond love no cure will have, seek no repose,
Delights in grief, nor any measure knows.
And now the Moon begins in clouds to rise;
The brightening stars increase within the skies;
The winds are hush; the dews distil; and sleep
Hath clos'd the eyelids of my weary sheep:
I only, with the prowling wolf, constrain'd
All night to wake: with hunger he is pain'd,
And I, with love. His hunger he may tame;
But who can quench, O cruel Love, thy flame?
Whilom did I, all as this poplar fair,
Up-raise my heedless head, then void of care,
'Mong rustic routs the chief for wanton game;
Nor could they merry make, till Lobbin came.
Who better seen than I in shepherds' arts,
To please the lads and win the lasses' hearts!
How deftly, to mine oaten-reed so sweet,
Wont they upon the green to shift their feet!
And, wearied in the dance, how would they yearn
Some well-devised tale from me to learn!

31

For many songs and tales of mirth had I,
To chase the loitering Sun adown the sky:
But, ah! since Lucy coy, deep-wrought her spite
Within my heart, unmindful of delight,
The jolly grooms I fly, and, all alone,
To rocks and woods pour forth my fruitless moan.
Oh, quit thy wonted scorn, relentless fair!
Ere, lingering long, I perish through despair.
Had Rosalind been mistress of my mind,
Though not so fair, she would have prov'd more kind.
O think, unwitting maid, while yet is time,
How flying years impair thy youthful prime!
Thy virgin-bloom will not for ever stay,
And flowers, though left ungather'd, will decay:
The flowers, anew, returning seasons bring!
But beauty faded has no second spring.
My words are wind! She, deaf to all my cries,
Takes pleasure in the mischief of her eyes;
Like frisking heifer, loose in flow'ry meads,
She gads where'er her roving fancy leads,
Yet still from me.   Ah me, the tiresome chase!
Shy as the fawn, she flies my fond embrace:
She flies, indeed, but ever leaves behind,
Fly where she will, her likeness in my mind.
No cruel purpose, in my speed, I bear;
'Tis only love; and love why shouldst thou fear?
What idle fears a maiden-breast alarm!
Stay, simple girl; a lover cannot harm.
Two sportive kidlings, both fair-fleck'd, I rear;
Whose shooting horns like tender buds appear:
A lambkin too, of spotless fleece, I breed,
And teach the fondling from my hand to feed:
Nor will I cease betimes to cull the fields
Of every dewy sweet the morning yields:
From early spring to autumn late shalt thou
Receive gay girlonds, blooming o'er thy brow:
And when——But why these unavailing pains?
The gifts, alike, and giver she disdains:
And now, left heiress of the glen, she'll deem
Me, landless lad, unworthy her esteem:
Yet, was she born, like me, of shepherd-sire;
And I may fields and lowing herds acquire.
O! would my gifts but win her wanton heart,
Or could I half the warmth I feel impart,
How would I wander, every day, to find
The choice of wildings, blushing through the rind!
For glossy plums how lightsome climb the tree,
How risk the vengeance of the thrifty bee!

32

Or! if thou deign to live a shepherdess,
Thou Lobbin's flock and Lobbin shalt possess:
And, fair my flock, nor yet uncomely I,
If liquid fountains flatter not; and why
Should liquid fountains flatter us, yet show
The bordering flowers less beauteous than they grow?
O! come, my love; nor think th' employment mean,
The dams to milk, and little lambkins wean,
To drive a-field, by morn, the fattening ewes,
Ere the warm Sun drink-up the cooly dews,
While, with my pipe and with my voice, I cheer
Each hour, and through the day detain thy ear.
How would the crook beseem thy lily-hand!
How would my younglings round thee gazing stand!
Ah, witless younglings! gaze not on her eye,
Thence all my sorrow; thence the death I die.
O, killing beauty! and O, sore desire!
Must then my sufferings, but with life, expire?
Though blossoms every year the trees adorn,
Spring after spring I wither, nipt with scorn:
Nor trow I when this bitter blast will end,
Or if yon stars will e'er my vows befriend.
Sleep, sleep my flock; for, happy, ye may take
Sweet nightly rest, though still your master wake."
　　Now to the waning Moon the nightingale,
In slender warblings, tun'd her piteous tale;
The love-sick shepherd, listening, felt relief,
Pleas'd with so sweet a partner in his grief,
Till, by degrees, her notes and silent Night
To slumbers soft his heavy heart invite.

THE HAPPY SWAIN

Have ye seen the morning sky,
When the dawn prevails on high,
When, anon, some purply ray
Gives a sample of the day,
When, anon, the lark, on wing,
Strives to soar, and strains to sing?
　　Have ye seen th' ethereal blue
Gently shedding silvery dew,
Spangling o'er the silent green,
While the nightingale, unseen,
To the Moon and stars, full bright,
Lonesome chants the hymn of night?

Have ye seen the broider'd May
All her scented bloom display,
Breezes opening, every hour,
This, and that, expecting flower,
While the mingling birds prolong,
From each bush, the vernal song?
Have ye seen the damask-rose
Her unsullied blush disclose,
Or the lily's dewy bell,
In her glossy white, excell,
Or a garden varied o'er
With a thousand glories more?
By the beauties these display,
Morning, evening, night, or day,
By the pleasures these excite,
Endless sources of delight!
Judge, by them, the joys I find,
Since my Rosalind was kind,
Since she did herself resign
To my vows, for ever mine.

A SONG

From White's and Will's,
    To purling Rills
The Love-sick Strephon flies;
    There, full of Woe,
    His Numbers flow,
And all in Rhyme he dies.

    The fair Coquett,
    With feign'd Regret,
Invites him back to Town;
    But when, in Tears,
    The Youth appears,
She meets him with a Frown.

    Full oft' the Maid
    This Prank had play'd,
'Till angry Strephon swore;
    And, what is strange,
    Tho' loath to change,
Would never see her more.

UPON THE TOASTS OF THE HANOVER CLUB

The reigning fair on polish'd crystal shine,
Enrich our glasses, and improve our wine.
The favourite names we to our lips apply,
Indulge our thoughts, and drink with ecstasy.
While these, the chosen beauties of our isle,
Propitious on the cause of freedom smile,
The rash Pretender's hopes we may despise,
And trust Britannia's safety to their eyes.

EPIGRAM

George came to the crown without striking a blow:
Ah, quoth the Pretender, would I could do so!

WILLIAM SOMERVILE (1675-1742)

EPITAPH

Upon Hugh Lumber, Husbandman

In Cottages and homely cells,
True Piety neglected dwells:
Till call'd to Heaven, her native seat,
Where the good man alone is great:
'Tis then this humble dust shall rise,
And view his Judge with joyful eyes;
While haughty tyrants shrink afraid,
And call the mountains to their aid.

THE HIP

To William Colmore, Esq.,
the Day after the Great Meteor, in March 1715

This dismal morn, when east winds blow,
And every languid pulse beats low,
With face most sorrowfully grim,
And head oppress'd with wind and whim,
Grave as an owl, and just as witty,
To thee I twang my doleful ditty;
And in mine own dull rhymes would find
Music to soothe my restless mind:
But oh! my friend, I sing in vain,
No doggrel can relieve my pain;
Since thou art gone my heart's desire,
And Heaven, and Earth, and Sea conspire,
To make my miseries compleat;
Where shall a wretched Hip retreat?
What shall a drooping mortal do,
Who pines for sunshine and for you?
If in the dark alcove I dream,
And you, or Phillis, is my theme,
While love or friendship warm my soul,
My shins are burning to a coal.
If rais'd to speculations high,
I gaze the stars and spangled sky,
With heart devout and wondering eye,

Amaz'd I view strange globes of light,
Meteors with horrid lustre bright,
My guilty trembling soul affright.
To mother Earth's prolific bed,
Pensive I stoop my giddy head,
From thence too all my hopes are fled.
Nor flowers, nor grass, nor shrubs appear,
To deck the smiling infant year;
But blasts my tender blossoms wound,
And desolation reigns around.
If sea-ward my dark thoughts I bend,
O! where will my misfortunes end?
My loyal soul distracted meets
Attainted dukes, and Spanish fleets.
Thus jarring elements unite;
Pregnant with wrongs, and arm'd with spite,
Successive mischiefs every hour
On my devoted head they pour.
Whate'er I do, wheree'er I go,
'Tis still an endless scene of woe.
'Tis thus disconsolate I mourn,
I faint, I die, till thy return:
'Till thy brisk wit, and humorous vein,
Restore me to my self again.
Let others vainly seek for ease,
From Galen and Hippocrates,
I scorn such nauseous aids as these.
Haste then, my dear, unbrib'd attend,
The best elixir is a friend.

PRESENTING TO A LADY A WHITE ROSE AND A RED,

On the Tenth of June

If this pale Rose offend your Sight,
    It in your Bosom wear;
'Twill blush to find itself less white,
    And turn <u>Lancastrian</u> there.

But, <u>Celia</u>, should the Red be chose,
    With gay Vermilion bright;
'Twou'd sicken at each Blush that glows,
    And in Despair turn White.

Let Politicians idly prate,
    Their <u>Babels</u> build in vain;

37

As uncontrolable as Fate,
    Imperial Love shall reign.

Each haughty Faction shall obey,
    And Whigs, and Tories join,
Submit to your Despotick Sway,
    Confess your Right Divine.

Yet this (my gracious Monarch) own,
    They're Tyrants that oppress;
'Tis Mercy must support your Throne,
    And 'tis like Heav'n to Bless.

ADDRESS TO HIS ELBOW-CHAIR, NEW CLOATHED

My dear companion, and my faithful friend!
If Orpheus taught the listening oaks to bend:
If stones and rubbish, at Amphion's call,
Danc'd into form, and built the Theban wall;
Why should not thou attend my humble lays,
And hear my grateful harp resound thy praise?
    True, thou art spruce and fine, a very beau;
But what are trappings and external show?
To real worth alone I make my court;
Knaves are my scorn, and coxcombs are my sport.
Once I beheld thee far less trim and gay;
Ragged, disjointed, and to worms a prey;
The safe retreat of every lurking mouse;
Derided, shunn'd; the lumber of my house!
Thy robe how chang'd from what it was before!
Thy velvet robe, which pleas'd my sires of yore!
'Tis thus capricious Fortune wheels us round;
Aloft we mount——then tumble to the ground.
Yet grateful then, my constancy I prov'd;
I knew thy worth; my friend in rags I lov'd;
I lov'd thee more; nor, like a courtier, spurn'd
My benefactor, when the tide was turn'd.
With conscious shame, yet frankly, I confess,
That in my youthful days——I lov'd thee less.
Where vanity, where pleasure call'd, I stray'd;
And every wayward appetite obey'd.
But sage Experience taught me how to prize
My self; and how, this world: she bade me rise
To nobler flights regardless of a race
Of factious emmets; pointed where to place
My bliss, and lodg'd me in thy soft embrace.

Here on thy yielding down I sit secure;
And, patiently, what Heaven has sent, endure;
From all the futile cares of business free;
Not fond of life, but yet content to be:
Here mark the fleeting hours; regret the past;
And seriously prepare to meet the last.
So safe on shore the pension'd sailor lies;
And all the malice of the storm defies:
With ease of body blest, and peace of mind,
Pities the restless crew he left behind;
Whilst, in his cell, he meditates alone
On his great voyage, to the world unknown.

A SONG

As o'er Asteria's fields I rove,
The blisful seat of peace and love,
Ten thousand beauties round me rise,
And mingle pleasure with surprise.
By Nature blest in every part,
Adorn'd with every grace of Art,
This paradise of blooming joys
Each raptur'd sense, at once, employs.

But when I view the radiant queen,
Who form'd this fair enchanting scene;
Pardon, ye grots! ye crystal floods!
Ye breathing flowers! ye shady woods!
Your coolness now no more invites;
No more your murmuring stream delights;
Your sweets decay, your verdure's flown;
My soul's intent on her alone.

ANACREONTIC

To Cloe Drinking

When, my dear Cloe, you resign
One happy hour to mirth and wine,
Each glass you drink still paints your face
With some new victorious grace:
Charms in reserve my soul surprise,
And by fresh wounds your lover dies.
Who can resist thee, lovely fair!

That wit! that soft engaging air!
Each panting heart its homage pays,
And all the vassal world obeys.
God of the grape, boast now no more
Thy triumphs on far Indus' shore:
Each useless weapon now lay down,
Thy tigers, car, and ivy-crown;
Give but this juice in full supplies,
And trust thy fame to Cloe's eyes.

HUNTING-SONG

Behold, my friend, the rosy-finger'd Morn,
    With blushes on her face
    Peeps o'er yon azure hill;
    Rich gems the trees enchase,
    Pearls from each bush distil,
Arise, arise, and hail the light new-born.

Hark! hark! the merry horn calls, come away:
    Quit, quit thy downy bed;
    Break from Amynta's arms;
    Oh! let it ne'er be said,
    That all, that all her charms,
Though she's as Venus fair, can tempt thy stay.

Perplex thy soul no more with cares below,
    For what will pelf avail!
    Thy courser paws the ground,
    Each beagle cocks his tail,
    They spend their mouths around,
While health, and pleasure, smiles on every brow.

Try, huntsmen, all the brakes, spread all the plain,
    Now, now, she's gone away,
    Strip, strip, with speed pursue;
    The jocund god of day,
    Who fain our sport would view,
See, see, he flogs his fiery steeds in vain.

Pour down, like a flood from the hills, brave boys,
    On the wings of the wind
    The merry beagles fly;
    Dull Sorrow lags behind:
    Ye shrill echoes, reply;
Catch each flying sound, and double our joys.

Ye rocks, woods, and caves, our music repeat:
  The bright spheres thus above,
  A gay refulgent train,
  Harmoniously move,
  O'er yon celestial plain
Like us whirl along, in concert so sweet.

Now Puss threads the brakes, and heavily flies,
  At the head of the pack
  Old Fidler bears the bell,
  Every foil he hunts back,
  And aloud rings her knell,
Till, forc'd into view, she pants, and she dies.

In life's dull round thus we toil and we sweat;
  Diseases, grief, and pain,
  An implacable crew,
  While we double in vain,
  Unrelenting pursue,
Till, quite hunted down, we yield with regret.

This moment is ours, come live while ye may,
  What's decreed by dark Fate
  Is not in our own power,
  Since to morrow's too late,
  Take the present kind hour:
With wine cheer the night, as sports bless the day.

THE INCURIOUS BENCHER

At Jenny Mann's, where heroes meet,
And lay their laurels at her feet;
The modern Pallas, at whose shrine
They bow, and by whose aid they dine:
Colonel Brocade among the rest
Was every day a welcome guest.
One night as carelessly he stood,
    Chearing his reins before the fire,
(So every true-born Briton should)
    Like that, he chaf'd, and fum'd, with ire.
"Jenny," said he, " 'tis very hard,
That no man's honour can be spar'd;
If I but sup with lady dutchess,
Or play a game at ombre, such is
The malice of the world, 'tis said,
Although his grace lay drunk in bed,

'Twas I that caus'd his aching head.
If madam Doodle would be witty,
And I am summon'd to the city,
To play at blind-man's-buff, or so,
What won't such hellish malice do?
If I but catch her in a corner,
Hump——'tis, 'Your servant, colonel Horner:'
But rot the sneering fops, if e'er
I prove it, it shall cost them dear;
I swear by this dead-doing blade,
Dreadful examples shall be made:
What——can't they drink bohea and cream,
But (d—n them) I must be their theme?
Other mens business let alone,
Why should not coxcombs mind their own?"
    And thus he rav'd with all his might
(How insecure from Fortune's spite
Alas! is every mortal wight!)
To show his antient spleen to Mars,
Fierce Vulcan caught him by the a—,
Stuck to his skirts, insatiate varlet!
And fed with pleasure on the scarlet.
Hard by, and in the corner, sate
A Bencher grave, with look sedate,
Smoking his pipe, warm as a toast,
And reading over last week's post;
He saw the foe the fort invade,
And soon smelt out the breach he made:
But not a word——a little sly
He look'd, 'tis true, and from each eye
A side-long glance sometimes he sent,
To bring him news, and watch th' event.
At length, upon that tender part
    Where Honour lodges (as of old
    Authentic Hudibras has told)
The blustering colonel felt a smart,
Sore griev'd for his affronted bum,
Frisk'd, skip'd, and bounc'd about the room;
Then turning short, "Zounds, sir!" he cries——
"Pox on him had the fool no eyes?
What! let a man be burnt alive!"
    "I am not, sir, inquisitive"
(Reply'd sir Gravity) "to know
Whate'er your honour's pleas'd to do;
If you will burn your tail to tinder,
Pray what have I to do to hinder?
Other mens business let alone,
Why should not coxcombs mind their own?"

42

Then, knocking out his pipe with care,
Laid down his penny at the bar;
And, wrapping round his frieze surtout,
Took up his crab-tree, and walk'd out.

JOHN HUGHES (1677-1720)

BARN-ELMS

Let Phoebus his late happiness rehearse,
And grace Barn-Elms with never-dying verse!
Smooth was the Thames, his waters sleeping lay,
Unwak'd by winds that o'er the surface play;
When th' early god, arising from the east,
Disclos'd the golden dawn, with blushes drest.
First in the stream his own bright form he sees,
But brighter forms shine through the neighbouring trees.
He speeds the rising day, and sheds his light
Redoubled on the grove, to gain a nearer sight.
Not with more speed his Daphne he pursu'd,
Nor fair Leucothoe with such pleasure view'd;
Five dazzling nymphs in graceful pomp appear;
He thinks his Daphne and Leucothoe here,
Join'd with that heavenly three, who on mount Ide
Descending once the prize of beauty try'd.
  Ye verdant Elms, that towering grace this grove,
Be sacred still to Beauty and to Love!
No thunder break, nor lightning glare between
Your twisted boughs, but such as then was seen.
The grateful Sun will every morning rise
Propitious here, saluting from the skies
Your lofty tops, indulg'd with sweetest air,
And every spring your losses he'll repair;
Nor his own laurels more shall be his care.

A SONG

Fame of Dorinda's conquest brought
    The god of Love her charms to view;
To wound th' unwary maid he thought,
    But soon became her conquest too.

He dropp'd, half drawn, his feeble bow,
    He look'd, he rav'd, and sighing pin'd;
And wish'd in vain he had been now,
    As painters falsely draw him, blind.

Disarm'd, he to his mother flies;
    Help, Venus, help thy wretched son!

44

Who no will pay us sacrifice?
   For Love himself's, alas! undone.

To Cupid now no lover's prayer
   Shall be address'd in suppliant sighs;
My darts are gone, but oh! beware,
   Fond mortals, of Dorinda's eyes.

ON LUCINDA'S TEA-TABLE

January 1st, 1701

Poets invoke, when they rehearse
   In happy strains their pleasing dreams,
Some Muse unseen to crown their verse,
   And boast of Heliconian streams:

But here, a real Muse inspires
   (Who more reviving streams imparts)
Our fancies with the poets' fires,
   And with a nobler flame our hearts.

While from her hand each honour'd guest
   Receives his cup with liquor crown'd,
He thinks 'tis Jove's immortal feast,
   And Venus deals the nectar round.

As o'er each fountain, poets sing,
   Some lovely guardian nymph has sway,
Who from the consecrated spring,
   Wild beasts and satyrs drives away;

So hither dares no savage press,
   Who Beauty's sovereign power defies;
All, drinking here, her charms confess,
   Proud to be conquer'd by her eyes.

When Phoebus try'd his herbs in vain
   On Hyacinth, had she been there,
With tea she would have cur'd the swain,
   Who only then had dy'd for her.

ODE ON THE SPRING

For the Month of May

Wanton Zephyr, come away!
On this sweet, this silent grove,
Sacred to the Muse and Love,
In gentle whisper'd murmurs play!
Come, let thy soft, thy balmy breeze
Diffuse thy vernal sweets around
From sprouting flowers, and blossom'd trees;
While hills and echoing vales resound
With notes, which wing'd musicians sing
In honour to the bloom of Spring.

Lovely season of desire!
Nature smiles with joy to see
The amorous Months led on by thee,
That kindly wake her genial fire.
The brightest object in the skies,
The fairest lights that shine below,
The Sun, and Mira's charming eyes,
At thy return more charming grow:
With double glory they appear,
To warm and grace the infant Year.

A LETTER TO A FRIEND IN THE COUNTRY

Whilst thou art happy in a blest retreat,
And free from care dost rural songs repeat,
Whilst fragrant air fans thy poetic fire,
And pleasant groves with sprightly notes inspire,
(Groves whose recesses and refreshing shade
Indulge th' invention, and the judgment aid)
I, midst the smoke and clamours of the town,
That choke my Muse, and weigh my fancy down,
Pass my unactive hours;——
In such an air, how can soft numbers flow,
Or in such soil the sacred laurel grow?
All we can boast of the poetic fire,
Are but some sparks that soon as born expire.
Hail happy Woods! harbours of Peace and Joy!
Where no black cares the mind's repose destroy!
Where grateful Silence unmolested reigns,
Assists the Muse, and quickens all her strains.

Such were the scenes of our first parents' love,
In Eden's groves with equal flames they strove,
While warbling birds, soft whispering breaths of wind,
And murmuring streams, to grace their nuptials join'd.
All nature smil'd; the plains were fresh and green,
Unstain'd the fountains, and the heavens serene.
  Ye blest remains of that illustrious age!
Delightful Springs and Woods! —
Might I with you my peaceful days live o'er,
You, and my friend, whose absence I deplore,
Calm as a gentle brook's unruffled tide
Should the delicious flowing minutes glide;
Discharg'd of care, on unfrequented plains,
We'd sing of rural joys in rural strains.
No false corrupt delights our thoughts should move,
But joys of friendship, poetry, and love.
While others fondly feed ambition's fire,
And to the top of human state aspire,
That from their airy eminence they may
With pride and scorn th' inferior world survey,
Here we should dwell obscure, yet happier far than they.

A THOUGHT IN A GARDEN

1704

Delightful mansion! blest retreat!
Where all is silent, all is sweet!
Here Contemplation prunes her wings,
The raptur'd Muse more tuneful sings,
While May leads on the cheerful hours,
And opens a new world of flowers.
Gay Pleasure here all dresses wears,
And in a thousand shapes appears.
Pursu'd by Fancy, how she roves
Through airy walks, and museful groves;
Springs in each plant and blossom'd tree,
And charms in all I hear and see!
In this elysium while I stray,
And Nature's fairest face survey,
Earth seems new-born, and life more bright;
Time steals away, and smooths his flight;
And Thought's bewilder'd in delight.
Where are the crowds I saw of late?
What are those tales of Europe's fate?
Of Anjou, and the Spanish crown;

And leagues to pull usurpers down?
Of marching armies, distant wars;
Of factions, and domestic jars?
Sure these are last night's dreams, no more;
Or some romance, read lately o'er;
Like Homer's antique tale of Troy,
And powers confederate to destroy
Priam's proud house, the Dardan name,
With him that stole the ravish'd dame,
And, to possess another's right,
Durst the whole world to arms excite.
Come, gentle Sleep, my eye-lids close,
These dull impressions to help me lose;
Let Fancy take her wing, and find
Some better dreams to sooth my mind;
Or waking let me learn to live;
The prospect will instruction give.
For see, where beauteous Thames does glide
Serene, but with a fruitful tide;
Free from extremes of ebb and flow,
Not swell'd too high, nor sunk too low:
Such let my life's smooth current be,
Till from Time's narrow shore set free,
It mingle with th' eternal sea;
And, there enlarg'd, shall be no more
That trifling thing it was before.

THE TOASTERS

While circling healths inspire your sprightly wit,
And on each glass some beauty's praise is writ,
You ask, my friends, how can my silent Muse
To Montague's soft name a verse refuse?
Bright though she be, of race victorious sprung,
By wits ador'd, and by court-poets sung;
Unmov'd I hear her person call'd divine,
I see her features uninspiring shine;
A softer fair my soul to transport warms,
And, she once nam'd, no other nymph has charms.

THE MORNING APPARITION

Written at Wallington-House, in Surry, the Seat of Mr. Bridges

All things were hush'd, as Noise itself were dead;
No midnight mice stirr'd round my silent bed;
Not e'en a gnat disturb'd the peace profound,
Dumb o'er my pillow hung my watch unwound;
No ticking death-worm told a fancy'd doom,
Nor hidden cricket chirrup'd in the room;
No breeze the casement shook, or fann'd the leaves,
Nor drops of rain fell soft from off the eaves;
Nor noisy splinter made the candle weep,
But the dim watchlight seem'd itself asleep,
When, tir'd, I clos'd my eyes——how long I lay
In slumber wrapp'd, I list not now to say:
When hark! a sudden noise——See! open flies
The yielding door——I, starting, rubb'd my eyes,
Fast clos'd awhile; and, as their lids I rear'd,
Full at my feet a tall thin form appear'd,
While through my parted curtains rushing broke
A light like day, ere yet the figure spoke.
Cold sweat bedew'd my limbs——nor did I dream;
Hear, mortals, hear! for real truth's my theme.
And now, more bold, I rais'd my trembling bones
To look——when, lo! 'twas honest master Jones;
Who wav'd his hand, to banish fear and sorrow,
Well charg'd with toast and sack, and cry'd——"Good morrow!"

ABEL EVANS (1679-1737)

ON BLENHEIM HOUSE

See, Sir, here's the grand approach,
This way is for his Grace's coach;
There lies the bridge, and here's the clock:
Observe the lion and the cock,
The spacious court, the colonade,
And mark how wide the hall is made!
The chimneys are so well design'd,
They never smoke in any wind.
This gallery's contriv'd for walking,
The windows to retire and talk in;
The council-chamber for debate,
And all the rest are rooms of state.
   Thanks, Sir, cry'd I, 'tis very fine,
But where d'ye sleep, or where d'ye dine?
I find, by all you have been telling,
That 'tis a house, but not a dwelling.

THOMAS PARNELL (1679-1718)

A SONG

"When thy beauty appears
    In its graces and airs,
All bright as an angel new dropt from the sky;
    At distance I gaze, and am aw'd by my fears,
    So strangely you dazzle my eye!

"But when, without art,
    Your kind thought you impart,
When your love runs in blushes through every vein:
    When it darts from your eyes, when it pants in your heart,
    Then I know you're a woman again."

"There's a passion and pride
    In our sex," she reply'd,
"And thus, might I gratify both, I would do:
    Still an angel appear to each lover beside,
    But still be a woman to you."

LOVE AND INNOCENCE

A Song

My days have been so wond'rous free,
    The little birds that fly
With careless ease from tree to tree,
    Were but as bless'd as I.

Ask gliding waters, if a tear
    Of mine encreas'd their stream?
Or ask the flying gales, if e'er
    I lent one sigh to them?

But now my former days retire,
    And I'm by beauty caught,
The tender chains of sweet desire
    Are fix'd upon my thought.

Ye nightingales, ye twisting pines!
    Ye swains that haunt the grove!
Ye gentle echoes, breezy winds!
    Ye close retreats of love!

With all of nature, all of art,
   Assist the dear design;
O teach a young, unpractis'd heart,
   To make fair Nancy mine.

The very thought of change I hate,
   As much as of despair;
Nor ever covet to be great,
   Unless it be for her.

'Tis true, the passion in my mind
   Is mix'd with soft distress;
Yet, while the fair I love is kind,
   I cannot wish it less.

ON A LADY WITH FOUL BREATH

Art thou alive? It cannot be,
There's so much rottenness in thee,
Corruption only is in death;
And what's more putrid than thy breath?
Think not you live because you speak,
For graves such hollow sounds can make;
And respiration can't suffice,
For vapours do from caverns rise:
From thee such noisome stenches come,
Thy mouth betrays thy breast a tomb.
Thy body is a corpse that goes,
By magic rais'd from its repose:
A pestilence that walks by day,
But falls at night to worms and clay.
But I will to my Chloris run,
Who will not let me be undone:
The sweets her virgin-breath contains
Are fitted to remove my pains;
There will I healing nectar sip,
And, to be sav'd, approach her lip,
Though, if I touch the matchless dame,
I'm sure to burn with inward flame.
Thus, when I would one danger shun,
I'm straight upon another thrown:
I seek a cure, one sore to ease,
Yet in that cure's a new disease:
But love, though fatal, still can bless.
And greater dangers hide the less;
I'll go where passion bids me fly,

And choose my death, since I must die;
As doves pursued by birds of prey,
Venture with milder man to stay.

A NIGHT-PIECE ON DEATH

By the blue Tapers trembling Light,
No more I waste the wakeful Night,
Intent with endless view to pore
The Schoolmen and the Sages o'er:
Their Books from Wisdom widely stray,
Or point at best the longest Way.
I'll seek a readier Path, and go
Where Wisdom's surely taught below.

How deep yon Azure dies the Sky!
Where Orbs of Gold unnumber'd lye,
While thro' their Ranks in silver pride
The nether Crescent seems to glide.
The slumb'ring Breeze forgets to breathe,
The Lake is smooth and clear beneath,
Where once again the spangled Show
Descends to meet our Eyes below.
The Grounds which on the right aspire,
In dimness from the View retire:
The Left presents a Place of Graves,
Whose Wall the silent Water laves.
That Steeple guides thy doubtful sight
Among the livid gleams of Night.
There pass with melancholy State,
By all the solemn Heaps of Fate,
And think, as softly-sad you tread
Above the venerable Dead,
Time was, like thee they Life possest,
And Time shall be, that thou shalt Rest.

Those Graves, with bending Osier bound,
That nameless heave the crumbled Ground,
Quick to the glancing Thought disclose
Where Toil and Poverty repose.

The flat smooth Stones that bear a Name,
The Chissels slender help to Fame,
(Which e'er our Sett of Friends decay
Their frequent Steps may wear away.)

A middle Race of Mortals own,
Men, half ambitious, all unknown.

The Marble Tombs that rise on high,
Whose dead in vaulted Arches lye,
Whose Pillars swell with sculptur'd Stones,
Arms, Angels, Epitaphs and Bones,
These (all the poor Remains of State)
Adorn the Rich, or praise the Great;
Who while on Earth in Fame they live,
Are sensless of the Fame they give.

Ha! while I gaze, pale Cynthia fades,
The bursting Earth unveils the Shades!
All slow, and wan, and wrap'd with Shrouds,
They rise in visionary Crouds,
And all with sober Accent cry,
Think, Mortal, what it is to dye.

Now from yon black and fun'ral Yew,
That bathes the Charnel House with Dew,
Methinks I hear a Voice begin;
(Ye Ravens, cease your croaking Din,
Ye tolling Clocks, no Time resound
O'er the long Lake and midnight Ground)
It sends a Peal of hollow Groans,
Thus speaking from among the Bones.

When Men my Scythe and Darts supply,
How great a King of Fears am I!
They view me like the last of Things:
They make, and then they dread, my Stings.
Fools! if you less provok'd your Fears,
No more my Spectre-Form appears.
Death's but a Path that must be trod,
If Man wou'd ever pass to God:
A Port of Calms, a State of Ease
From the rough Rage of swelling Seas.

Why then thy flowing sable Stoles,
Deep pendent Cypress, mourning Poles,
Loose Scarfs to fall athwart thy Weeds,
Long Palls, drawn Herses, cover'd Steeds,
And Plumes of black, that as they tread,
Nod o'er the 'Scutcheons of the Dead?

Nor can the parted Body know,
Nor wants the Soul, these Forms of Woe:

54

As Men who long in Prison dwell,
With Lamps that glimmer round the Cell,
When e'er their suffering Years are run,
Spring forth to greet the glitt'ring Sun:
Such Joy, tho' far transcending Sense,
Have pious Souls at parting hence.
On Earth, and in the Body plac't,
A few, and evil Years, they wast:
But when their Chains are cast aside,
See the glad Scene unfolding wide,
Clap the glad Wing and tow'r away,
And mingle with the Blaze of Day.

BARTON BOOTH (1681-1733)

A SONG

from THE HIVE

Sweet are the Charms of her I love,
  More fragrant than the Damask Rose;
Soft as the Down on Turtle-Dove;
  Gentle as Air when Zephir blows;
Refreshing as descending Rains,
To Sun-burnt Climes and thirsty Plains.

True as the Needle to the Pole,
  Or as the Dial to the Sun;
Constant as gliding Waters roll,
  Whose swelling Tides obey the Moon:
From ev'ry other Charmer free,
My Life and Love shall follow thee.

The Lamb the flow'ry Thyme devours,
  The Dam the tender Kid pursues;
Sweet Philomel, in shady Bowers
  Of verdant Spring, his Note renews:
All follow what they most admire,
As I pursue my Soul's Desire.

Nature must change her beauteous Face,
  And vary as the Seasons rise;
As Winter to the Spring gives place,
  Summer th' Approach of Autumn flies:
No Change in Love the Seasons bring,
Love only knows perpetual Spring.

Devouring Time, with stealing Pace,
  Makes lofty Oaks and Cedars bow;
And marble Tow'rs, and Walls of Brass,
  In his rude March he levels low:
But Time, destroying far and wide,
Love from the Soul can ne'er divide.

Death only, with his cruel Dart,
  The gentle Godhead can remove;
And drive him from the bleeding Heart,
  To mingle with the Bless'd above:

Where, known to all his kindred Train,
He finds a lasting Rest from Pain.

Love, and his Sister fair, the Soul,
    Twin-born, from Heav'n together came;
Love will the Universe controul,
    When dying Seasons lose their Name:
Divine Abodes shall own his Pow'r,
When Time and Death shall be no more.

CUPID AND HYMEN

Cupid resign'd to Sylvia's care
  His bow and quiver stor'd with darts;
Commissioning the matchless fair
  To fill his shrine with bleeding hearts.

His empire thus secur'd, he flies
  To sport amid th' Idalian grove;
Whose feather'd choirs proclaim'd the joys,
  And bless'd the pleasing power of love.

The god their grateful songs engage,
  To spread his nets which Venus wrought;
Whilst Hymen held the golden cage,
  To keep secure the game they caught.

The warblers, brisk with genial flame,
  Swift from the myrtle shades repair;
A willing captive each became,
  And sweetlier carol'd in the snare.

When Hymen had receiv'd the prey,
  To Cytherea's fane they flew,
Regardless, while they wing'd their way,
  How sullen all the songsters grew.

Alas! no sprightly note is heard,
  But each with silent grief consumes;
Though to celestial food preferr'd,
  They pining droop their painted plumes.

Cupid, afflicted at the change,
  To beg her aid to Venus run;
She heard the tale, nor thought it strange,
  But, smiling, thus advis'd her son:

"Pleasure grows languid with restraint,
  'Tis Nature's privilege to roam:
If you'll not have your linnets faint,
  Leave Hymen with his cage at home."

OLIVIA

Olivia's lewd, but looks devout,
And scripture-proofs she throws about,
    When first you try to win her:
Pull your fob of guineas out;
Fee Jenny first, and never doubt
    To find the saint a sinner.

Baxter by day is her delight:
No chocolate must come in sight
    Before two morning chapters:
But, lest the spleen should spoil her quite,
She takes a civil friend at night,
    To raise her holy raptures.

Thus oft we see a glow-worm gay,
At large her fiery tail display,
    Encourag'd by the dark:
And yet the sullen thing all day
Snug in the lonely thicket lay,
    And hid the native spark.

TO A LADY, SITTING BEFORE HER GLASS

So smooth and clear the fountain was,
    In which his face Narcissus spy'd,
When, gazing in that liquid glass,
    He for himself despair'd and dy'd:
Now, Chloris, can you safer see
Your own perfections here than he.

The lark before the mirror plays,
    Which some deceitful swain has set,
Pleas'd with herself, she fondly stays
    To die deluded in the net.
Love may such frauds for you prepare,
Yourself the captive, and the snare.

But, Chloris, whilst you there review
    Those graces opening in their bloom,
Think how disease and age pursue,
    Your riper glories to consume.
Then sighing you would wish your glass
Could show to Chloris what she was.

Let Pride no more give Nature law,
    But free the youth your power enslaves
Her form, like yours, bright Cynthia saw,
    Reflected on the crystal waves;
Yet priz'd not all her charms above
The pleasure of Endymion's love.

No longer let your glass supply
    Too just an emblem of your breast,
Where oft to my deluded eye
    Love's image has appear'd imprest;
But play'd so lightly on your mind,
It left no lasting print behind.

THE ROSE

See, Sylvia, see, this new-blown rose,
The image of thy blush,
Mark how it smiles upon the bush,
    And triumphs as it grows!
"Oh, pluck it not! we'll come anon,"
Thou say'st.   Alas! 'twill then be gone.

Now its purple beauty's spread,
Soon it will droop and fall,
And soon it will not be at all;
    No fine things draw a length of thread.
Then tell me, seems it not to say,
"Come on, and crop me whilst you may?"

JOHN GAY (1685-1732)

SWEET WILLIAM'S FAREWELL TO BLACK-EY'D SUSAN

A Ballad

All in the Downs the fleet was moor'd,
   The streamers waving in the wind,
When black-ey'd Susan came aboard.
   Oh! where shall I my true love find!
Tell me, ye jovial sailors, tell me true,
If my sweet William sails among the crew.

William, who high upon the yard,
   Rock'd with the billow to and fro,
Soon as her well-known voice he heard,
   He sigh'd, and cast his eyes below:
The cord slides swiftly through his glowing hands,
And, (quick as lightning,) on the deck he stands.

So the sweet lark, high-pois'd in air,
   Shuts close his pinions to his breast,
(If, chance, his mate's shrill call he hear)
   And drops at once into her nest.
The noblest Captain in the British fleet,
Might envy William's lip those kisses sweet.

O Susan, Susan, lovely dear,
   My vows shall ever true remain;
Let me kiss off that falling tear,
   We only part to meet again.
Change, as ye list, ye winds; my heart shall be
The faithful compass that still points to thee.

Believe not what the landmen say,
   Who tempt with doubts thy constant mind:
They'll tell thee, sailors, when away,
   In ev'ry port a mistress find.
Yes, yes, believe them when they tell thee so,
For thou art present wheresoe'er I go.

If to far India's coast we sail,
   Thy eyes are seen in di'monds bright,
Thy breath is Africk's spicy gale,
   Thy skin is ivory, so white.

Thus ev'ry beauteous object that I view,
Wakes in my soul some charm of lovely Sue.

Though battel call me from thy arms,
    Let not my pretty Susan mourn;
Though cannons roar, yet safe from harms,
    William shall to his Dear return.
Love turns aside the balls that round me fly,
Lest precious tears should drop from Susan's eye.

The boatswain gave the dreadful word,
    The sails their swelling bosom spread,
No longer must she stay aboard:
    They kiss'd, she sigh'd, he hung his head.
Her less'ning boat, unwilling rows to land:
Adieu, she cries! and wav'd her lilly hand.

MOLLY MOG: OR, THE FAIR MAID OF THE INN

A Ballad

Says my Uncle, I pray you discover
    What hath been the Cause of your Woes,
Why you pine, and you whine, like a Lover?
    I have seen Molly Mog of the Rose.

O Nephew! Your Grief is but Folly,
    In Town you may find better Prog;
Half a Crown there will get you a Molly,
    A Molly much better than Mog.

I know that by Wits 'tis recited,
    That Women at best are a Clog;
But I am not so easily frighted,
    From loving of sweet Molly Mog.

The School-Boy's desire is a Play-Day,
    The School-Master's joy is to flog;
The Milk-Maid's delight is on May-Day,
    But mine is on sweet Molly Mog.

Will-a-wisp leads the Trav'ler a gadding
    Thro' Ditch, and thro' Quagmire and Bog;
But no Light can set me a madding,
    Like the Eyes of my sweet Molly Mog.

For Guineas in other Mens Breeches
    Your Gamesters will palm and will cog;
But I envy them none of their Riches,
    So I may win sweet Molly Mog.

The Heart, when half-wounded, is changing,
    It here and there leaps like a Frog;
But my Heart can never be ranging,
    'Tis so fix'd upon sweet Molly Mog.

Who follows all Ladies of Pleasure,
    In Pleasure is thought but a Hog;
All the Sex cannot give so good measure
    Of Joys, as my sweet Molly Mog.

I feel I'm in Love to Distraction,
    My Senses all lost in a Fog;
And nothing can give Satisfaction
    But thinking of sweet Molly Mog.

A Letter when I am inditing,
    Comes Cupid and gives me a Jog,
And I fill all the Paper with writing
    Of nothing but sweet Molly Mog.

If I would not give up the three Graces,
    I wish I were hang'd like a Dog,
And at Court all the Drawing-Room Faces,
    For a Glance of my sweet Molly Mog.

Those Faces want Nature and Spirit,
    And seem as cut out of a Log;
Juno, Venus, and Pallas's Merit
    Unite in my sweet Molly Mog.

Those who toast all the Family Royal,
    In Bumpers of Hogan and Nog,
Have Hearts not more true or more loyal
    Than mine to my sweet Molly Mog.

Were Virgil alive with his Phillis,
    And writing another Eclogue;
Both his Phillis and fair Amaryllis
    He'd give up for sweet Molly Mog.

When she smiles on each Guest, like her Liquor,
    Then Jealousy sets me agog.

63

To be sure she's a Bit for the Vicar,
And so I shall lose Molly Mog.

THOUGHT ON ETERNITY

Ere the foundations of the world were laid,
Ere kindling light th' Almighty word obey'd,
Thou wert; and when the subterraneous flame
Shall burst its prison, and devour this frame,
From angry Heaven when the keen lightning flies,
When fervent heat dissolves the melting skies,
Thou still shalt be; still as thou wert before,
And know no change, when time shall be no more.
O endless thought! divine Eternity
Th' immortal soul shares but a part of thee;
For thou wert present when our life began,
When the warm dust shot up in breathing man.
      Ah! what is life? with ills encompass'd round,
Amidst our hopes, Fate strikes the sudden wound:
To day the statesman of new honour dreams,
To morrow Death destroys his airy schemes;
Is mouldy treasure in thy chest confin'd?
Think, all that treasure thou must leave behind;
Thy heir with smiles shall view thy blazon'd hearse,
And all thy hoards with lavish hand disperse.
Should certain Fate th' impending blow delay,
Thy mirth will sicken, and thy bloom decay;
Then feeble age will all thy nerves disarm,
No more thy blood its narrow channels warm.
Who then would wish to stretch this narrow span,
To suffer life beyond the date of man?
      The virtuous soul pursues a nobler aim,
And life regards but as a fleeting dream:
She longs to wake, and wishes to get free,
To launch from Earth into Eternity.
For, while the boundless theme extends our thought,
Ten thousand thousand rolling years are nought.

A RECEIPT FOR STEWING VEAL

Take a knuckle of veal;
    You may buy it, or steal.
In a few pieces cut it:
In a stewing-pan put it.

Salt, pepper, and mace,
    Must season this knuckle;
Then what's join'd to a place
    With other herbs muckle;
That which killed king Will;
And what never stands still.
Some prigs of that bed
Where children are bred,
Which much you will mend, if
Both spinnage and endive,
And lettuce, and beet,
With marygold meet.
Put no water at all;
For it maketh things small,
Which, lest it should happen,
A close cover clap on.
Put this pot of Wood's metal
In a hot boiling kettle,
And there let it be
    (Mark the doctrine I teach)
About——let me see——
    Thrice as long as you preach;
So skimming the fat off,
Say grace with your hat off.
O, then! with what rapture
Will it fill dean and chapter!

THE MASTIFF

A Fable

    Those who in quarrels interpose,
Must often wipe a bloody nose.
    A Mastiff, of true English blood,
Lov'd fighting better than his food.
When dogs were snarling for a bone,
He long'd to make the war his own.
And often found (when two contend)
To interpose obtain'd his end.
He glory'd in his limping pace;
The scars of honour seam'd his face;
In every limb a gash appears,
And frequent fights retrench'd his ears.
    As on a time he heard from far
Two dogs engag'd in noisy war,
Away he scours, and lays about him,

Resolv'd no fray should be without him.
Forth from his yard a tanner flies,
And to the bold intruder cries:
"A cudgel shall correct your manners:
Whence sprung this cursed hate to tanners?
While on my dog you vent your spite,
Sirrah! 'tis me you dare not bite."
To see the battle thus perplex'd,
With equal rage a butcher, vex'd,
Hoarse-screaming from the circled crowd,
To the curs'd Mastiff cries aloud:
"Both Hockleyhole and Marybone
The combats of my dog have known:
He ne'er, like bullies, coward-hearted,
Attacks in public, to be parted.
Think not, rash fool, to share his fame;
Be his the honour, or the shame."
Thus said, they swore, and rav'd like thunder,
Then dragg'd their fasten'd dogs asunder;
While clubs and kicks from every side
Rebounded from the Mastiff's hide.
All reeking now with sweat and blood,
Awhile the parted warriors stood;
Then pour'd upon the meddling foe,
Who, worried, howl'd and sprawl'd below.
He rose; and limping from the fray,
By both sides mangled, sneak'd away.

THE BARLEY-MOW AND THE DUNGHILL

A Fable

How many saucy airs we meet
From Temple-bar to Aldgate-street!
Proud rogues, who shared the South-sea prey,
And sprung like mushrooms in a day!
They think it mean to condescend
To know a brother or a friend;
They blush to hear their mother's name,
And by their pride expose their shame.
As cross his yard, at early day,
A careful farmer took his way,
He stopp'd; and, leaning on his fork,
Observ'd the flail's incessant work.
In thought he measur'd all his store,
His geese, his hogs, he number'd o'er;

66

In fancy weigh'd the fleeces shorn,
And multiply'd the next year's corn.
   A Barley-mow, which stood beside,
Thus to its musing master cry'd:
   "Say, good sir, is it fit or right
To treat me with neglect and slight?
Me, who contribute to your cheer,
And raise your mirth with ale and beer?
Why thus insulted, thus disgrac'd,
And that vile Dunghill near me plac'd?
Are those poor sweepings of a groom,
That filthy sight, that nauseous fume,
Meet objects here? Command it hence;
A thing so mean must give offence."
   The humble Dunghill thus reply'd:
"Thy master hears, and mocks thy pride:
Insult not thus the meek and low;
In me thy benefactor know;
My warm assistance gave thee birth,
Or thou hadst perish'd low in earth;
But upstarts, to support their station,
Cancel at once all obligation."

THE GARDENER AND THE HOG

A Fable

   A gardener, of peculiar taste,
On a young Hog his favour plac'd,
Who fed not with the common herd;
His tray was to the hall preferr'd.
He wallow'd underneath the board,
Or in his master's chamber snor'd,
Who fondly strok'd him every day,
And taught him all the puppy's play.
Where'er he went, the grunting friend
Ne'er fail'd his pleasure to attend.
   As on a time the loving pair
Walk'd forth to tend the garden's care,
The master thus address'd the swine:
   "My house, my garden, all is thine.
On turnips feast whene'er you please,
And riot in my beans and pease;
If the potatoe's taste delights,
Or the red carrot's sweet invites,
Indulge thy morn and evening hours;

67

But let due care regard my flowers:
My tulips are my garden's pride:
What vast expense those beds supply'd!"
    The Hog by chance one morning roam'd,
Where with new ale the vessels foam'd:
He munches now the steaming grains,
Now with full swill the liquor drains.
Intoxicating fumes arise;
He reels, he rolls his winking eyes;
Then staggering through the garden scours,
And treads down painted ranks of flowers.
With delving snout he turns the soil,
And cools his palate with the spoil.
    The master came, the ruin spy'd;
"Villain! suspend thy rage," he cry'd.
"Hast thou, thou most ungrateful sot,
My charge, my only charge, forgot?
What, all my flowers!" No more he said,
But gaz'd, and sigh'd, and hung his head.
    The Hog with stuttering speech returns:
"Explain, sir, why your anger burns.
See there, untouch'd, your tulips strown,
For I devour'd the roots alone."
    At this the Gardener's passion grows;
From oaths and threats he fell to blows.
The stubborn brute the blows sustains,
Assaults his legs, and tears the veins.
    "Ah! foolish swain! too late you find
That sties were for such friends design'd!"
    Homeward he limps with painful pace,
Reflecting thus on past disgrace:
"Who cherishes a brutal mate,
Shall mourn the folly soon or late."

MY OWN EPITAPH

Life is a jest, and all things show it;
I thought so once, but now I know it.

ALLAN RAMSAY (1686-1758)

POLWART ON THE GREEN

At Polwart on the Green
If you'll meet me the Morn,
Where Lasses do conveen
To dance about the Thorn;
A kindly welcome you shall meet
Frae her wha likes to view
A Lover and a Lad complete,
The Lad and Lover you.

Let dorty Dames say Na,
As lang as e'er they please,
Seem caulder than the Sna',
While inwardly they Bleez;
But I will frankly shaw my Mind,
And yield my Heart to thee;
Be ever to the Captive kind,
That langs na to be free.

At Polwart on the Green,
Amang the new mawn Hay,
With Sangs and dancing keen
We'll pass the heartsome Day:
At Night if Beds be o'er thrang laid,
And thou be twin'd of thine,
Thou shalt be welcome, my dear Lad,
To take a Part of mine.

A SONG

At setting day and rising morn,
    With soul that still shall love thee,
I'll ask of Heaven thy safe return,
    With all that can improve thee.
I'll visit aft the birken bush,
    Where first thou kindly told me
Sweet tales of love, and hid thy blush,
    Whilst round thou didst enfold me.
To all our haunts I will repair,
    By greenwood shaw or fountain;
Or where the summer day I'd share

69

With thee upon yon mountain:
There will I tell the trees and flowers,
From thoughts unfeigned and tender;
By vows you're mine, by love is yours
A heart that cannot wander.

THE HIGHLAND LADDIE

The Lawland lads think they are fine,
But oh they're vain and idly gaudy!
How much unlike the gracefu' mien,
And manly looks of my Highland laddie?

CHORUS

O my bonny, bonny Highland laddie;
My handsome, charming Highland laddie:
May Heaven still guard, and love reward
Our Lawland lass and her Highland laddie.

If I were free at will to chuse
To be the wealthiest Lawland lady,
I'd take young Donald without trews,
With bonnet blew, and belted plaidy.

The brawest beau in borrows-town
In a' his airs, with art made ready,
Compar'd to him, he's but a clown;
He's finer far in 's tartan plaidy.

O'er benty hill with him I'll run,
And leave my Lawland kin and dady;
Frae winter's cauld and summer's sun
He'll screen me with his Highland plaidy.

A painted room and silken bed
May please a Lawland laird and lady;
But I can kiss, and be as glad
Behind a bush in 's Highland plaidy.

Few compliments between us pass,
I ca' him my dear Highland laddie;
And he ca's me his Lawland lass:
Syne rows me in his Highland plaidy.

70

Nae greater joy I'll e'er pretend,
Than that his love prove true and steady,
Like mine to him; which ne'er shall end,
While Heaven preserve my Highland laddie.

LOCHABER NO MORE

Farewell to Lochaber, and farewell, my Jean,
Where heartsome with thee I've mony day been;
For Lochaber no more, Lochaber no more,
We'll maybe return to Lochaber no more.
These tears that I shed they are a' for my dear,
And no for the dangers attending on weir;
Though borne on rough seas to a far bloody shore,
Maybe to return to Lochaber no more.

Though hurricanes rise, and rise every wind,
They'll ne'er make a tempest like that in my mind;
Though loudest of thunder on louder waves roar,
That's naething like leaving my love on the shore.
To leave thee behind me my heart is sair pained;
By ease that's inglorious no fame can be gained;
And beauty and love's the reward of the brave,
And I must deserve it before I can crave.

Then glory, my Jeany, maun plead my excuse;
Since honour commands me, how can I refuse?
Without it I ne'er can have merit for thee,
And without thy favour I'd better not be.
I gae then, my lass, to win honour and fame,
And if I should luck to come gloriously hame,
I'll bring a heart to thee with love running o'er,
And then I'll leave thee and Lochaber no more.

GIVE ME A LASS WITH A LUMP OF LAND

Gi'e me a lass with a lump of land,
    And we for life shall gang thegither;
Tho' daft or wise I'll never demand,
    Or black or fair it maks na whether.
I'm aff with wit, and beauty will fade,
    And blood alane is no worth a shilling;
But she that's rich her market's made,
    For ilka charm about her is killing.

71

Gi'e me a lass with a lump of land,
    And in my bosom I'll hug my treasure;
Gin I had anes her gear in my hand,
    Should love turn dowf, it will find pleasure.
Laugh on wha likes, but there's my hand,
    I hate with poortith, though bonny, to meddle;
Unless they bring cash or a lump of land,
    They'se never get me to dance to their fiddle.

There's meikle good love in bands and bags,
    And siller and gowd's a sweet complexion;
But beauty, and wit, and virtue in rags,
    Have tint the art of gaining affection.
Love tips his arrows with woods and parks,
    And castles, and riggs, and moors, and meadows;
And naithing can catch our modern sparks,
    But well-tocher'd lasses or jointur'd widows.

THOMAS TICKELL (1686-1740)

TO THE EARL OF WARWICK
ON THE DEATH OF MR. ADDISON

1721

If, dumb too long, the drooping Muse hath stay'd,
And left her debt to Addison unpaid;
Blame not her silence, Warwick, but bemoan,
And judge, oh judge, my bosom by your own.
What mourner ever felt poetic fires!
Slow comes the verse, that real woe inspires:
Grief unaffected suits but ill with art,
Or flowing numbers with a bleeding heart.
  Can I forget the dismal night, that gave
My soul's best part for-ever to the grave!
How silent did his old companions tread,
By mid-night lamps, the mansions of the dead,
Through breathing statues, then unheeded things,
Through rowes of warriors, and through walks of kings!
What awe did the slow solemn knell inspire;
The pealing organ, and the pausing choir;
The duties by the lawn-robed prelate pay'd;
And the last words, that dust to dust convey'd!
While speechless o'er thy closing grave we bend,
Accept these tears, thou dear departed friend,
Oh gone for-ever, take this long adieu;
And sleep in peace, next thy lov'd Montagu!
  To strew fresh laurels let the task be mine,
A frequent pilgrim, at thy sacred shrine;
Mine with true sighs thy absence to bemoan,
And grave with faithful epitaphs thy stone.
If e'er from me thy lov'd memorial part,
May shame afflict this alienated heart;
Of thee forgetful if I form a song,
My lyre be broken, and untun'd my tongue,
My grief be doubled, from thy image free,
And mirth a torment, unchastised by thee.
  Oft let me range the gloomy Iles alone
(Sad luxury! to vulgar minds unknown)
Along the walls where speaking marbles show
What worthies form the hallow'd mold below:
Proud names, who once the reins of empire held;
In arms who triumph'd; or in arts excell'd;
Chiefs, grac'd with scars, and prodigal of blood;

Stern patriots, who for sacred freedom stood;
Just men, by whom impartial laws were given;
And saints, who taught, and led, the way to heaven.
Ne'er to these chambers, where the mighty rest,
Since their foundation, came a nobler guest,
Nor e'er was to the bowers of bliss convey'd
A fairer spirit, or more welcome shade.
In what new region, to the just assign'd,
What new employments please th' unbody'd mind?
A winged Virtue thro' th' ethereal sky,
From world to world unweary'd does he fly?
Or curious trace the long laborious maze
Of heaven's decrees where wond'ring angels gaze?
Does he delight to hear bold Seraphs tell
How Michael battel'd, and the Dragon fell?
Or, mixt with milder Cherubim, to glow
In hymns of love, not ill essay'd below?
Or do'st thou warn poor mortals left behind,
A task well suited to thy gentle mind?
Oh, if sometimes thy spotless form descend,
To me thy aid, thou guardian Genius, lend!
When rage misguides me, or when fear alarms,
When pain distresses, or when pleasure charms,
In silent whisperings purer thoughts impart,
And turn from Ill a frail and feeble heart;
Lead through the paths thy virtue trode before,
'Till bliss shall join, nor death can part us more.
   That awful form (which, so ye heavens decree,
Must still be lov'd and still deplor'd by me)
In nightly visions seldom fails to rise,
Or, rous'd by fancy, meets my waking eyes.
If business calls, or crowded courts invite,
Th' unblemish'd statesman seems to strike my sight;
If in the stage I seek to soothe my care,
I meet his soul, which breathes in Cato there;
If pensive to the rural shades I rove,
His shape o'ertakes me in the lonely grove:
'Twas there of Just and Good he reason'd strong,
Clear'd some great truth, or rais'd some serious song;
There patient show'd us the wise course to steer,
A candid censor, and a friend severe;
There taught us how to live; and (oh! too high
The price for knowledge) taught us how to die.
   Thou Hill, whose brow the antique structures grace,
Rear'd by bold chiefs of Warwick's noble race,
Why, once so lov'd, when-e'er thy bower appears,
O'er my dim eye-balls glance the sudden tears!
How sweet were once thy Prospects fresh and fair,

Thy sloping walks, and unpolluted air!
How sweet the glooms beneath thy aged trees,
Thy noon-tide shadow, and thy evening breeze!
His image thy forsaken bowers restore
Thy walks and airy prospects charm no more,
No more the summer in thy gloomes allay'd,
Thy ev'ning breezes, and thy noon-day shade.
From other ills, however fortune frown'd,
Some refuge in the Muse's art I found:
Reluctant now I touch the trembling string,
Bereft of him, who taught me how to sing,
And these sad accents, murmur'd o'er his urn,
Betray that absence, they attempt to mourn.
Oh! must I then (now fresh my bosom bleeds,
And Craggs in death to Addison succeeds)
The verse, begun to one lost friend, prolong,
And weep a second in th' unfinish'd song!
These works divine, which on his death-bed laid
To thee, O Craggs, th' expiring Sage convey'd,
Great, but ill-omen'd monument of fame,
Nor he surviv'd to give, nor thou to claim.
Swift after him thy social spirit flies,
And close to his, how soon! thy coffin lies.
Blest pair! whose union future bards shall tell
In future tongues: each other's boast! farewel.
Farewel! whom join'd in fame, in friendship try'd,
No chance could sever, nor the grave divide.

COLIN AND LUCY

1725

Of Leinster, fam'd for maidens fair,
  Bright Lucy was the grace;
Nor e'er did Liffy's limpid stream
  Reflect so sweet a face:
Till luckless love, and pining care,
  Impair'd her rosy hue,
Her coral lips, and damask cheeks,
  And eyes of glossy blue.

Oh! have you seen a lilly pale,
  When beating rains descend?
So droop'd the slow-consuming maid,
  Her life now near its end.

By Lucy warn'd, of flatt'ring swains
   Take heed, ye easy fair;
Of vengeance due to broken vows,
   Ye perjur'd swains, beware.

Three times, all in the dead of night,
   A bell was heard to ring;
And shrieking at her window thrice,
   The raven flap'd his wing.
Too well the love-lorn maiden knew
   The solemn-boding sound:
And thus, in dying words, bespoke
   The virgins weeping round:

"I hear a voice, you cannot hear,
   Which says, I must not stay;
I see a hand, you cannot see,
   Which beckons me away.
By a false heart, and broken vows,
   In early youth I die:
Was I to blame, because his bride
   Was thrice as rich as I?

"Ah, Colin! give not her thy vows,
   Vows due to me alone;
Nor thou, fond maid, receive his kiss,
   Nor think him all thy own.
To-morrow, in the church to wed,
   Impatient, both prepare!
But know, fond maid, and know, false man,
   That Lucy will be there!

"Then bear my corse, my comrades, bear,
   This bridegroom blythe to meet,
He in his wedding-trim so gay,
   I in my winding-sheet."
She spoke; she dy'd; her corse was born,
   The bridegroom blythe to meet,
He in his wedding-trim so gay,
   She in her winding-sheet.

Then what were perjur'd Colin's thoughts?
   How were these nuptials kept?
The bridesmen flock'd round Lucy dead,
   And all the village wept.
Confusion, shame, remorse, despair,
   At once his bosom swell:

The damps of death bedew'd his brow,
    He shook, he groan'd, he fell.

From the vain bride (ah bride no more!)
    The varying crimson fled,
When stretch'd before her rival's corse,
    She saw her husband dead.
Then to his Lucy's new-made grave,
    Convey'd by trembling swains,
One mould with her, beneath one sod,
    For ever he remains.

Oft at this grave, the constant hind,
    And plighted maid are seen;
With garlands gay, and true-love knots,
    They deck the sacred green;
But, swain forsworn, whoe'er thou art,
    This hallow'd spot forbear;
Remember Colin's dreadful fate,
    And fear to meet him there.

WILLIAM BROOME (1689-1745)

THE COQUETTE

Sillia, with uncontested sway,
    Like Rome's fam'd tyrant reigns;
Beholds adoring crowds obey,
    And heroes proud to wear her chains:
Yet stoops, like him, to every prize,
Busy to murder beaux and flies.

She aims at every trifling heart,
    Attends each flatterer's vows;
And, like a picture drawn with art,
    A look on all that gaze bestows.
O! may the power who lovers rules,
Grant rather scorn, than hope with fools.

Mistaken nymph! the crowds that gaze
    Adore thee into shame;
Unguarded beauty is disgrace,
    And coxcombs, when they praise, defame.
O! fly such brutes in human shapes,
Nor, like th' Egyptians, worship apes.

TO A LADY OF THIRTY

No more let youth its beauty boast,
S——n at thirty reigns a toast,
An, like the Sun as he declines,
More mildly, but more sweetly shines.

The hand of Time alone disarms
Her face of its superfluous charms:
But adds, for every grace resign'd,
A thousand to adorn her mind.

Youth was her too inflaming time;
This, her more habitable clime:
How must she then each heart engage,
Who blooms like youth, is wise like age!

Thus the rich orange-trees produce
At once both ornament, and use:

Here opening blossoms we behold,
There fragrant orbs of ripen'd gold.

THE ROSE-BUD

To the Lady Jane Wharton

Queen of Fragrance, lovely Rose,
The Beauties of thy Leaves disclose!
The Winter's past, the Tempests fly,
Soft Gales breathe gently thro' the Sky;
The Lark sweet warbling on the Wing
Salutes the gay Return of Spring:
The silver Dews, the vernal Show'rs,
Call forth a bloomy Waste of Flow'rs;
The joyous Fields, the shady Woods,
Are cloath'd with Green, or swell with Buds;
Then haste thy Beauties to disclose,
Queen of Fragrance, lovely Rose!
    Thou, beauteous Flow'r, a welcome Guest,
Shalt flourish on the Fair-One's Breast,
Shalt grace her Hand, or deck her Hair,
The Flow'r most sweet, the Nymph most fair;
Breathe soft, ye Winds! be calm, ye Skies!
Arise ye flow'ry Race, arise!
And haste thy Beauties to disclose,
Queen of Fragrance, lovely Rose!
    But thou, fair Nymph, thy self survey
In this sweet Offspring of a Day;
That Miracle of Face must fail,
Thy Charms are sweet, but Charms are frail:
Swift as the short-liv'd Flow'r they fly,
At Morn they bloom, at Evening die:
Tho' Sickness yet a while forbears,
Yet Time destroys, what Sickness spares;
Now Helen lives alone in Fame,
And Cleopatra's but a Name;
Time must indent that heav'nly Brow,
And thou must be, what Helen's now.
    This Moral to the Fair disclose,
Queen of Fragrance, lovely Rose.

TO A GENTLEMAN OF SEVENTY

who Married a Lady of Sixteen

What woes must such unequal union bring,
When hoary Winter weds the youthful Spring!
You, like Mezentius, in the nuptial bed,
Once more unite the living to the dead.

LADY MARY WORTLEY MONTAGU (1689-1762)

FAREWELL TO BATH

To all you ladies now at Bath,
　　And eke, ye beaus, to you,
With aking heart, and wat'ry eyes,
　　I bid my last adieu.

Farewell ye nymphs, who waters sip
　　Hot reeking from the pumps,
While music lends her friendly aid,
　　To cheer you from the dumps.

Farewell, ye wits, who prating stand,
　　And criticise the fair;
Yourselves the joke of men of sense,
　　Who hate a coxcomb's air.

Farewell to Deard's, and all her toys,
　　Which glitter in her shop,
Deluding traps to girls and boys,
　　The warehouse of the fop.

Lindsay's and Hayes's, both farewell,
　　Where in the spacious hall,
With bounding steps, and sprightly air,
　　I've led up many a ball.

When Somerville, of courteous mien,
　　Was part'ner in the dance,
With swimming Hawes, and Brownlow blithe,
　　And Britton, pink of France.

Poor Nash, farewell! may fortune smile,
　　Thy drooping soul revive:
My heart is full, I can no more——
　　John, bid the coachman drive.

JOHN BYROM (1692-1763)

CARELESS CONTENT

I am Content, I do not care,
    Wag as it will the World for me;
When Fuss and Fret was all my Fare,
    It got no ground, as I could see:
So when away my Caring went,
I counted Cost, and was Content.

With more of Thanks, and less of Thought,
    I strive to make my Matters meet;
To seek what ancient Sages sought,
    Physic and Food, in sour and sweet:
To take what passes in good Part,
And keep the Hiccups from the Heart.

With good and gentle-humour'd Hearts
    I choose to chat where e'er I come,
Whate'er the Subject be that starts;
    But if I get among the Glum,
I hold my Tongue to tell the Troth,
And keep my Breath to cool my Broth.

For Chance or Change, of Peace or Pain,
    For Fortune's Favour, or her Frown,
For Lack or Glut, for Loss or Gain,
    I never dodge, nor up nor down:
But swing what Way the Ship shall swim,
Or tack about, with equal Trim.

I suit not where I shall not speed,
    Nor trace the Turn of ev'ry Tide;
If simple Sense will not succeed,
    I make no Bustling, but abide:
For shining Wealth, or scaring Woe,
I force no Friend, I fear no Foe.

Of Ups and Downs, of Ins and Outs,
    Of they're i' th' wrong, and we're i' th' right,
I shun the Rancours, and the Routs,
    And wishing well to every Wight,
Whatever Turn the Matter takes,
I deem it all but Ducks and Drakes.

With whom I feast I do not fawn,
    Nor if the Folks should flout me, faint
If wonted Welcome be withdrawn,
    I cook no Kind of a Complaint,
With none dispos'd to disagree,
But like them best, who best like me.

Not that I rate myself the Rule
    How all my Betters should behave;
But Fame shall find me no Man's Fool,
    Nor to a Set of Men a Slave:
I love a Friendship free and frank,
And hate to hang upon a Hank.

Fond of a true and trusty Tie,
    I never loose where'er I link;
Tho' if a Bus'ness budges by,
    I talk thereon just as I think:
My Word, my Work, my Heart, my Hand,
Still on a Side together stand.

If Names or Notions make a noise,
    Whatever Hap the Question hath,
The Point impartially I poise,
    And read, or write, but without Wrath;
For should I burn or break my Brains,
Pray, who will pay me for my Pains?

I love my Neighbour as myself,
    Myself like him too, by his Leave;
Nor to his Pleasure, Pow'r, or Pelf,
    Came I to crouch, as I conceive:
Dame Nature doubtless has design'd
A Man the Monarch of his Mind.

Now taste and try this Temper, Sirs,
    Mood it, and brood it in your Breast;
Or if ye ween, for worldly Stirs,
    That Man does right to mar his Rest,
Let me be deft, and debonair:
I am Content, I do not care.

JACOBITE TOAST

God bless the king!——I mean the Faith's Defender;
God bless (no harm in blessing) the Pretender!

But who Pretender is, or who is king,
God bless us all!——that's quite another thing.

ON INOCULATION

Written when it First Began to be Practised in England

I heard two neighbours talk, the other night,
About this new distemper-giving plan,
Which some so wrong, and others think so right;
Short was the dialogue——and thus it ran.

"If I had twenty children of my own,
I would inoculate them ev'ry one."
"Ay, but should any of them die! what moan
Would then be made, for vent'ring thereupon?"

"No; I should think that I had done the best;
And be resign'd, whatever should befall."
"But could you really be so, quite at rest?"
"I could"——"Then why inoculate at all?

"Since to resign a child to God, who gave,
Is full as easy, and as just a part,
When sick, and led by Nature to the grave,
As when in health, and driv'n to it by Art."

THE NIMMERS

Two foot companions once in deep discourse,
"Tom," says the one——"let's go and steal a horse."
"Steal!" says the other, is a huge surprise,
"He that says I'm a thief——I say he lies."
"Well, well," replies his friend, "no such affront,
I did but ask ye——if you won't——you won't."
So they jogg'd on——till, in another strain,
The querist mov'd to honest Tom again;
"Suppose," says he, "for supposition sake, —
'Tis but a supposition that I make, —
Suppose——that we should filch a horse, I say?"
"Filch! filch!" quoth Tom, demurring by the way;
"That's not so bad as downright theft——I own——
But——yet——methinks——'twere better let alone:
It soundeth something pitiful and low;

84

Shall we go filch a horse, you say——why no——
I'll filch no filching; and I'll tell no lie:
Honesty's the best policy——say I."
    Struck with such vast integrity quite dumb
His comrade paus'd——at last, says he, "Come, come;
Thou art an honest fellow——I agree——
Honest and poor;——alas! that should not be:
And dry into the bargain——and no drink!
Shall we go nim a horse, Tom, what dost' think?"
    How clear things are when liquor's in the case!
Tom answers quick, with casuistic grace,
"Nim? yes, yes, yes, let's nim with all my heart,
I see no harm in nimming, for my part;
Hard is the case, now I look sharp into't,
That honesty should trudge i' th' dirt a foot;
So many empty houses round about,
That honesty should wear its bottoms out;
Besides——shall honesty be chok'd with thirst?
Were it my lord mayor's horse——I'd nim it first.
And——by the by——my lad——no scrubby tit——
There is the best that ever wore a bit,
Not far from hence,"——"I take ye," quoth his friend,
"Is not yon stable, Tom, our journey's end."
    Good wits will jump——both meant the very steed;
The top o' th' country, both for shape and speed:
So to't they went——and, with an halter round
His feather'd neck, they nimm'd him off the ground.
    And now, good people, we should next relate
Of these adventurers the luckless fate:
Poor Tom!——but here the sequel is to seek,
Not being yet translated from the Greek:
Some say, that Tom would honestly have peach'd.
But by his blabbing friend was over reach'd;
Others insist upon't that both the elves
Were, in like manner, halter-nimm'd themselves.
    It matters not——the moral is the thing,
For which our purpose, neighbours, was to sing.
If it should hit some few amongst the throng,
Let 'em not lay the fault upon the song.
Fair warning all: he that has got a cap,
Now put it on——or else beware a rap:
'Tis but a short one, it is true, but yet
Has a long reach with it——videlicet,
'Twixt right and wrong how many gentle trimmers
Will neither steal nor filch, but will be plaguy Nimmers!

GEORGE LILLO (1693-1739)

A SONG

from "Fatal Curiosity"

Cease, cease, heart-easing tears!
Adieu, you flatt'ring fears,
Which seven long tedious years
    Taught me to bear.
Tears are for lighter woes;
Fear no such danger knows,
As fate remorseless shows,
    Endless despair!
Dear cause of all my pain,
On the wide stormy main,
Thou wast preserv'd in vain,
    Though still ador'd.
Hadst thou dy'd there unseen,
My wounded eyes had been
Sav'd from the direst scene
    Maid e'er deplor'd.

ROBERT CRAWFORD (1695?-1733)

THE BUSH ABOON TRAQUAIR

Hear me, ye nymphs, and every swain,
    I'll tell how Peggy grieves me;
Though thus I languish and complain,
    Alas! she ne'er believes me.
My vows and sighs, like silent air,
    Unheeded, never move her;
At the bonny Bush aboon Traquair,
    'Twas there I first did love her.

That day she smiled and made me glad,
    No maid seemed ever kinder;
I thought myself the luckiest lad,
    So sweetly there to find her;
I tried to soothe my amorous flame,
    In words that I thought tender;
If more there passed, I'm not to blame—
    I meant not to offend her.

Yet now she scornful flees the plain,
    The fields we then frequented;
If e'er we meet she shews disdain,
    She looks as ne'er acquainted.
The bonny bush bloomed fair in May,
    Its sweets I'll aye remember;
But now her frowns make it decay—
    It fades as in December.

Ye rural powers, who hear my strains,
    Why thus should Peggy grieve me?
O make her partner in my pains,
    Then let her smiles relieve me:
If not, my love will turn despair,
    My passion no more tender;
I'll leave the Bush aboon Traquair—
    To lonely wilds I'll wander.

TWEEDSIDE

What beauties does Flora disclose!
    How sweet are her smiles upon Tweed!

Yet Mary's, still sweeter than those,
　　Both nature and fancy exceed.
No daisy, nor sweet blushing rose,
　　Not all the gay flowers of the field,
Not Tweed, gliding gently through those,
　　Such beauty and pleasure does yield.

The warblers are heard in the grove,
　　The linnet, the lark, and the thrush;
The blackbird, and sweet cooing dove,
　　With music enchant every bush.
Come, let us go forth to the mead;
　　Let us see how the primroses spring;
We'll lodge in some village on Tweed,
　　And love while the feathered folk sing.

How does my love pass the long day?
　　Does Mary not tend a few sheep?
Do they never carelessly stray
　　While happily she lies asleep?
Should Tweed's murmurs lull her to rest,
　　Kind nature indulging my bliss,
To ease the soft pains of my breast,
　　I'd steal an ambrosial kiss.

'Tis she does the virgins excel;
　　No beauty with her may compare;
Love's graces around her do dwell;
　　She's fairest where thousands are fair.
Say, charmer, where do thy flocks stray?
　　Oh, tell me at morn where they feed?
Shall I seek them on sweet-winding Tay?
　　Or the pleasanter banks of the Tweed?

MATTHEW GREEN (1696-1737)

from THE SPLEEN

Thus, thus I steer my bark, and sail
On even keel with gentle gale,
At helm I make my reason sit,
My crew of passions all submit.
If dark and blust'ring prove some nights,
Philosophy puts forth her lights,
Experience holds the cautious glass,
To shun the breakers, as I pass,
And frequent throws the wary lead,
To see what dangers may be hid:
And once in seven years I'm seen
At Bath, or Tunbridge to careen;
Though pleas'd to see the dolphins play,
I mind my compass and my way,
With store sufficient for relief,
And wisely still prepar'd to reef,
Nor wanting the dispersive bowl
Of cloudy weather in the soul,
I make (may Heav'n propitious send
Such wind and weather to the end)
Neither becalm'd, nor overblown,
Life's voyage to the world unknown.

WILLIAM OLDYS (1696-1761)

SONG

Occasioned by a Fly Drinking Out of a Cup of Ale

Busy, curious, thirsty fly,
Drink with me, and drink as I;
Freely welcome to my cup,
Couldst thou sip and sip it up.
Make the most of life you may—
Life is short, and wears away.

Both alike are mine and thine,
Hastening quick to their decline:
Thine's a summer, mine no more,
Though repeated to threescore;
Threescore summers, when they're gone,
Will appear as short as one.

RICHARD SAVAGE (1698?-1743)

TO A YOUNG LADY

Polly, from me, tho' now a love-sick youth,
Nay, tho' a poet, hear the voice of truth!
Polly, you're not a beauty, yet you're pretty;
So grave, yet gay; so silly, yet so witty;
A heart of softness, yet a tongue of satire;
You've cruelty, yet, ev'n in that, good-nature:
Now you are free, and now reserv'd a while;
Now a forc'd frown betrays a willing smile.
Reproach'd for absence, yet your sight deny'd;
My tongue you silence, yet my silence chide.
How wou'd you praise me, shou'd your sex defame!
Yet, shou'd they praise, grow jealous, and exclaim.
If I despair, with some kind look you bless;
But if I hope, at once all hope suppress.
You scorn; yet shou'd my passion change or fail,
Too late you'd whimper out a softer tale.
You love; yet from your lover's wish retire;
Doubt, yet discern; deny, and yet desire,
Such, Polly, are your sex——part truth, part fiction,
Some thought, much whim, and all a contradiction.

ALEXANDER ROSS (1698-1784)

WOO'D, AND MARRIED, AND A'

The bride cam out o' the byre,
    And, oh, as she dighted her cheeks:
"Sirs, I'm to be married the night,
    And have neither blankets nor sheets;
Have neither blankets nor sheets,
    Nor scarce a coverlet too;
The bride that has a' thing to borrow,
    Has e'en right muckle ado."
      Woo'd, and married, and a',
        Married, and woo'd, and a'!
    And was she nae very weel off,
      That was woo'd, and married, and a'?

Out spake the bride's father,
    As he cam in frae the pleugh:
"Oh, haud your tongue, my dochter,
    And ye 'se get gear eneugh;
The stirk stands i' the tether,
    And our braw bawsint yaud,
Will carry ye hame your corn——
What wad ye be at, ye jaud?"

Out spake the bride's mither:
    "What deil needs a' this pride?
I had nae a plack in my pouch
    That night I was a bride;
My gown was linsey-woolsey,
    And ne'er a sark ava;
And ye hae ribbons and buskins,
    Mae than ane or twa." ...

Out spake the bride's brither,
    As he cam in wi' the kye:
"Poor Willie wad ne'er hae ta'en ye,
    Had he kent ye as weel as I;
For ye're baith proud and saucy,
    And no for a poor man's wife;
Gin I canna get a better,
    I'se ne'er tak ane i' my life."

Out spake the bride's sister,
    As she cam in frae the byre:

"O gin I were but married,
    It's a' that I desire;
But we poor folk maun live single,
    And do the best that we can;
I dinna care what I should want,
    If I could get but a man."

THE ROCK AN' THE WEE PICKLE TOW

There was an auld wife had a wee pickle tow,
    And she wad gae try the spinnin' o't;
But lootin' her doun, her rock took a-lowe,
    And that was an ill beginnin' o't.
She spat on't, she flat on't, and tramped on its pate,
But a' she could do it wad ha'e its ain gate;
At last she sat down on't and bitterly grat,
    For e'er ha'in' tried the spinnin' o't.

Foul fa' them that ever advised me to spin,
    It minds me o' the beginnin' o't;
I weel might ha'e ended as I had begun,
    And never ha'e tried the spinnin' o't.
But she's a wise wife wha kens her ain weird,
I thought ance a day it wad never be spier'd,
How let ye the lowe tak' the rock by the beard,
    When ye gaed to try the spinnin' o't?

The spinnin', the spinnin', it gars my heart sab
    To think on the ill beginnin' o't;
I took 't in my head to mak' me a wab,
    And that was the first beginnin' o't.
But had I nine daughters, as I ha'e but three,
The safest and soundest advice I wad gi'e,
That they wad frae spinnin' aye keep their heads free,
    For fear o' an ill beginnin' o't.

But if they, in spite o' my counsel, wad run
    The dreary, sad task o' the spinnin' o't;
Let them find a lown seat by the light o' the sun,
    And syne venture on the beginnin' o't.
For wha's done as I've done, alake and awowe!
To busk up a rock at the cheek o' a lowe;
They'll say that I had little wit in my pow——
    O the muckle black deil tak' the spinnin' o't.

93

JOHN DYER (1699?-1758)

GRONGAR HILL

Silent Nymph, with curious eye!
Who, the purple ev'ning, lie
On the mountain's lonely van,
Beyond the noise of busy man,
Painting fair the form of things,
While the yellow linet sings;
Or the tuneful nightingale
Charms the forest with her tale;
Come with all thy various hues,
Come, and aid thy sister Muse;
Now while Phoebus riding high
Gives lustre to the land and sky!
Grongar Hill invites my song,
Draw the landskip bright and strong;
Grongar, in whose mossy cells
Sweetly-musing Quiet dwells;
Grongar, in whose silent shade,
For the modest Muses made,
So oft I have, the evening still,
At the fountain of a rill,
Sate upon a flow'ry bed,
With my hand beneath my head;
While stray'd my eyes o'er Towy's flood,
Over mead, and over wood,
From house to house, from hill to hill,
'Till Contemplation had her fill.
   About his chequer'd sides I wind,
And leave his brooks and meads behind,
And groves, and grottoes where I lay,
And vistoes shooting beams of day:
Wide and wider spreads the vale;
As circles on a smooth canal:
The mountains round, unhappy fate!
Sooner or later, of all height,
Withdraw their summits from the skies,
And lessen as the others rise:
Still the prospect wider spreads,
Adds a thousand woods and meads,
Still it widens, widens still,
And sinks the newly-risen hill.
   Now, I gain the mountain's brow,
What a landskip lies below!

94

No clouds, no vapours intervene
But the gay, the open scene
Does the face of nature show,
In all the hues of heaven's bow!
And, swelling to embrace the light,
Spreads around beneath the sight.
   Old castles on the cliffs arise,
Proudly tow'ring in the skies!
Rushing from the woods, the spires
Seem from hence ascending fires!
Half his beams Apollo sheds
On the yellow mountain-heads!
Gilds the fleeces of the flocks:
And glitters on the broken rocks!
   Below me trees unnumber'd rise,
Beautiful in various dyes:
The gloomy pine, the poplar blue,
The yellow beech, the sable yew,
The slender fir, that taper grows,
The sturdy oak with broad-spread boughs.
And beyond the purple grove,
Haunt of Phillis, queen of love!
Gaudy as the op'ning dawn,
Lies a long and level lawn
On which a dark hill, steep and high,
Holds and charms the wand'ring eye!
Deep are his feet in Towy's flood,
His sides are cloath'd with waving wood,
And ancient towers crown his brow,
That cast an aweful look below;
Whose ragged walls the ivy creeps,
And with her arms from falling keeps;
So both a safety from the wind
On mutual dependence find.
   'Tis now the raven's bleak abode;
'Tis now th' apartment of the toad;
And there the fox securely feeds;
And there the pois'nous adder breeds
Conceal'd in ruins, moss and weeds;
While, ever and anon, there falls
Huge heaps of hoary moulder'd walls.
Yet time has seen, that lifts the low,
And level lays the lofty brow,
Has seen this broken pile compleat,
Big with the vanity of state;
But transient is the smile of fate!
A little rule, a little sway,
A sun beam in a winter's day,

Is all the proud and mighty have
Between the cradle and the grave.
And see the rivers how they run,
Thro' woods and meads, in shade and sun,
Sometimes swift, sometimes slow,
Wave succeeding wave, they go
A various journey to the deep,
Like human life to endless sleep!
Thus is nature's vesture wrought,
To instruct our wand'ring thought;
Thus she dresses green and gay,
To disperse our cares away.
Ever charming, ever new,
When will the landskip tire the view!
The fountain's fall, the river's flow,
The woody vallies, warm and low;
The windy summit, wild and high,
Roughly rushing on the sky!
The pleasant seat, the ruin'd tow'r,
The naked rock, the shady bow'r;
The town and village, dome and farm,
Each give each a double charm,
As pearls upon an Ethiop's arm.
See on the mountain's southern side,
Where the prospect opens wide,
Where the evening gilds the tide;
How close and small the hedges lie!
What streaks of meadows cross the eye!
A step methinks may pass the stream,
So little distant dangers seem;
So we mistake the future's face,
Ey'd thro' hope's deluding glass;
As yon summits soft and fair
Clad in colours of the air,
Which to those who journey near,
Barren, brown, and rough appear;
Still we tread the same coarse way,
The present's still a cloudy day.
O may I with myself agree,
And never covet what I see:
Content me with an humble shade,
My passions tam'd, my wishes laid;
For while our wishes wildly roll,
We banish quiet from the soul:
'Tis thus the busy beat the air,
And misers gather wealth and care.
Now, ev'n now, my joys run high,
As on the mountain-turf I lie;

While the wanton Zephyr sings,
And in the vale perfumes his wings;
While the waters murmur deep;
While the shepherd charms his sheep;
While the birds unbounded fly,
And with musick fill the sky,
Now, ev'n now, my joys run high.
  Be full, ye courts, be great who will;
Search for Peace with all your skill:
Open wide the lofty door,
Seek her on the marble floor,
In vain you search, she is not there;
In vain ye search the domes of care!
Grass and flowers Quiet treads,
On the meads, and mountain-heads,
Along with Pleasure, close ally'd,
Every by each other's side:
And often, by the murm'ring rill,
Hears the thrush, while all is still,
Within the groves of Grongar Hill.

AN EPISTLE TO A FRIEND IN TOWN

Have my friends in the town, in the gay busy town,
    Forgot such a man as John Dyer?
Or heedless despise they, or pity the clown,
    Whose bosom no pageantries fire?

No matter, no matter——content in the shades——
    (Contented?——why every thing charms me)
Fall in tunes all adown the green steep, ye cascades,
    Till hence rigid Virtue alarms me.

Till Outrage arises, or Misery needs
    The swift, the intrepid avenger;
Till sacred Religion or Liberty bleeds,
    Then mine be the deed and the danger.

Alas! what a folly, that wealth and domain
    We heap up in sin and in sorrow!
Immense is the toil, yet the labour how vain!
    Is not life to be over tomorrow?

Then glide on my moments, the few that I have,
    Smooth-shaded, and quiet, and even;
While gently the body descends to the grave,
    And the spirit arises to Heaven.

97

CHRISTOPHER PITT (1699-1748)

ODE ON A SHADOW

How are deluded human kind
    By empty shows betray'd?
In all their hopes and schemes they find
    A nothing or a shade.

The prospects of a truncheon cast
    The soldier on the wars;
Dismist with shatter'd limbs at last,
    Brats, poverty, and scars.

The fond philosophers for gain
    Will leave unturn'd no stone;
But though they toil with endless pain,
    They never find their own.

By the same rock the chymists drown,
    And find no friendly hold,
But melt their ready specie down,
    In hopes of fancy'd gold.

What is the mad projector's care?
    In hopes elate and swelling,
He builds his castles in the air,
    Yet wants an house to dwell in.

At court the poor dependants fail,
    And damn their fruitless toil,
When complimented thence to jail,
    And ruin'd with a smile.

How to philosophers will sound
    So strange a truth display'd?
"There's not a substance to be found,
    But every where a shade."

VERSES ON A FLOWERED CARPET

On this fair ground, with ravish'd eyes,
We see a second Eden rise,
As gay and glorious as the first,

Before th' offending world was curst.
While these bright nymphs the needle guide,
To paint the rose in all her pride,
Nature, like her, may blush to own
Herself so far by Art out-done.
These flowers she rais'd with all her care,
So blooming, so divinely fair!
The glorious children of the Sun,
That David's regal heir out-shone,
Were scarce like one of these array'd;
They died, but these shall never fade.

BENJAMIN STILLINGFLEET (1702-1771)

A SONNET

When I behold thee, blameless Williamson,
　　Wreck'd like an infant on a savage shore,
　　While others round on borrow'd pinions soar,
My busy fancy calls thy thread misspun;
Till Faith instructs me the deceit to shun,
　　While thus she speaks: "Those wings that from the store
　　Of virtue were not lent, howe'er they bore
In this gross air, will melt when near the sun.
The truly ambitious wait for Nature's time,
　　Content by certain though by slow degrees
　　　　To mount above the reach of vulgar flight:
Nor is that man confin'd to this low clime,
　　Who but the extremest skirts of glory sees,
　　　　And hears celestial echoes with delight."

ROBERT DODSLEY (1703-1764)

THE KINGS OF EUROPE

A Jest

Why pray, of late, do Europe's kings
   No jester in their courts admit?
They're grown such stately solemn things,
   To bear a joke they think not fit.

But tho' each court a jester lacks,
   To laugh at monarchs to their face:
All mankind behind their backs
   Supply the honest jester's place.

AN EPIGRAM

Cries Sylvia to a reverend dean,
   "What reason can be given,
Since marriage is a holy thing,
   That there are none in Heaven?"

"There are no women," he reply'd;
   She quick returns the jest—
"Women there are, but I'm afraid
   They cannot find a priest."

A SONG

Man's a poor deluded bubble,
   Wand'ring in a mist of lies,
Seeing false, or seeing double,
   Who wou'd trust to such weak eyes?
Yet presuming on his senses,
   On he goes most wond'rous wise;
Doubts of truth, believes pretences;
   Lost in error, lives and dies.

KITTY

A Pastoral

Beneath a cool shade, by the side of a stream,
Thus breath'd a fond shepherd, his Kitty his theme:
"Thy beauties comparing, my dearest," said he,
"There's nothing in Nature so lovely as thee.

"Tho' distance divides us, I view thy dear face,
And wander in transport o'er every grace;
Now, now I behold thee, sweet-smiling and pretty,
O gods! you've made nothing so fair as my Kitty!

"Come, lovely idea, come fill my fond arms,
And whilst in soft rapture I gaze on thy charms,
The beautiful objects which round me arise,
Shall yield to those beauties that live in thine eyes.

"Now Flora the meads and the groves does adorn,
With flowers and blossoms on every thorn;
But look on my Kitty! ——there sweetly does blow,
A spring of more beauties than Flora can show.

"See, see how that rose there adorns the gay bush,
And proud of its color, would view with her blush.
Vain boaster! thy beauties shall quickly decay,
She blushes——and see how it withers away.

"Observe that fair lily, the pride of the vale,
In whiteness unrivall'd, now droop and look pale;
It sickens, and changes its beautiful hue,
And bows down its head in submission to you.

"The Zephyrs that fan me beneath the cool shade,
When panting with heat on the ground I am laid,
Are less grateful and sweet than the heavenly air
That breathes from her lips when she whispers——"My dear."

"I hear the gay lark, as she mounts in the skies,
How sweet are her notes! how delightful her voice!
Go dwell in the air, little warbler, go!
I have music enough while my Kitty's below.

"With pleasure I watch the industrious bee,
Extracting her sweets from each flower and tree;

102

Ah fools! thus to labour, to keep you alive;
Fly, fly to her lips, and at once fill your hive.

"See there, on the top of that oak, how the doves
Sit brooding each other, and cooing their loves:
Our loves are thus tender, thus mutual our joy,
When folded on each other's bosom we lie.

"It glads me to see how the pretty young lambs
Are fondled and cherish'd, and lov'd by their dams:
The lambs are less pretty, my dearest, than thee;
Their dams are less fond, nor so tender as me.

"As I gaze on the river that smoothly glides by,
Thus even and sweet is her temper, I cry;
Thus clear is her mind, thus calm and serene,
And virtues, like gems, at the bottom are seen.

"Here various flowers still paint the gay scene,
And as some fade and die, others bud and look green;
The charms of my Kitty are constant as they;
Her virtues will bloom as her beauties decay.

"But in vain I compare her, here's nothing so bright,
And darkness approaches to hinder my sight:
To bed I will hasten, and there all her charms,
In softer ideas, I'll bring to my arms."

ON THE DEATH OF MR. POPE

Come, ye whose souls harmonious sounds inspire,
    Friends to the Muse, and judges of her song;
Who, catching from the bard his heavenly fire,
    Soar as he soars, sublimely rapt along;
Mourn, mourn your loss: he's gone who had the art,
With sounds to soothe the ear, with sense to warm the heart.

Who now shall dare to lift the sacred rod,
    Truth's faithful guard, where vice escapes the law?
Who now, high-soaring to the throne of God,
    In Nature's moral cause his pen shall draw?
Let none pretend! he's gone, who had the art,
With sounds to soothe the ear, with sense to warm the heart.

Vice now, secure, her blushless front shall raise,
    And all her triumph be thro' Britain borne;

103

Whose worthless sons from guilt shall purchase praise,
    Nor dread the hand that pointed them to scorn;
No check remains; he's gone, who had the art,
    With sounds to soothe the ear, with sense to warm the heart.

Ye tuneless bards, now tire each venal quill,
    And from the public gather idle pence;
Ye tasteless peers, now build and plant your fill,
    Tho' splendor borrows not one ray from sense:
Fear no rebuke; he's gone, who had the art,
    With sounds to soothe the ear, with sense to warm the heart.

But, come, ye chosen, ye selected few,
    Ye next in genius, as in friendship, join'd,
The social virtues of his heart who knew,
    And tasted all the beauties of his mind;
Drop, drop a tear; he's gone, who had the art,
    With sounds to soothe the ear, with sense to warm the heart.

And, O great shade! permit thy humblest friend
    His sigh to waft, his grateful tear to pay
Thy honour'd memory; and condescend
    To hear, well-pleas'd, the weak yet well-meant lay,
Lamenting thus; he's gone, who had the art,
    With sounds to soothe the ear, with sense to warm the heart.

104

GILBERT WEST (1703-1756)

FATHER FRANCIS' PRAYER

Written in Lord Westmorland's Hermitage

Ne gay attire, ne marble hall,
Ne arched roof, ne pictur'd wall;
Ne cook of Fraunce, ne dainty board
Bestow'd with pyes of Perigord;
Ne power, ne such like idle fancies,
Sweet Agnes, grant to Father Francis:
Let me ne more myself deceive;
Ne more regret the toys I leave:
The world I quit, the proud, the vain,
Corruption's and Ambition's train;
But not the good, perdie, nor fair,
'Gainst them I make ne vow, ne prayer;
But such aye welcome to my cell,
And oft, not always, with me dwell;
Then cast, sweet saint, a circle round,
And bless from fools this holy ground;
From all the foes to worth and truth,
From wanton old, and homely youth;
The gravely dull, and pertly gay,
Oh banish these; and, by my fay,
Right well I ween that in this age,
Mine house shall prove an hermitage.

SOAME JENYNS (1704-1787)

TO A YOUNG LADY, GOING TO THE WEST INDIES

For universal sway design'd,
    To distant realms Clorinda flies,
And scorns, in one small isle confin'd,
    To bound the conquests of her eyes.

From our cold climes to India's shore
    With cruel haste she wings her way,
To scorch their sultry plains still more,
    And rob us of our only day.

Whilst ev'ry streaming eye o'erflows
    With tender floods of parting tears,
Thy breast, dear cause of all our woes,
    Alone unmov'd and gay appears.

But still, if right the Muses tell,
    The fated point of time is nigh,
When grief shall that fair bosom swell,
    And trickle from thy lovely eye.

Though now, like Philip's son, whose arms
    Did once the vassal world command,
You rove with unresisted charms,
    And conquer both by sea and land;

Yet when (as soon they must) mankind
    Shall all be doom'd to wear your chain,
You too, like him, will weep to find
    No more unconquer'd worlds remain.

EPITAPH ON DR. SAMUEL JOHNSON

Here lies Sam Johnson:——Reader, have a care,
Tread lightly, lest you wake a sleeping bear:
Religious, moral, generous, and humane
He was; but self-sufficient, proud, and vain,
Fond of, and overbearing in dispute,
A Christian, and a scholar——but a brute.

106

ON SEEING THE EARL OF CHESTERFIELD AT A BALL
AT BATH

1770

In times of selfishness and faction sour'd,
When dull importance has all wit devour'd;
When rank, as if t' insult alone design'd,
Affects a proud seclusion from mankind;
And greatness, to all social converse dead,
Esteems it dignity to be ill-bred:—
See! Chesterfield alone resists the tide,
Above all party, and above all pride,
Vouchsafes each night these brilliant scenes to grace,
Augments and shares th' amusements of the place;
Admires the fair, enjoys the sprightly ball,
Deigns to be pleas'd, and therefore pleases all.
Hence, though unable now this style to hit,
Learn what was once politeness, ease, and wit.

WILLIAM HAMILTON, OF BANGOUR (1704-1754)

ON A SUMMER-HOUSE IN MY OWN GARDEN

Whilst round my head the zephyrs gently play,
To calm reflection I resign the day;
From all the servitudes of life releast,
I bid mild Friendship to the sober feast,
Nor Beauty banish from the hallow'd ground,
She enters here to solace, not to wound;
All else excluded from the sacred spot,
One half detested, and one half forgot:
All the mad human tumult, what to me?
Here, chaste Calliope, I live with thee.

ON A DOG

Calm though not mean, courageous without rage,
Serious not dull, and without thinking sage;
Pleas'd at the lot that Nature has assign'd,
Snarl as I list, and freely bark my mind;
As churchman wrangle not with jarring spite,
Nor statesman-like caressing whom I bite;
View all the canine kind with equal eyes,
I dread no mastiff, and no cur despise:
True from the first, and faithful to the end,
I balk no mistress, and forsake no friend.
My days and nights one equal tenour keep,
Fast but to eat, and only wake to sleep:
Thus stealing along life I live incog,
A very plain and downright honest dog.

THE BRAES OF YARROW

A. Busk ye, busk ye, my bony bony bride,
    Busk ye, busk ye, my winsome marrow,
    Busk ye, busk ye, my bony bony bride,
    And think nae mair on the Braes of Yarrow.

B. Where gat ye that bony bony bride?
    Where gat ye that winsome marrow?
A. I gat her where I dare na weil be seen,
    Puing the birks on the Braes of Yarrow.

Weep not, weep not, my bony bony bride,
  Weep not, weep not, my winsome marrow,
Nor let thy heart lament to leave
  Puing the birks on the Braes of Yarrow.

B. Why does she weep, thy bony bony bride?
  Why does she weep, thy winsome marrow?
And why dare ye nae mair weil be seen
  Puing the birks on the Braes of Yarrow?

A. Lang maun she weep, lang maun she, maun she weep,
  Lang maun she weep with dule and sorrow,
And lang maun I nae mair weil be seen
  Puing the birks on the Braes of Yarrow.

For she has tint her luver luver dear,
  Her luver dear, the cause of sorrow,
And I hae slain the comliest swain
  That e'er pu'd birks on the Braes of Yarrow.

Why runs thy stream, O Yarrow, Yarrow red?
  Why on thy braes heard the voice of sorrow?
And why yon melancholeous weids
  Hung on the bony birks of Yarrow!

What yonder floats on the rueful rueful flude?
  What's yonder floats? O dule and sorrow!
'Tis he the comely swain I slew
  Upon the duleful Braes of Yarrow.

Wash, O wash his wounds his wounds in tears,
  His wounds in tears, with dule and sorrow,
And wrap his limbs in mourning weids,
  And lay him on the Braes of Yarrow.

Then build, then build, ye sisters sisters sad,
  Ye sisters sad, his tomb with sorrow,
And weep around in waeful wise,
  His helpless fate on the Braes of Yarrow.

Curse ye, curse ye, his useless useless shield,
  My arm that wrought the deed of sorrow,
The fatal spear that pierc'd his breast,
  His comely breast on the Braes of Yarrow.

Did I not warn thee not to, not to lue,
  And warn from fight, but to my sorrow,

109

O'er rashly bald a stronger arm
Thou met'st, and fell on the Braes of Yarrow.

Sweet smells the birk, green grows, green grows the
    grass,
  Yellow on Yarrow's bank the gowan,
Fair hangs the apple frae the rock,
  Sweet the wave of Yarrow flowan.

Flows Yarrow sweet? as sweet, as sweet flows Tweed,
  As green its grass, its gowan yellow,
As sweet smells on its braes the birk,
  The apple frae the rock as mellow.

Fair was thy luve, fair fair indeed thy luve,
  In floury bands thou him did'st fetter,
Tho' he was fair and weil beluv'd again,
  Than me, he never lued thee better.

Busk ye, then busk, my bony bony bride,
  Busk ye, busk ye, my winsome marrow,
Busk ye, and lue me on the banks of Tweed,
  And think nae mair on the Braes of Yarrow.

C. How can I busk a bony bony bride,
      How can I busk a winsome marrow,
    How lue him on the banks of Tweed,
      That slew my luve on the Braes of Yarrow?

  O Yarrow fields, may never never rain,
    No dew thy tender blossoms cover,
  For there was basely slain my luve,
    My luve, as he had not been a lover.

  The boy put on his robes, his robes of green,
    His purple vest, 'twas my awn seuing,
  Ah! wretched me! I little little ken'd
    He was in these to meet his ruin.

  The boy took out his milk-white milk-white steed,
    Unheedful of my dule and sorrow,
  But e'er the toofall of the night
    He lay a corps on the Braes of Yarrow.

  Much I rejoic'd that waeful waeful day;
    I sang, my voice the woods returning,
  But lang e'er night the spear was flown
    That slew my luve, and left me mourning.

110

What can my barbarous barbarous father do,
    But with his cruel rage pursue me?
My luver's blood is on thy spear,
    How can'st thou, barbarous man, then woo me?

My happy sisters may be may be proud,
    With cruel, and ungentle scoffin,
May bid me seek on Yarrow Braes
    My luver nailed in his coffin.

My brother Douglas may upbraid,
    And strive with threatning words to muve me,
My luver's blood is on thy spear,
    How can'st thou ever bid me luve thee?

Yes yes, prepare the bed, the bed of luve,
    With bridal sheets my body cover,
Unbar ye bridal maids the door,
    Let in the expected husband lover.

But who the expected husband husband is?
    His hands, methinks, are bath'd in slaughter,
Ah me! what ghastly spectre's yon,
    Comes, in his pale shroud, bleeding after.

Pale as he is, here lay him lay him down,
    O lay his cold head on my pillow;
Take aff take aff these bridal weids,
    And crown my careful head with willow.

Pale tho' thou art, yet best yet best beluv'd,
    O could my warmth to life restore thee,
Yet lye all night between my briests,
    No youth lay ever there before thee.

Pale pale indeed, O lovely lovely youth,
    Forgive, forgive so foul a slaughter,
And lye all night between my briests,
    No youth shall ever lye there after.

A. Return return, O mournful mournful bride,
    Return and dry thy useless sorrow,
Thy luver heeds nought of thy sighs,
    He lyes a corps on the Braes of Yarrow.

DAVID MALLET (1705?-1765)

A WINTER'S DAY

(Written in a State of Melancholy)

Now, gloomy soul! look out——now comes thy turn;
With thee, behold all ravag'd nature mourn.
Hail the dim empire of thy darling night,
That spreads, slow-shadowing, o'er the vanquish'd light.
Look out, with joy; the ruler of the day,
Faint, as thy hopes, emits a glimmering ray:
Already exil'd to the utmost sky,
Hither, oblique, he turn'd his clouded eye;
Lo! from the limits of the wintery pole,
Mountainous clouds, in rude confusion, roll:
In dismal pomp, now, hovering on their way,
To a sick twilight, they reduce the day.
And hark! imprison'd winds, broke loose, arise,
And roar their haughty triumph through the skies.
While the driven clouds, o'ercharg'd with floods of rain,
And mingled lightning, burst upon the plain.
Now see sad Earth——like thine, her alter'd state,
Like thee, she mourns her sad reverse of Fate!
Her smile, her wanton looks——where are they now?
Faded her face, and wrapt in clouds her brow!
    No more, th' ungrateful verdure of the plain;
No more, the wealth-crown'd labours of the swain;
These scenes of bliss, no more upbraid my fate,
Torture my pining thought, and rouze my hate.
The leaf-clad forest, and the tufted grove,
Erewhile the safe retreats of happy love,
Stript of their honours, naked, now appear;
This is——my soul! the winter of their year!
The little, noisy songsters of the wing,
All, shivering on the bough, forget to sing.
Hail! reverend Silence! with thy awful brow!
Be Music's voice, for ever mute——as now:
Let no intrusive joy my dead repose
Disturb: no pleasure disconcert my woes.
    In this moss-cover'd cavern, hopeless laid,
On the cold cliff, I'll lean my aching head;
And, pleas'd with Winter's waste, unpitying, see
All nature in an agony with me!
Rough, rugged rocks, wet marshes, ruin'd towers,
Bare trees, brown brakes, bleak heaths, and rushy moors,

Dead floods, huge cataracts, to my pleas'd eyes——
(Now I can smile!)——in wild disorder rise:
And now, the various dreadfulness combin'd,
Black Melancholy comes, to doze my mind.
 See! Night's wish'd shades rise, spreading through the air,
And the lone, hollow gloom, for me prepare!
Hail! solitary ruler of the grave!
Parent of terrours! from thy dreary cave!
Let thy dumb silence midnight all the ground,
And spread a welcome horrour wide around.
But hark! a sudden howl invades my ear!
The phantoms of the dreadful hour are near.
Shadows, from each dark cavern, now combine,
And stalk around, and mix their yells with mine.
 Stop, flying Time! repose thy restless wing;
Fix here——nor hasten to restore the spring:
Fix'd my ill fate, so fix'd let winter be——
Let never wanton season laugh at me!

A SONG

The smiling Morn, the breathing Spring,
Invite the tuneful Birds to sing:
And while they warble from each Spray,
Love melts the universal Lay.
Let us, Amanda, timely wise,
Like them improve the Hour that flies;
And in soft Raptures waste the Day,
Among the Birks of Endermay.

For soon the Winter of the Year,
And Age, Life's Winter, will appear:
At this, thy living Bloom will fade;
As that will strip the verdant Shade.
Our Taste of Pleasure then is o'er;
The feather'd Songsters love no more:
And when they droop, and we decay,
Adieu the Birks of Endermay.

A SONG

Where Thames, along the daisy'd meads,
His wave, in lucid mazes, leads,
Silent, slow, serenely flowing,
Wealth on either shore bestowing:

113

There, in a safe, though small retreat,
Content and Love have fix'd their seat:
Love, that counts his duty, pleasure;
Content, that knows and hugs his treasure.
From art, from jealousy secure;
As faith unblam'd, as friendship pure;
Vain opinion nobly scorning.
Virtue aiding, life adorning.
Fair Thames, along thy flow'ry side,
May those whom truth and reason guide,
All their tender hours improving,
Live like us, belov'd and loving!

ON AN AMOROUS OLD MAN

Still hovering round the fair at sixty-four,
Unfit to love, unable to give o'er;
A flesh-fly, that just flutters on the wing,
Awake to buz, but not alive to sting;
Brisk where he cannot, backward where he can;
The teazing ghost of the departed man.

WILLIAM AND MARGARET

'Twas at the silent, solemn hour,
    When night and morning meet;
In glided MARGARET's grimly ghost,
    And stood at WILLIAM's feet.

Her face was like an April morn,
    Clad in a wintry cloud:
And clay-cold was her lilly hand,
    That held her sable shroud.

So shall the fairest face appear,
    When youth and years are flown:
Such is the robe that kings must wear,
    When death has reft their crown.

Her bloom was like the springing flower,
    That sips the silver dew;
The rose was budded in her cheek,
    Just opening to the view.

114

But Love had, like the canker-worm,
    Consum'd her early prime:
The rose grew pale, and left her cheek;
    She dy'd before her time.

Aware! she cry'd, thy True Love calls,
    Come from her midnight grave;
Now let thy Pity hear the maid,
    Thy Love refus'd to save.

This is the dumb and dreary hour,
    When injur'd ghosts complain;
When yauning graves give up their dead
    To haunt the faithless swain.

Bethink thee, WILLIAM, of thy fault,
    Thy pledge, and broken oath:
And give me back my maiden vow,
    And give me back my troth.

Why did you promise love to me,
    And not that promise keep?
Why did you swear my eyes were bright,
    Yet leave those eyes to weep?

How could you say my face was fair,
    And yet that face forsake?
How could you win my virgin heart,
    Yet leave that heart to break?

Why did you say, my lip was sweet,
    And made the scarlet pale?
And why did I, young, witless maid!
    Believe the flattering tale?

That face, alas! no more is fair;
    Those lips no longer red:
Dark are my eyes, now clos'd in death,
    And every charm is fled.

The hungry worm my sister is;
    This winding-sheet I wear:
And cold and weary lasts our night,
    Till that last morn appear.

But hark! ——the cock has warn'd me hence;
    A long and late adieu!
Come, see, false man, how low she lies,

115

Who dy'd for love of you.

The lark sung loud; the morning smil'd,
    And rais'd her glistering head:
Pale WILLIAM quak'd in every limb,
    And raving left his bed.

He hy'd him to the fatal place
    Where MARGARET's body lay:
And stretch'd him on the grass-green turf,
    That wrap'd her breathless clay.

And thrice he call'd on MARGARET's name,
    And thrice he wept full sore:
Then laid his cheek to her cold grave,
    And word spake never more.

NATHANIEL COTTON (1705-1788)

THE SNAIL AND THE GARDENER

A Fable

When sons of fortune ride on high,
How do we point the admiring eye!
With foolish face of wonder gaze,
And often covet what we praise.
How do we partial Nature chide,
As deaf to every son beside!
Or censure the mistaken dame,
As if her optics were to blame!
Thus we deem Nature most unkind,
Or what's as bad, we deem her blind.
　　But when inferior ranks we see,
Who move in humbler spheres than we;
Men by comparisons are taught,
Nature is not so much in fault.
Yet mark my tale——the poet's pen
Shall vindicate her ways to men.
　　Within a garden, far from town,
There dwelt a snail of high renown;
Who, by tradition as appears,
Had been a tenant several years.
She spent her youth in wisdom's page——
Hence honour'd and rever'd in age.
Do snails at any time contend,
Insult a neighbour, or a friend;
Dispute their property, and share,
Or in a cherry, or a pear?
No lord chief justice, all agree,
So able, and so just as she!
Whichever way their causes went,
All parties came away content.
At length she found herself decay,
Death sent mementos every day.
Her drooping strength sustains no more
The shell, which on her back she bore.
The eye had lost its visual art,
The heavy ear refus'd its part;
The teeth perform'd their office ill,
And every member fail'd her will.
But no defects in mind appear,

117

Her intellects are strong and clear.
Thus when his glorious course is run,
How brightly shines the setting Sun!
The news thro' all the garden spread,
The neighbours throng'd about her bed;
Cheerful she rais'd her voice aloud,
And thus address'd the weeping crowd.
"My friends, I'm hast'ning to the grave,
And know, nor plum, nor peach can save.
Yes, to those mansions go I must,
Where our good fathers sleep in dust.
Nor am I backward to explore
That gloomy vale they trod before.
'Gainst Fate's decree what can I say?
Like other snails I've had my day.
Full many summer suns I've seen,
And now die grateful and serene.
"If men the higher pow'rs arraign,
Shall we adopt the plaintive strain?
Nature, profuse to us and ours,
Hath kindly built these stately tow'rs;
Where, when the skies in night are drest,
Secure from every ill we rest.
Survey our curious structure well—
How firm, and yet how light our shell!
Our refuge, when cold storms invade,
And in the dog-days' heat our shade.
"Thus when we see a fleeter race,
We'll not lament our languid pace.
Do dangers rise, or foes withstand?
Are not our castles close at hand?
For let a snail at distance roam,
The happy snail is still at home.
"Survey our gardens' blest retreats—
Oh! what a paradise of sweets!
With what variety it's stor'd!
Unnumber'd dainties spread our board.
The plums assume their glossy blue,
And cheeks of nectarines glow for you;
Peaches their lovely blush betray,
And apricots their gold display;
While for your beverage, when you dine,
There streams the nectar of the vine.
"Be not my dying words forgot;
Depart, contented with your lot;
Repress complaints when they begin,
Ingratitude's a crying sin.
And hold it for a truth, that we,

Are quite as blest as snails should be."
The gardener hears with great surprise
This sage discourse, and thus he cries——
"Oh! what a thankless wretch am I,
Who pass ten thousand favours by!
I blame, whene'er the linnet sings,
My want of song, or want of wings,
The piercing hawk, with towering flight,
Reminds me of deficient sight.
And when the generous steed I view,
Is not his strength my envy too?
I thus at birds and beasts repine,
And wish their various talents mine.
Fool as I am, who cannot see
Reason is more than all to me.

"My landlord boasts a large estate,
Rides in his coach, and eats in plate.
What! shall these lures bewitch my eye?
Shall they extort the murmuring sigh?
Say, he enjoys superior wealth——
Is not my better portion, health?
Before the Sun has gilt the skies,
Returning labour bids me rise;
Obedient to the hunter's horn,
He quits his couch at early morn.
By want compell'd, I dig the soil,
His is a voluntary toil.
For truth it is, since Adam's fall,
His sons must labour, one and all.
No man's exempted by his purse,
Kings are included in the curse.
Wou'd monarchs relish what they eat?
'Tis toil that makes the manchet sweet;
Nature enacts, before they're fed,
That prince and peasant earn their bread.

"Hence wisdom and experience show,
That bliss in equal currents flow;
That happiness is still the same,
How'er ingredients change their name.
Nor doth this theme our search defy,
'Tis level to the human eye.
Distinctions, introduc'd by men,
Bewilder, and obscure our ken.
I'll store these lessons in my heart,
And cheerful act my proper part.
If sorrows rise, as sorrows will,
I'll stand resign'd to every ill;

Convinc'd, that wisely every pack
Is suited to the bearer's back."

ON LORD COBHAM'S GARDEN

It puzzles much the sages' brains,
  Where Eden stood of yore,
Some place it in Arabia's plains,
  Some say it is no more.

But Cobham can these tales confute,
  As all the curious know;
For he hath prov'd, beyond dispute,
  That Paradise is Stow.

TO A CHILD OF FIVE YEARS OLD

Fairest flower, all flowers excelling,
  Which in Milton's page we see;
Flowers of Eve's embower'd dwelling
  Are, my fair one, types of thee.

Mark, my Polly, how the roses
  Emulate thy damask cheek;
How the bud its sweets discloses—
  Buds thy opening bloom bespeak.

Lilies are by plain direction
  Emblems of a double kind;
Emblems of thy fair complexion,
  Emblems of thy fairer mind.

But, dear girl, both flowers and beauty
  Blossom, fade, and die away;
Then pursue good sense and duty,
  Evergreens! which ne'er decay.

UPON MISS GEE

Who Died October 25, 1736, Aetat. 28

Beauteous, nor known to pride, to friends sincere,
Mild to thy neighbour, to thyself severe;
Unstain'd thy honour——and thy wit was such,
Knew no extremes, nor little, nor too much.
Few were thy years, and painful thro' the whole,
Yet calm thy passage, and serene thy soul.
  Reader, amidst these sacred crowds that sleep,
View this once lovely form, nor grudge to weep.
O Death, all terrible! how sure thy hour!
How wide thy conquests! and how fell thy pow'r!
When youth, wit, virtue, plead for longer reign,
When youth, when wit, when virtue plead in vain;
Stranger, then weep afresh, for know this clay
Was once the good, the wise, the beautiful, the gay.

ON SLEEP

Mysterious deity, impart
From whence thou com'st, and what thou art.
I feel thy pow'r, thy reign I bless,
But what I feel, I can't express.
Thou bind'st my limbs, but canst n't restrain
The busy workings of the brain.
  All nations of the air and land
Ask the soft blessing at thy hand.
The reptiles of the frozen zone
Are close attendants on thy throne;
Where painted basilisks enfold
Their azure scales in rolls of gold.
  The slave, that's destin'd to the oar,
In one kind vision swims to shore;
The lover meets the willing fair,
And fondly grasps impassive air.
Last night the happy miser told
Twice twenty thousand pounds in gold.
  The purple tenant of the crown
Implores thy aid on beds of down:
While Lubbin, and his healthy bride,
Obtain what monarchs are denied.
  The garter'd statesman thou wouldst own,
But rebel conscience spurns thy throne;

121

Braves all the poppies of the fields,
And the fam'd gum that Turkey yields.
    While the good man, oppress'd with pain,
Shall court thy smiles, nor sue in vain.
Propitious thou'lt his prayer attend,
And prove his guardian and his friend.
Thy faithful hands shall make his bed,
And thy soft arm support his head.

A SONG

Tell me, my Caelia, why so coy,
    Of men so much afraid;
Caelia, 'tis better far to die
    A mother than a maid.

The rose, when past its damask hue,
    Is always out of favour;
And when the plum hath lost its blue,
    It loses too its flavour.

To vernal flow'rs the rolling years
    Returning beauty bring;
But faded once, thou'lt bloom no more,
    Nor know a second spring.

HENRY FOX, LORD HOLLAND (1705-1774)

TO A LADY, WITH AN ARTIFICIAL ROSE

Fair copy of the fairest flower,
Thy colours equal Nature's power;
Thou hast the Rose's blushing hue,
Art full as pleasing to the view:
Go, then, to Chloe's lovely breast,
Whose sweetness can give all the rest.
But if at first thy artful make,
Her hasty judgment should mistake,
And she grow peevish at the cheat,
Urge 'twas an innocent deceit,
And safely too thou may'st aver,
The first I ever us'd to her.
Then bid her mark, that, as to view,
The Rose has nothing more than you;
That so, if to the eye alone
Her wondrous beauty she made known;
That, if she never will dispense
A trial to some sweeter sense;
Nature no longer we prefer,
Her very picture equals her.
Then whisper gently in her ear,
Say, softly, if the blushing fair
Should to such good advice incline,
How much I wish that trial mine.

STEPHEN DUCK (1705-1756)

ON POVERTY

There is no ill on earth which mortals fly
With so much dread as abject poverty.
Strange terrour of mankind! by thee misled,
Not conscience, quicksands, rocks, or death they dread.
And yet thou art no formidable foe,
Except to little souls, who think thee so!

SAMUEL BOYSE (1708-1749)

TO CLARISSA WITH A ROSE-BUD

An Ode

Quam longa una dies, aetas est tam longa rosarum.
— Anonymous

Clarissa, view this newly-nascent rose,
  How sweet its fragrance! but how short the date!
And think distinct the lovely emblem shows
  Thy equal beauty's bloom, its equal fate.

Like that in fair perfection's opening dawn,
  Your roseate charms the ravish'd sense delight;
Pass but a few short years, and then withdrawn,
  They all must fade, conceal'd in endless night!

Yet from the parent-plant's exhausted side,
  See yon fair shoot its lively odours spread!
Rising in early beauty's native pride,
  And softly blushing with maternal red!

Then haste, thou beauteous charmer! to employ
  The treasures which indulgent Nature gave;
Nor longer shun to taste the genial joy,
  Which youth alone can give——alone receive!

So when dark Fate, irrevocably cross,
  Shall snatch you hence to grace the radiant skies;
A self-born beauty may repair your loss,
  A new Clarissa charm succeeding eyes!

The phenix so, amidst the spicy blaze
  Consuming, does the fate of mortals shun;
The infant bird its radiant crest displays,
  And men enjoy the rival of the Sun!

APOLLO AND DAPHNE

Cease, thou bright god of poetry and light,
To urge relentless Daphne's rapid flight!

125

Think on th' inconstant source from whence she came,
Well might she run, whose parent was a stream!

WILLIAM PITT, EARL OF CHATHAM (1708-1778)

VERSES TO DAVID GARRICK

When on a Visit at Mt. Edgecomb

Leave, Garrick, the rich landscape, proudly gay,
Docks, forts, and navies bright'ning all the bay:
To my plain roof repair, primaeval seat!
Yet there no wonders your quick eyes can meet,
Save should you deem it wonderful to find
Ambition cur'd, and an unpassion'd mind;
A Statesman without pow'r, and without gall,
Hating no courtiers, happier than them all;
Bow'd to no yoke, nor crouching for applause,
Vot'ry alone to freedom and the laws;
Herds, flocks, and smiling Ceres deck our plain,
And, interspers'd, an heart-enlivening train
Of sportive children frolic o'er the green;
Mean time pure love looks on and consecrates the scene.
Come then, immortal spirit of the Stage,
Great Nature's proxy, glass of ev'ry age;
Come taste the simple life of Patriarchs old,
Who, rich in rural peace, ne'er thought of pomp or gold.

GEORGE, LORD LYTTELTON (1709-1773)

ON GOOD HUMOUR

1729

Tell me, ye sons of Phoebus, what is this
Which all admire, but few, too few possess?
A virtue 'tis to ancient maids unknown,
And prudes, who spy all faults except their own:
Lov'd and defended by the brave and wise,
Tho' knaves abuse it, and like fools despise.
Say, Wyndham, if 'tis possible to tell
What is the thing in which you most excel?
Hard is the question——for in all you please;
Yet sure good-nature is your noblest praise.
Secur'd by this, your parts no envy move;
For none can envy him whom all must love.
This magic pow'r can make e'en folly please:
This to Pitt's genius adds a brighter grace,
And sweetens ev'ry charm in Caelia's face.

A SONG

1732

Say, Myra, why is gentle love
    A stranger to that mind,
Which pity and esteem can move,
    Which can be just and kind?

Is it, because you fear to share
    The ills that love molest;
The jealous doubt, the tender care,
    That rack the amorous breast?

Alas! by some degree of woe
    We every bliss must gain:
The heart can ne'er a transport know,
    That never feels a pain.

A SONG

1732

When Delia on the plain appears,
Aw'd by a thousand tender fears,
I would approach, but dare not move;
Tell me, my heart, if this be love?

Whene'er she speaks, my ravish'd ear
No other voice but her's can hear,
No other wit but her's approve;
Tell me, my heart, if this be love?

If she some other youth commend,
Though I was once his fondest friend,
His instant enemy I prove;
Tell me, my heart, if this be love?

When she is absent, I no more
Delight in all that pleas'd before,
The clearest spring, or shadiest grove;
Tell me, my heart, if this be love?

When fond of pow'r, of beauty vain,
Her nets she spread for ev'ry swain,
I strove to hate, but vainly strove;
Tell me, my heart, if this be love.

A SONG

1733

The heavy hours are almost past
    That part my love and me:
My longing eyes may hope at last
    Their only wish to see.

But now, my Delia, will you meet
    The man you've lost so long?
Will love in all your pulses beat,
    And tremble on your tongue?

Will you in every look declare
    Your heart is still the same;

And heal each idly-anxious care
  Our fears in absence frame?

Thus, Delia, thus I paint the scene,
  When shortly we shall meet;
And try what yet remains between
  Of loitering time to cheat.

But, if the dream that soothes my mind
  Shall false and groundless prove;
If I am doom'd at length to find
  You have forgot to love:

All I of Venus ask, is this;
  No more to let us join:
But grant me here the flattering bliss,
  To die, and think you mine.

WALTER HARTE (1709-1774)

A SIMILIE

Upon a Set of Tea-Drinkers

So fairy elves their morning-table spread,
O'er a white mushroom's hospitable head:
In acorn cups the merry goblins quaff,
The pearly dews, they sing, they love, they laugh;
Melodious music trembles through the sky,
And airy sounds along the green-wood die.

A SOLILOQUY

Occasioned by the Chirping of a Grasshopper

Happy insect! ever blest
With a more than mortal rest,
Rosy dews the leaves among,
Humble joys, and gentle song!
Wretched poet! ever curst,
With a life of lives the worst,
Sad despondence, restless fears,
Endless jealousies and tears.
  In the burning summer, thou
Warblest on the verdant bough,
Meditating chearful play,
Mindless of the piercing ray;
Scorch'd in Cupid's fervours, I
Ever weep and ever die.
  Proud to gratify thy will,
Ready Nature waits thee still:
Balmy wines to thee she pours,
Weeping through the dewy flow'rs:
Rich as those by Hebe giv'n
To the thirsty sons of Heav'n.
  Yet alas, we both agree,
Miserable thou like me!
Each alike in youth rehearses
Gentle strains, and tender verses;
Ever wand'ring far from home;
Mindless of the days to come,
(Such as aged Winter brings

Trembling on his icy wings).
Both alike at last we die;
Thou art starv'd, and so am I!

PAUL WHITEHEAD (1710-1774)

THE BUTTERFLY AND BEE

To Flavia

See! Flavia, see! that flutt'ring thing,
Skim round yon flower with sportive wing,
      Yet ne'er its sweet explore;
While, wiser, the industrious bee
Extracts the honey from the tree,
      And hives the precious store.

So you, with coy, coquettish art,
Play wanton round your lover's heart,
      Insensible and free:
Love's balmy blessing would you try,
No longer sport a Butterfly,
      But imitate the Bee.

VERSES DROPT

In Mr. Garrick's Temple of Shakespeare

While here to Shakespeare Garrick pays
His tributary thanks and praise;
Invokes the animated stone,
To make the poet's mind his own;
That he each character may trace
With humour, dignity, and grace;
And mark, unerring mark, to men,
The rich creation of his pen;
    Preferr'd the pray'r——the marble god
Methinks I see, assenting, nod,
And, pointing to his laurell'd brow,
Cry——"Half this wreath to you I owe:
Lost to the stage, and lost to fame;
Murder'd my scenes, scarce known my name;
Sunk in oblivion and disgrace
Among the common, scribbling race,
Unnotic'd long thy Shakespeare lay,
To dulness and to time a prey:
But now I rise, I breathe, I live
In you——my representative!

133

Again the hero's breast I fire,
Again the tender sigh inspire;
Each side, again, with laughter shake,
And teach the villain-heart to quake;
All this, my son! again I do——
I?——No, my son!——'Tis I, and you."
  While thus the grateful statue speaks,
A blush o'erspreads the suppliant's cheeks——
  "What!——Half this wreath, wit's mighty chief?——
O grant," he cries, "one single leaf;
That far o'erpays his humble merit,
Who's but the organ of thy spirit."
  Phoebus the gen'rous contest heard——
When thus the god address'd the bard:
"Here, take this laurel from my brow,
On him your mortal wreath bestow;——
Each matchless, each the palm shall bear,
In Heav'n the bard, on Earth the play'r."

CUPID BAFFLED

Diana, hunting on a day,
Beheld where Cupid sleeping lay,
    His quiver by his head:
One of his darts she stole away,
And one of her's did close convey
    Into the other's stead.

When next the archer through the grove,
In search of prey, did wanton rove,
    Aurelia fair he 'spy'd;
Aurelia, who to Damon's pray'r
Disdain'd to lend a tender ear,
    And Cupid's pow'r defy'd.

Soon as he ey'd the rebel maid,
"Now know my pow'r!" enrag'd he said;
    Then levell'd at her heart:
Full to the head the shaft he drew;
But harmless to her breast it flew,
    For, lo!——'twas Dian's dart.

Exulting, then the fair-one cry'd,
"Fond urchin, lay your bow aside;
    Your quiver be unbound:

134

Would you Aurelia's heart subdue,
Thy play-thing arrows ne'er will do;
    Bid Damon give the wound."

DEATH AND THE DOCTOR

'Twixt Death and Schomberg, t'other day,
    A contest did arise;
Death swore his prize he'd bear away;
    The Doctor, Death defies.

Enrag'd to hear his pow'r defy'd,
    Death drew his keenest dart;
But wond'ring saw it glance aside,
    And miss the vital part.

JAMES HAMMOND (1710-1742)

ELEGY III

Should Jove descend in floods of liquid ore,
And golden torrents stream from every part,
That craving bosom still would heave for more,
Not all the gods could satisfy thy heart:

But may thy folly, which can thus disdain
My honest love, the mighty wrong repay,
May midnight fire involve thy sordid gain,
And on the shining heaps of rapine prey:

May all the youths, like me, by love deceiv'd,
Not quench the ruin, but applaud the doom;
And, when thou dy'st, may not one heart be griev'd,
May not one tear bedew the lonely tomb.

But the deserving, tender, generous maid,
Whose only care is her poor lover's mind,
Though ruthless age may bid her beauty fade,
In every friend to love, a friend shall find:

And, when the lamp of life will burn no more,
When dead she seems as in a gentle sleep,
The pitying neighbour shall her loss deplore,
And round the bier assembled lovers weep:

With flow'ry garlands, each revolving year,
Shall strow the grave where truth and softness rest,
Then home returning, drop the pious tear,
And bid the turf lie easy on her breast.

ELEGY IV

While calm you sit beneath your secret shade,
And lose in pleasing thought the summer-day,
Or tempt the wish of some unpractis'd maid,
Whose heart at once inclines and fears to stray:

The sprightly vigour of my youth is fled,
Lonely and sick, on death is all my thought,

Oh, spare, Persephone, this guiltless head,
Love, too much love, is all thy suppliant's fault.

No virgin's easy faith I e'er betray'd,
My tongue ne'er boasted of a feign'd embrace;
No poisons in the cup have I convey'd,
Nor veil'd destruction with a friendly face:

No secret horrours gnaw this quiet breast,
This pious hand ne'er robb'd the sacred fane,
I ne'er disturb'd the gods' eternal rest
With curses loud, —but oft have pray'd in vain.

No stealth of Time has thinn'd my flowing hair,
Nor Age yet bent me with his iron hand:
Ah! why so soon the tender blossom tear!
Ere autumn yet the ripen'd fruit demand?

Ye gods, whoe'er in gloomy shades below,
Now slowly tread your melancholy round;
Now wandering view the paleful rivers flow,
And musing hearken to their solemn sound:

O, let me still enjoy the chearful day,
Till, many years unheeded o'er me roll'd,
Pleas'd in my age, I trifle life away,
And tell how much we lov'd, ere I grew old.

But you, who now, with festive garlands crown'd,
In chase of pleasure they gay moments spend,
By quick enjoyment heal love's pleasing wound,
And grieve for nothing but your absent friend.

ELEGY X

This day, which saw my Delia's beauty rise,
Shall more than all our sacred days be blest,
The world enamour'd of her lovely eyes,
Shall grow as good and gentle as her breast.

By all our guarded sighs, and hid desires,
Oh, may our guiltless love be still the same!
I burn, and glory in the pleasing fires,
If Delia's bosom share the mutual flame.

Thou happy genius of her natal hour,
Accept her incense, if her thoughts be kind;
But let her court in vain thy angry power,
If all our vows are blotted from her mind.

And thou, O Venus, hear my righteous prayer,
Or bind the shepherdess, or loose the swain,
Yet rather guard them both with equal care,
And let them die together in thy chain:

What I demand, perhaps her heart desires,
But virgin fears her nicer tongue restrain;
The secret thought, which blushing love inspires,
The conscious eye can full as well explain.

RICHARD GLOVER (1712-1785)

ADMIRAL HOSIER'S GHOST

As near Porto-Sello lying
  On the gently swelling flood,
At midnight with streamers flying,
  Our triumphant navy rode;
There while Vernon sat all-glorious
  From the Spaniard's late defeat;
And his crews, with shouts victorious,
  Drank success to England's fleet:

On a sudden shrilly sounding,
  Hideous yells and shrieks were heard:
Then each heart with fear confounding,
  A sad troop of ghosts appear'd,
All in dreary hammocks shrouded,
  Which for winding-sheets they wore,
And with looks by sorrow clouded,
  Frowning on that hostile shore.

On them gleamed the Moon's wan lustre,
  When the shade of Hosier brave
His pale bands was seen to muster,
  Rising from their watry grave:
O'er the glimm'ring wave he hy'd him,
  Where the Burford rear'd her sail,
With three thousand ghosts beside him,
  And in groans did Vernon hail.

"Heed, O heed, our fatal story,
  I am Hosier's injur'd ghost,
You, who now have purchas'd glory
  At this place where I was lost;
Though in Porto-Bello's ruin
  You now triumph free from fears,
When you think on our undoing,
  You will mix your joy with tears.

"See these mournful spectres, sweeping
  Ghastly o'er this hated wave,
Whose wan cheeks are stain'd with weeping;
  These were English captains brave:
Mark those numbers pale and horrid,
  Those were once my sailors bold,

139

Lo! each hangs his drooping forehead,
    While his dismal tale is told.

"I, by twenty sail attended,
    Did this Spanish town affright:
Nothing then its wealth defended
    But my orders not to fight:
O! that in this rolling ocean
    I had cast them with disdain,
And obey'd my heart's warm motion,
    To have quell'd the pride of Spain.

"For resistance I could fear none,
    But with twenty ships had done
What thou, brave and happy Vernon,
    Hast achiev'd with six alone.
Then the Bastimentos never
    Had our foul dishonour seen,
Nor the sea the sad receiver
    Of this gallant train had been.

"Thus, like thee, proud Spain dismaying,
    And her galleons leading home,
Though condemn'd for disobeying,
    I had met a traitor's doom;
To have fall'n, my country crying
    He has play'd an English part,
Had been better far than dying
    Of a griev'd and broken heart.

"Unrepining at thy glory,
    Thy successful arms we hail;
But remember our sad story,
    And let Hosier's wrongs prevail.
Sent in this foul clime to languish,
    Think what thousands fell in vain,
Wasted with disease and anguish,
    Not in glorious battle slain.

"Hence, with all my train attending
    From their oozy toombs below,
Through the hoary foam ascending,
    Here I feed my constant woe:
Here the Bastimentos viewing,
    We recall our shameful doom,
And our plaintive cries renewing,
    Wander through the midnight gloom.

140

"O'er these waves for ever mourning
    Shall we roam depriv'd of rest,
If to Britain's shores returning,
    You neglect my just request.
After this proud foe subduing,
    When your patriot friends you see,
Think on vengeance for my ruin,
    And for England sham'd in me."

EDWARD MOORE (1712-1757)

THE OWL AND THE NIGHTINGALE

A Fable

To know the mistress' humour right,
See if her maids are clean and tight;
If Betty waits without her stays,
She copies but her lady's ways.
When miss comes in with boist'rous shout,
And drops no curtsy going out,
Depend upon 't, mamma is one,
Who reads, or drinks too much alone.
If bottled beer her thirst assuage,
She feels enthusiastic rage,
And burns with ardour to inherit
The gifts, and workings of the spirit.
If learning crack her giddy brains,
No remedy, but death, remains.
Sum up the various ills of life,
And all are sweet, to such a wife.
At home, superior wit she vaunts,
And twits her husband with his wants;
Her ragged offspring all around,
Like pigs, are wallowing on the ground:
Impatient ever of control,
She knows no order, but of soul;
With books her litter'd floor is spread,
Of nameless authors, never read;
Foul linen, petticoats, and lace
Fill up the intermediate space.
Abroad, at visitings, her tongue
Is never still, and always wrong;
All meanings she defines away,
And stands, with truth and sense, at bay.
    If e'er she meets a gentle heart,
Skill'd in the housewife's useful art,
Who makes her family her care,
And builds Contentment's temple there,
She starts at such mistakes in Nature,
And cries, "Lord help us! what a creature!"
    Melissa, if the moral strike,
YOU'll find the fable not unlike.

    An Owl, puff'd up with self-conceit,

142

Lov'd learning better than his meat;
Old manuscripts he treasur'd up,
And rummag'd every grocer's shop;
At pastry-cooks was known to ply,
And strip, for science, every pie.
For modern poetry and wit,
He had read all that Blackmore writ;
So intimate with Curl was grown,
His learned treasures were his own;
To all his authors had access,
And sometimes would correct the press.
In logic he acquir'd such knowledge,
You'd swear him fellow of a college;
Alike to every art and science,
His daring genius bid defiance,
And swallow'd wisdom, with that haste,
That cits do custards at a feast.
    Within the shelter of a wood,
One ev'ning, as he musing stood,
Hard by, upon a leafy spray,
A Nightingale began his lay.
Sudden he starts, with anger stung,
And, screeching, interrupts the song.
    "Pert, busy thing, thy airs give o'er,
And let my contemplation soar.
What is the music of thy voice,
But jarring dissonance and noise?
Be wise. True harmony, thou'lt find,
Not in the throat, but in the mind;
By empty chirping not attain'd,
But by laborious study gain'd.
Go read the authors Pope explodes,
Fathom the depth of Cibber's odes,
With modern plays improve thy wit,
Read all the learning Henley writ;
And, if thou needs must sing, sing then,
And emulate the ways of men;
So shalt thou grow, like me, refin'd,
And bring improvement to thy kind."
    "Thou wretch," the little warbler cry'd,
"Made up of ignorance and pride,
Ask all the birds, and they'll declare,
A greater blockhead wings not air.
Read o'er thyself, thy talents scan,
Science was only meant for man.
No useless authors me molest,
I mind the duties of my nest;
With careful wing protect my young,

143

And cheer their ev'nings with a song.

"Thus, following Nature, and her laws,
From men and birds I claim applause;
While, nurs'd in pedantry and sloth,
An Owl is scorn'd alike by both."

THE BEE

Leave wanton Bee, those blossoms leave,
Thou buzzing harbinger of Spring,
To Stella fly, and sweeter spoils
Shall load thy thigh, and gild thy wing.

Her cheeks, her lips with roses swell,
Not Paphian roses deeper glow;
And lillies o'er her bosom spread
Their spotless sweets, and balmy snow.

Then, grateful for the sacred dews,
Invite her, humming round, to rest;
Soft dreams may tune her soul to love,
Tho' coldness arm her waking breast.

But if she still obdurate prove,
O shoot thy sting. The little smart
May teach her then to pity me
Transfix'd with Love's and Beauty's dart.

Ah no, forbear, to sting forbear;
Go, fly unto thy hive again,
Much rather let me die for her,
Than she endure the least of pain.

Go, fly unto thy hive again,
With more than Hybla-honey blest:
For Pope's sweet lips prepare the dew,
Or else for Love a nectar-feast.

THE MORNING LARK

Feather'd lyric! warbling high,
Sweetly gaining on the sky,
Op'ning with thy matin-lay
(Nature's hymn!) the eye of day,
Teach my soul, on early wing,
Thus to soar and thus to sing.

While the bloom of orient light

145

Gilds thee in thy tuneful flight,
May the Day-spring from on high,
Seen by Faith's religious eye,
Cheer me with his vital ray,
Promise of eternal day!

EPITAPH ON MY FATHER

Dear to the wise and good by all approv'd,
The joy of Virtue, and Heaven's well-belov'd!
His life inspir'd with every better art,
A learned head, clear soul, and honest heart.
Each science chose his breast her favourite seat,
Each language, but the language of deceit.
Severe his virtues, yet his manners kind,
A manly form, and a seraphic mind.
So long he walk'd in Virtue's even road,
In him at length, 'twas natural to do good.
Like Eden, his old age (a sabbath rest!)
Flow'd without noise, yet all around him blest!
His patron, Jesus! with no titles grac'd,
But that best title, a good parish priest.
Peace with his ashes dwell. And, mortals, now,
The saint's above; the dust alone below.
The wise and good shall pay their tribute here,
The modest tribute of one thought and tear;
Then pensive sigh, and say, "To me be given
By living thus on Earth, to reign in Heaven."

WILLIAM SHENSTONE (1714-1763)

ODE TO HEALTH

1730

O health, capricious maid!
Why dost thou shun my peaceful bower,
Where I had hope to share thy power,
    And bless thy lasting aid?

Since thou, alas! art flown,
It 'vails not whether Muse or Grace,
With tempting smile, frequent the place:
    I sigh for thee alone.

Age not forbids thy stay;
Thou yet might'st act the friendly part;
Thou yet might'st raise this languid heart;
    Why speed so swift away?

Thou scorn'st the city-air;
I breathe fresh gales o'er furrow'd ground,
Yet hast not thou my wishes crown'd,
    O false! O partial fair!

I plunge into the wave:
And though with purest hand I raise
A rural altar to thy praise,
    Thou wilt not deign to save.

Amid my well-known grove,
Where mineral fountains vainly bear
Thy boasted name, and titles fair,
    Why scorns thy foot to rove?

Thou hear'st the sportsman's claim;
Enabling him, with idle noise,
To drown the Muse's melting voice,
    And fright the timorous game.

Is thought thy foe? adieu,
Ye midnight lamps! ye curious tomes!
Mine eye o'er hills and valleys roams,
    And deals no more with you.

147

Is it the clime you flee?
Yet, 'midst his unremitting snows,
The poor Laponian's bosom glows;
　　And shares bright rays from thee.

There was, there was a time,
When, though I scorn'd thy guardian care,
Nor made a vow, nor said a prayer,
　　I did not rue the crime.

Who then more blest than I?
When the glad school-boy's task was done,
And forth, with jocund sprite, I run
　　To freedom, and to joy?

How jovial then the day!
What since have all my labours found,
Thus climbing life, to gaze around,
　　That can thy loss repay?

Wert thou, alas! but kind,
Methinks no frown that Fortune wears,
Nor lessen'd hopes, nor growing cares,
　　Could sink my cheerful mind.

Whate'er my stars include;
What other breasts convert to pain,
My towering mind shall soon disdain,
　　Should scorn——Ingratitude!

Repair this mouldering cell,
And blest with objects found at home,
And envying none their fairer dome,
　　How pleas'd my soul should dwell:

Temperance should guard the doors;
From room to room should Memory stray,
And ranging all in neat array,
　　Enjoy her pleasing stores——

There let them rest unknown,
The types of many a pleasing scene:
But to preserve them bright or clean,
　　Is thine, fair queen! alone.

FLIRT AND PHIL

A Decision for the Ladies

A wit, by learning well refined,
A beau, but of the rural kind,
    To Silvia made pretences;
They both profess'd an equal love,
Yet hoped by different means to move
    Her judgment or her senses.

Young sprightly Flirt, of blooming mien,
Watch'd the best minutes to be seen,
    Went——when his glass advised him;
While meagre Phil of books inquired,
A wight for wit and parts admired,
    A witty ladies prized him.

Silvia had wit, had spirits too;
To hear the one, the other view,
    Suspended held the scales;
Her wit, her youth too, claim'd its share;
Let none the preference declare,
    But turn up——heads or tails.

THE RAPE OF THE TRAP

A Ballad.　1737

'Twas in a land of learning,
    The Muses' favourite city,
Such pranks of late
Were play'd by a rat,
    As tempt one to be witty.

All in a college study,
    Where books were in great plenty;
This rat would devour
More sense in an hour,
    Than I could write in twenty.

Corporeal food, 'tis granted,
    Serves vermin less refin'd, sir;
But this, a rat of taste,

149

All other rats surpass'd,
  And he prey'd on the food of the mind, sir.

His breakfast, half the morning,
  He constantly attended:
And when the bell rung
For evening song,
  His dinner scarce was ended.

He spar'd not e'en heroics,
  On which we poets pride us;
And wou'd make no more
Of king Arthurs, by the score,
  Than all the world beside does.

In books of geo-graphy,
  He made the maps to flutter:
A river or a sea
Was to him a dish of tea;
  And a kingdom, bread and butter.

But if some mawkish potion
  Might chance to over-dose him,
To check its rage,
He took a page
  Of logic——to compose him.

A trap, in haste and anger,
  Was bought, you need not doubt on't:
And such was the gin,
Were a lion once got in,
  He could not, I think, get out on't.

With cheese, not books, 't was baited,
  The fact I'll not belye it,
Since none——I'll tell you that,
Whether scholar or rat,
  Mind books, when he has other diet.

But more of trap and bait, sir,
  Why should I sing, or either?
Since the rat, who knew the sleight,
Came in the dead of night,
  And dragg'd them away together.

Both trap and bait were vanish'd
  Through a fracture in the flooring:
Which, though so trim

It now may seem,
    Had then——a dozen or more in.

Then answer this, ye sages,
    Nor deem a man to wrong ye,
Had the rat which thus did seize on
The trap, less claim to reason,
    Than many a scull among ye?

Dan Prior's mice, I own it,
    Were vermin of condition:
But this rat, who merely learn'd
What rats alone concern'd,
    Was the greater politician.

That England's topsy-turvy,
    Is clear from these mishaps, sir;
Since traps, we may determine,
Will no longer take our vermin,
    But vermin take our traps, sir!

Let sophs, by rats infested,
    Then trust in cats to catch'em;
Lest they grow as learn'd as we,
In our studies; where, d'ye see,
    No mortal sits to watch 'em.

Good luck betide our captains!
    Good luck betide our cats, sir!
And grant that the one
May quell the Spanish Don,
    And the other destroy our rats, sir!

ON CERTAIN PASTORALS

So rude and tuneless are thy lays,
    The weary audience vow,
'T is not th' Arcadian swain that sings,
    But 't is his herds that low.

151

THE LANDSKIP

A Song

How pleas'd within my native bowers
    Erewhile I pass'd the day!
Was ever scene so deck'd with flowers?
    Were ever flowers so gay?

How sweetly smil'd the hill, the vale,
    And all the landskip round!
The river gliding down the dale!
    The hill with beeches crown'd!

But now, when urg'd by tender woes,
    I speed to meet my dear,
That hill and stream my zeal oppose,
    And check my fond career.

No more, since Daphne was my theme,
    Their wonted charms I see:
That verdant hill, and silver stream,
    Divide my love and me.

THE SKY-LARK

A Song

Go, tuneful bird, that glad'st the skies,
    To Daphne's window speed thy way;
And there on quivering pinions rise,
    And there thy vocal art display.

And if she deign thy notes to hear,
    And if she praise thy matin song,
Tell her the sounds that sooth her ear,
    To Damon's native plains belong.

Tell her, in livelier plumes array'd,
    The bird from Indian groves may shine;
But ask the lovely partial maid,
    What are his notes compar'd to thine?

Then bid her treat yon witless beau,
    And all his flaunting race with scorn;

And lend an ear to Damon's woe,
Who sings her praise, and sings forlorn.

THE EXTENT OF COOKERY

Aliusque et idem.

When Tom to Cambridge first was sent,
    A plain brown bob he wore;
Read much, and look'd as though he meant
    To be a fop no more.

See him to Lincoln's Inn repair,
    His resolution flag;
He cherishes a length of hair,
    And tucks it in a bag.

Nor Coke nor Salkeld he regards,
    But gets into the house,
And soon a judge's rank rewards
    His pliant votes and bows.

Adieu, ye bobs! ye bags, give place!
    Full bottoms come instead!
Good Lord! to see the various ways
    Of dressing——a calf's head.

A SONG

1742

When Bright Roxana treads the green,
In all the pride of dress and mien;
Averse to freedom, love, and play,
The dazzling rival of the day:
None other beauty strikes mine eye,
The lillies droop, the roses die.

But when, disclaiming art, the fair
Assumes a soft engaging air;
Mild as the opening morn of May,
Familiar, friendly, free, and gay; .
The scene improves, where'er she goes,
More sweetly smile the pink and rose.

O lovely Maid! propitious hear,
Nor deem thy shepherd insincere;
Pity a wild illusive flame,
That varies objects still the same;
And let their very changes prove
The never-varied force of love.

ELEGY I

To a Friend

For rural virtues, and for native skies,
    I bade Augusta's venal sons farewell;
Now, 'mid the trees, I see my smoke arise,
    Now hear the fountains bubbling round my cell.

O may that genius which secures my rest,
    Preserve this villa for a friend that's dear!
Ne'er may my vintage glad the sordid breast;
    Ne'er tinge the lip that dares be unsincere!

Far from these paths, ye faithless friends, depart!
    Fly my plain board, abhor my hostile name!
Hence! the faint verse that flows not from the heart,
    But mourns in labour'd strains, the price of fame!

O lov'd Simplicity, be thine the prize!
    Assiduous Art correct her page in vain!
His be the palm who, guiltless of disguise,
    Contemns the power, the dull resource to feign!

Still may the mourner, lavish of his tears,
    For lucre's venal meed invite my scorn!
Still may the bard, dissembling doubts and fears,
    For praise, for flattery sighing, sigh forlorn!

Soft as the line of love-sick Hammond flows, ——
    'T was his fond heart effus'd the meling theme;
Ah! never could Aonia's hill disclose
    So fair a fountain, or so lov'd a stream.

Ye loveless bards! intent with artful pains
    To form a sigh, or to contrive a tear,
Forego your Pindus, and on —— plains
    Survey Camilla's charms, and grow sincere.

154

But thou, my friend! while in thy youthful soul
    Love's gentle tyrant seats his aweful throne,
Write from thy bosom——Let not art control
    The ready pen, that makes his edicts known.

Pleasing, when youth is long expir'd, to trace
    The forms our pencil or our pen design'd!
"Such was our youthful air, and shape, and face!
    Such the soft image of our youthful mind!"

Soft, whilst we sleep beneath the rural bowers,
    The Loves and Graces steal unseen away;
And where the turf diffus'd its pomp of flowers,
    We wake to wintry scenes of chill decay!

Curse the sad fortune that detains thy fair;
    Praise the soft hours that gave thee to her arms;
Paint thy proud scorn of every vulgar care,
    When Hope exalts thee, or when Doubt alarms.

Where with Oenone thou hast worn the day,
    Near fount or stream, in meditation, rove;
If in the grove Oenone lov'd to stray,
    The faithful Muse shall meet thee in the grove.

ODE TO A YOUNG LADY

Somewhat Too Solicitous about her Manner of Expression

Survey, my fair! that lucid stream,
    Adown the smiling valley stray;
Would Art attempt, or Fancy dream,
    To regulate its winding way?

So pleas'd I view thy shining hair
    In loose dishevell'd ringlets flow:
Not all thy art, not all thy care,
    Can there on single grace bestow.

Survey again that verdant hill,
    With native plants enamell'd o'er;
Say, can the painter's utmost skill
    Instruct one flower to please us more?

As vain it were, with artful dye
    To change the bloom thy cheeks disclose;

155

And oh may Laura, ere she try,
    With fresh vermilion paint the rose.

Hark how the wood-lark's tuneful throat
    Can every study'd grace excel;
Let Art constrain the rambling note,
    And will she, Laura, please so well?

Oh ever keep thy native ease,
    By no pedantic law confin'd!
For Laura's voice is form'd to please,
    So Laura's words be not unkind.

NANCY OF THE VALE

A Ballad

Nerine Galatea! thymo mihi dulcior Hyblae!
Candidior cygnis! hedera formosior alba!   ——VIRGIL

The western sky was purpled o'er
    With every pleasing ray;
And flocks, reviving, felt no more
    The sultry heats of day:

When from a hazle's artless bower
    Soft warbled Strephon's tongue;
He blest the scene, he blest the hour,
    While Nancy's praise he sung.

"Let fops with fickle falsehood range
    The paths of wanton Love,
While weeping maids lament their change,
    And sadden every grove;

"But endless blessings crown the day
    I saw fair Esham's dale!
And every blessing find its way
    To Nancy of the Vale.

" 'T was from Avona's banks the maid
    Diffus'd her lovely beams;
And every shining glance display'd
    The Naiad of the streams.

"Soft as the wild-duck's tender young,
156

That floats on Avon's tide;
Bright as the water-lily, sprung,
And glittering near its side.

"Fresh as the bordering flowers, her bloom;
    Her eye, all mild to view;
The little halcyon's azure plume
    Was never half so blue.

"Her shape was like the reed so sleek,
    So taper, straight, and fair;
Her dimpled smile, her blushing cheek,
    How charming sweet they were!

"Far in the winding vale retir'd,
    This peerless bud I found;
And shadowing rock and woods conspir'd
    To fence her beauties round.

"That Nature is so lone a dell
    Should form a nymph so sweet;
Or Fortune to her secret cell
    Conduct my wandering feet!

"Gay lordlings sought her for their bride,
    But she would ne'er incline:
'Prove to your equals true,' she cried,
    'As I will prove to mine.

" ' 'Tis Strephon, on the mountain's brow,
    Has won my right good will;
To him I gave my plighted vow,
    With him I'll climb the hill.'

"Struck with her charms and gentle truth,
    I clasp'd the constant fair;
To her alone I gave my youth,
    And vow my future care.

"And when this vow shall faithless prove,
    Or I those charms forgo;
The stream that saw our tender love,
    That stream shall cease to flow."

ODE TO INDOLENCE

1750

Ah! why, for ever on the wing,
  Persists my wearied soul to roam?
Why, ever cheated, strives to bring
  Or pleasure or contentment home?

Thus the poor bird, that draws his name
  From Paradise's honour'd groves,
Careless, fatigues his little frame,
  Nor finds the resting-place he loves.

Lo! on the rural mossy bed
  My limbs with careless ease reclin'd;
Ah, gentle Sloth! indulgent spread
  The same soft bandage o'er my mind.

For why should lingering thought invade,
  Yet every wordly prospect cloy?
Lend me, soft Sloth, thy friendly aid,
  And give me peace, debarr'd of joy.

Lov'st thou yon calm and silent flood,
  That never ebbs, that never flows;
Protected by the circling wood
  From each tempestuous wind that blows?

An altar on its bank shall rise,
  Where oft thy votary shall be found;
What time pale Autumn lulls the skies,
  And sickening verdure fades around.

Ye busy race, ye factious train,
  That haunt Ambition's guilty shrine;
No more perplex the world in vain,
  But offer here your vows with mine.

And thou, puissant queen! be kind:
  If e'er I shar'd thy balmy power;
If e'er I sway'd my active mind
  To weave for thee the rural bower.

Dissolve in sleep each anxious care;
  Each unavailing sigh remove;

And only let me wake to share
  The sweets of friendship and of love.

KANE O'HARA (1714?-1782)

AN AIR

from "Tom Thumb"

We kings, who are in our senses,
Mock our consorts violences;
Pishing at their moods and tenses,
   Our own will we follow.
If the husband once gives way
To his wife's capricious sway,
For his breeches he next day
   May go whoop and hollow.

WILLIAM WHITEHEAD (1715-1785)

TO THE REVEREND MR. WRIGHT

1751

Prithee tease me no longer, dear troublesome friend,
    On a subject which wants not advice:
You may make me unhappy, but never can mend
    Those ills I have learnt to despise.

You say I'm dependent; what then?——if I make
    That dependence quite easy to me,
Say why should you envy my lucky mistake,
    Or why should I wish to be free?

Many men of less worth, you partially cry,
    To splendour and opulence soar:
Suppose I allow it; yet, pray sir, am I
    Less happy because they are more?

But why said I happy? I aim not at that,
    Mere ease is my humble request;
I would neither repine at a niggardly fate,
    Nor stretch my wings far from my nest.

Nor e'er may my pride or my folly reflect
    On the fav'rites whom fortune has made,
Regardless of thousands who pine with neglect
    In pensive obscurity's shade;

With whom, when comparing the merit I boast,
    Though rais'd by indulgence to fame,
I sink in confusion bewilder'd and lost,
    And wonder I am what I am!

And what are these wonders, these blessings refin'd,
    Which splendour and opulence shower?
The health of the body, and peace of the mind,
    Are things which are out of their power.

To contentment's calm sunshine, the lot of the few,
    Can insolent greatness pretend?
Or can it bestow, what I boast of in you,
    That blessing of blessings, a friend?

We may pay some regard to the rich and the great,
     But how seldom we love them you know;
Or if we do love them, it is not their state,
     The tinsel and plume of the show.

But some secret virtues we find in the heart
     When the mask is laid kindly aside,
Which birth cannot give them, nor riches impart,
     And which never once heard of their pride.

A flow of good spirits I've seen with a smile
     To worth make a shallow pretence;
And the chat of good breeding with ease, for a while,
     May pass for good nature and sense;

But where is the bosom untainted by art,
     The judgment so modest and stay'd,
That union so rare of the head and the heart,
     Which fixes the friends it has made?

For those whom the great and the wealthy employ
     Their pleasure or vanity's slaves,
Whate'er they can give I without them enjoy,
     And am rid of just so many knaves.

For the many whom titles alone can allure,
     And the blazon of ermine and gules,
I wrap myself round in my lowness secure,
     And am rid of just so many fools.

Then why should I covet what cannot increase
     My delights, and may lessen their store;
My present condition is quiet and ease,
     And what can my future be more?

Should Fortune capriciously cease to be coy,
     And in torrents of plenty descend,
I doubtless, like others, should clasp her with joy,
     And my wants and my wishes extend.

But since 't is denied me, and Heaven best knows
     Whether kinder to grant it or not,
Say, why should I vainly disturb my repose,
     And peevishly carp at my lot?

No; still let me follow sage Horace's rule,
     Who tried all things, and held fast the best;

Learn daily to put all my passions to school,
And keep the due poise of my breast.

Thus, firm at the helm, I glide calmly away
Like the merchant long us'd to the deep,
Nor trust for my safety on life's stormy sea
To the gilding and paint of my ship.

Nor yet can the giants of honour and pelf
My want of ambition deride,
He who rules his own bosom is lord of himself,
And lord of all nature beside.

ELEGY I

Written at the Convent of Haut Villers in Champagne, 1754

Silent and clear, through yonder peaceful vale,
While Marne's slow waters weave their mazy way,
See, to th' exulting Sun, and fost'ring gale,
What boundless treasures his rich banks display!

Fast by the stream, and at the mountain's base,
The lowing herds through living pastures rove;
Wide waving harvests crown the rising space;
And still superior nods the viny grove.

High on the top, as guardian of the scene,
Imperial Sylvan spreads his umbrage wide;
Nor wants there many a cot, and spire between,
Or in the vale, or on the mountain's side.

To mark that man, as tenant of the whole,
Claims the just tribute of his culturing care,
Yet pays to Heaven, in gratitude of soul,
The boon which Heaven accepts, of praise and prayer.

O dire effects of war! the time has been
When desolation vaunted here her reign;
One ravag'd desert was yon beauteous scene,
And Marne ran purple to the frighted Seine.

Oft at his work, the toilsome day to cheat,
The swain still talks of those disastrous times
When Guise's pride, and Conde's ill-star'd heat,
Taught Christian zeal to authorize their crimes:

163

Oft to his children sportive on the grass
   Does dreadful tales of worn tradition tell,
Oft points to Epernay's ill-fated pass,
   Where force thrice triumph'd, and where Biron fell.

O dire effects of war! —— may ever more
   Through this sweet vale the voice of discord cease!
A British bard to Gallia's fertile shore
   Can wish the blessings of eternal peace.

Yet say, ye monks, (beneath whose moss-grown seat,
   Within whose cloister'd cells th' indebted Muse
Awhile sojourns, for meditation meet,
   And these loose thoughts in pensive strain pursues,)

Avails it aught, that war's rude tumults spare
   Yon cluster'd vineyard, or yon golden field,
If, niggards to yourselves, and fond of care,
   You slight the joys their copious treasures yield?

Avails it aught, that Nature's liberal hand
   With every blessing grateful man can know,
Clothes the rich bosom of yon smiling land,
   The mountain's sloping side, or pendent brow,

If meagre famine paint your pallid cheek,
   If breaks the midnight bell your hours of rest,
If, midst heart-chilling damps, and winter bleak,
   You shun the cheerful bowl, and moderate feast?

Look forth, and be convinc'd! 'tis Nature pleads,
   Her ample volume opens on your view:
The simple-minded swain, who running reads,
   Feels the glad truth, and is it hid from you?

Look forth, and be convinc'd. Yon prospects wide
   To reason's ear how forcibly they speak:
Compar'd with those how dull is letter'd pride,
   And Austin's babbling eloquence how weak!

Temp'rance, not abstinence, in every bliss
   Is man's true joy, and therefore Heaven's command.
The wretch who riots thanks his God amiss:
   Who starves, rejects the bounties of his hand.

Mark, while the Marne in yon full channel glides,
   How smooth his course, how Nature smiles around!

164

But should impetuous torrents swell his tides,
    The fairy landskip sinks in oceans drown'd.

Nor less disastrous, should his thrifty urn
    Neglected leave the once well-water'd land,
To dreary wastes yon paradise would turn,
    Polluted ooze, or heaps of barren sand.

ODE TO THE TIBER

On Entering the Campania of Rome, at Otricoli, 1755

Hail sacred stream, whose waters roll
    Immortal through the classic page!
To thee the Muse-devoted soul,
    Though destin'd to a later age
And less indulgent clime, to thee,
    Nor thou disdain, in Runic lays,
Weak mimic of true harmony,
    His grateful homage pays.
Far other strains thine elder ear
With pleas'd attention wont to hear,
When he, who strung the Latian lyre,
    And he, who led th' Aonian quire
From Mantua's reedy lakes with osiers crown'd,
Taught Echo from thy banks with transport to resound.
    Thy banks?—alas! is this the boasted scene,
This dreary, wide, uncultivated plain,
Where sick'ning Nature wears a fainter green,
And Desolation spreads her torpid reign?
    Is this the scene where Freedom breath'd,
    Her copious horn where Plenty wreath'd,
        And Health at opening day
    Bade all her roseate breezes fly,
    To wake the sons of industry,
        And make their fields more gay?
    Where is the villa's rural pride,
        The swelling dome's imperial gleam,
    Which lov'd to grace thy verdant side,
        And tremble in thy golden stream?
    Where are the bold, the busy throngs,
        That rush'd impatient to the war,
    Or tun'd to peace triumphal songs,
        And hail'd the passing car?
    Along the solitary road,
    Th' eternal flint by consuls trod,

165

We muse, and mark the sad decays
Of mighty works, and mighty days!
For these vile wastes, we cry, had Fate decreed
That Veii's sons should strive, for these Camillus bleed?
Did here, in after-times of Roman pride,
The musing shepherd from Soracte's height
See towns extend where'er thy waters glide,
And temples rise, and peopled farms unite?
They did. For this deserted plain
The hero strove, nor strove in vain;
And here the shepherd saw
Unnumber'd towns and temples spread,
While Rome majestic rear'd her head,
And gave the nations law.

Yes, thou and Latium once were great;
And still, ye first of human things,
Beyond the grasp of time or fate
Her fame and thine triumphant springs.
What though the mould'ring columns fall,
And strow the desert earth beneath,
Though ivy round each nodding wall
Entwine its fatal wreath,
Yet say, can Rhine or Danube boast
The numerous glories thou hast lost?
Can ev'n Euphrates' palmy shore,
Or Nile, with all his mystic lore,
Produce from old records of genuine fame
Such heroes, poets, kings, or emulate thy name?
Ev'n now the Muse, the conscious Muse is here;
From every ruin's formidable shade
Eternal music breathes on fancy's ear,
And wakes to more than form th' illustrious dead.
Thy Caesars, Scipios, Catos rise,
The great, the virtuous, and the wise,
In solemn state advance!
They fix the philosophic eye,
Or trail the robe, or lift on high
The lightning of the lance.

But chief that humbler happier train,
Who knew those virtues to reward
Beyond the reach of chance or pain
Secure, th' historian and the bard.
By them the hero's generous rage
Still warm in youth immortal lives;
And in their adamantine page
Thy glory still survives.

166

Through deep savannahs wild and vast,
Unheard, unknown through ages past,
Beneath the Sun's directer beams,
What copious torrents pour their streams!
No fame have they, no fond pretence to mourn,
No annals swell their pride, or grace their storied urn.
While thou, with Rome's exalted genius join'd,
Her spear yet lifted, and her corslet brac'd,
Canst tell the waves, canst tell the passing wind,
Thy wondrous tale, and cheer the list'ning waste.
Though from his caves th' unfeeling North
Pour'd all his legion'd tempests forth,
Yet still thy laurels bloom:
One deathless glory still remains,
Thy stream has roll'd through Latian plains,
Has wash'd the walls of Rome.

ODE FOR THE YEAR 1777

Again imperial Winter's sway
Bids the earth and air obey;
Throws o'er yon hostile lakes his icy bar,
And, for a while, suspends the rage of war.
O may it ne'er revive! ——Ye wise,
Ye just, ye virtuous, and ye brave,
Leave fell contention to the sons of vice,
And join your powers to save!

Enough of slaughter have ye known,
Ye wayward children of a distant clime,
For you we heave the kindred groan,
We pity your misfortune, and your crime.
Stop, parricides, the blow,
O find another foe!
And hear a parent's dear request,
Who longs to clasp you to her yielding breast.

What change would ye require? What form
Ideal floats in fancy's sky?
Ye fond enthusiasts break the charm,
And let cool reason clear the mental eye.
On Britain's well-mix'd state alone,
True liberty has fix'd her throne,
Where law, not man, an equal rule maintains:
Can freedom e'er be found where many a tyrant reigns?

United, let us all those blessings find,
The God of Nature meant mankind,
Whate'er of errour, ill redrest;
Whate'er of passion, ill represt;
Whate'er the wicked have conceiv'd,
And folly's heedless sons believ'd,
Let all lie buried in oblivion's flood
And our great cement be the public good.

INSCRIPTION ON AN OAK

Once was I fam'd, an awful sage,
The silent wonder of my age!
To me was every science known,
And every language was my own.
The Sun beheld my daily toil,
I labour'd o'er the midnight oil,
And, hid in woods, conceal'd from view
Whate'er I was, whate'er I knew.
In short, consum'd with learned care
I liv'd, I died——I rooted here!
For Heaven, that's pleased with doing good,
To make me useful made me wood.

RICHARD JAGO (1715-1781)

ABSENCE

With leaden foot Time creeps along
   While Delia is away,
With her, nor plaintive was the song,
   Nor tedious was the day.

Ah! envious pow'r! reverse my doom,
   Now double thy career,
Strain ev'ry nerve, stretch ev'ry plume,
   And rest them when she's here.

TO A LADY

When Nature joins a beauteous face
With shape, and air, and life, and grace,
To ev'ry imperfection blind,
I spy no blemish in the mind.

When wit flows pure from Stella's tongue,
Or animates the sprightly song,
Our hearts confess the pow'r divine,
Nor lightly prize its mortal shrine.

Good-nature will a conquest gain,
Though wit and beauty sigh in vain.
When gen'rous thoughts the breast inspire,
I wish its rank and fortunes higher.

When Sidney's charms again unite
To win the soul, and bless the sight,
Fair, and learn'd, and good, and great!
An earthly goddess is complete.

But when I see a sordid mind
With affluence and ill-nature join'd,
And pride without a grain of sense,
And without beauty insolence,
The creature with contempt I view,
And sure 't is like Miss——you know who.

169

THE MISTAKE

On Captain Bluff

Says a gosling, almost frighten'd out of her wits,
"Help, mother, or else I shall go into fits.
I have had such a fright, I shall never recover,
O! that <u>hawke</u>, that you've told us of over and over.
See, there, where he sits, with his terrible face,
And his coat how it glitters all over with lace.
With his sharp hooked nose, and his sword at his heel,
How my heart it goes pit-a-pat, pray, mother, feel."
Says the goose, very gravely, "Pray don't talk so wild,
Those looks are as harmless as mine are, my child.
And as for his sword there, so bright and so nice,
I'll be sworn 't will hurt nothing besides frogs and mice.
Nay, prithee do n't hang so about me, let loose,
I tell thee he dares not say——bo to a goose.
In short there is not a more innocent fowl,
Why, instead of a <u>hawke</u>, look ye child, 't is an <u>owl</u>."

TO A LADY WITH A BASKET OF FRUIT

Once of forbidden fruit the mortal taste
Chang'd beauteous Eden to a dreary waste.
Here you may freely eat, secure the while
From latent poison, or insidious guile.
Yet O! could I but happily infuse
Some secret charm into the sav'ry juice,
Of pow'r to tempt your gentle breast to share
With me the peaceful cot, and rural fare:
A diff'rent fate should crown the blest device,
And change my desert to a paradise.

PEYTOE'S GHOST

To Craven's health, and social joy,
    The festive night was kept,
While mirth and patriot spirit flow'd,
    And Dullness only slept.

When from the jovial crowd I stole,
    And homeward shap'd my way;

170

And pass'd along by Chesterton,
    All at the close of day.

The sky with clouds was overcast,
    An hollow tempest blow'd,
And rains and foaming cataracts
    Had delug'd all the road;

When through the dark and lonesome shade
    Shone forth a sudden light;
And soon distinct an human form
    Engag'd my wondering sight.

Onward it mov'd with graceful port,
    And soon o'ertook my speed;
Then thrice I lifted up my hands,
    And thrice I check'd my steed.

"Who art thou, passenger," it cry'd,
    "From yonder mirth retir'd?
That here pursu'st thy cheerless way,
    Benighted, and be-mir'd."

"I am," said I, "a country clerk,
    A clerk of low degree,
And yonder gay and gallant scene
    Suits not a curacy.

"But I have seen such sights to day
    As make my heart full glad,
Although it is but dark, 't is true,
    And eke——my road is bad.

"For I have seen lords, knights, and 'squires,
    Of great and high renown,
To choose a knight for this fair shire,
    All met at Warwick town.

"A wight of skill to ken our laws,
    Of courage to defend,
Of worth to serve the public cause
    Before a private end.

"And such they found, if right I guess——
    Of gentle blood he came;
Of morals firm, of manners mild,
    And Craven is his name.

171

"Did half the British tribunes share
    Experienc'd Mordaunt's truth,
Another half, like Craven boast
    A free unbiass'd youth:

"The Sun I trow, in all his race,
    No happier realms should find;
Nor Britons hope for aught in vain,
    From warmth with prudence join'd.

"Go on, my country, favour'd soil,
    Such patriots to produce!"
"Go on, my countrymen," he cry'd,
    "Such patriots still to choose."

This said, the placid form retir'd
    Behind the veil of night;
Yet bade me, for my country's good,
    The solemn tale recite.

TO WILLIAM SHENSTONE, ESQ.

On Receiving a Gilt Pocket-Book, 1751

These spotless leaves, this neat array,
    Might well invite your charming quill,
In fair assemblage to display
    The power of learning, wit, and skill.

But since you carelessly refuse,
    And to my pen the task assign;
O! let your genius guide my Muse,
    And every vulgar thought refine.

Teach me your best, your best lov'd art,
    With frugal care to store my mind;
In this to play the miser's part,
    And give mean lucre to the wind:

To shun the coxcomb's empty noise,
    To scorn the villain's artful mask;
Nor trust gay pleasure's fleeting joys,
    Nor urge ambition's endless task.

Teach me to stem youth's boisterous tide,
    To regulate its giddy rage;

172

By reason's aid my bark to guide,
   Into the friendly port of age:

To share what classic culture yields,
   Through rhetoric's painted meads to roam;
With you to reap historic fields,
   And bring the golden harvest home.

To taste the genuine sweets of wit;
   To quaff in humour's sprightly bowl;
The philosophic mean to hit,
   And prize the dignity of soul.

Teach me to read fair nature's book,
   Wide opening in each flow'ry plain;
And with judicious eye to look
   On all the glories of her reign.

To hail her, seated on her throne,
   By awful woods encompass'd round,
Or her divine extraction own,
   Though with a wreath of rushes crown'd.

Through arched walks, o'er spreading lawns,
   Near solemn rocks, with her to rove;
Or court her, mid her gentle fawns,
   In mossy cell, or maple grove.

Whether the prospect strain the sight,
   Or in the nearer landskips charm,
Where hills, vales, fountains, woods unite,
   To grace your sweet Arcadian farm:

There let me sit, and gaze with you,
   On Nature's works by art refin'd;
And own, while we their contest view,
   Both fair, but fairest, thus combin'd!

AN ELEGY ON MAN

January, 1752

Behold Earth's lord, imperial man,
   In ripen'd vigour gay;
His outward form attentive scan,
   And all within survey.

Behold his plans of future life,
  His care, his hope, his love,
Relations dear of child and wife,
  The dome, the lawn, the grove.

Now see within his active mind,
  More gen'rous passions share,
Friend, neighbour, country, all his kind,
  By turns engage his care.

Behold him range with curious eye,
  O'er Earth from pole to pole,
And through th' illimitable sky
  Explore with daring soul.

Yet pass some twenty fleeting years,
  And all his glory flies,
His languid eye is bath'd in tears,
  He sickens, groans, and dies.

And is this all his destin'd lot,
  This all his boasted sway?
For ever now to be forgot,
  Amid the mould'ring clay!

Ah, gloomy thought! ah, worse than death!
  Life sickens at the sound;
Better it were not draw our breath,
  Than run this empty round.

Hence, cheating Fancy, then, away;
  O let us better try,
By reason's more enlighten'd ray,
  What 't is indeed to die.

Observe yon mass of putrid earth,
  It holds an embryo-brood
Ev'n now the reptiles crawl to birth,
  And seek their leafy food.

Yet stay till some few suns are past,
  Each forms a silken tomb,
And seems, like man, imprison'd fast,
  To meet his final doom.

Yet from this silent mansion too
  Anon you see him rise,

Nor more a crawling worm to view,
  But tenant of the skies.

And what forbids that man should share,
  Some more auspicious day,
To range at large in open air,
  As light and free as they?

There was a time when life first warm'd
  Our flesh in shades of night,
Then was th' imperfect substance form'd,
  And sent to view this light.

There was a time, when ev'ry sense
  In straiter limits dwelt,
Yet each its task could then dispense,
  We saw, we heard, we felt.

And times there are, when through the veins
  The blood forgets to flow,
Yet then a living pow'r remains,
  Though not in active show.

Times too there be, when friendly sleep's
  Soft charms the senses bind,
Yet fancy then her vigils keeps,
  And ranges unconfin'd.

And reason holds her sep'rate sway,
  Though all the senses wake,
And forms in mem'ry's storehouse play,
  Of no materials make.

What are these then, this eye, this ear,
  But nicer organs found,
A glass to read, a trump to hear,
  The modes of shape, or sound?

And blows may maim, or time impair
  These instruments of clay,
And Death may ravish what they spare,
  Completing their decay.

But are these then that living pow'r
  That thinks, compares, and rules?
Then say a scaffold is a tow'r,
  A workman is his tools.

175

For aught appears that Death can do,
    That still survives his stroke,
Its workings plac'd beyond our view,
    Its present commerce broke.

But what connections it may find,
    Boots much to hope and fear,
And if instruction courts the mind,
    'T is madness not to hear.

ON RECEIVING A LITTLE IVORY BOX

(from a Lady, Curiously Wrought by Her Own Hands)

Little box of matchless grace!
Fairer than the fairest face,
Smooth as was her parent-hand,
That did thy wondrous form command.
Spotless as her infant mind,
As her riper age refin'd,
Beauty with the graces join'd.
    Let me clothe the lovely stranger,
Let me lodge thee safe from danger.
Let me guard thy soft repose,
From giddy fortune's random blows.
From thoughtless mirth, barbaric hate,
From the iron hand of Fate,
And oppression's deadly weight.
    Thou art not of a sort, or number,
Fashion'd for a poet's lumber;
Though more capacious than his purse,
Too small to hold his store of verse.
Too delicate for homely toil,
Too neat for vulgar hands to soil.
O! would the Fates permit the Muse
Thy future destiny to choose!
In thy circle's fairy round,
With a golden fillet bound:
Like the snow-drop silver white,
Like the glow-worm's humid light,
Like the dew at early dawn,
Like the moon-light on the lawn,
Lucid rows of pearls should dwell,
Pleas'd as in their native shell;
Or the brilliant's sparkling rays,
Should emit a starry blaze.

And if the fair, whose magic skill
Wrought thee passive to her will,
Deign to regard thy poet's love,
Nor his aspiring suit reprove,
Her form should crown the fair design,
Goddess fit for such a shrine!

DAVID GARRICK (1717-1779)

A SONG

from "The Country Girl"

Tell not me of the roses and lilies,
Which tinge the fair cheek of your Phillis,
Tell not me of the dimples, and eyes,
For which silly Corydon dies:
Let all whining lovers go hang;
 My heart would you hit,
 Tip your arrow with wit,
And it comes to my heart with a twang, twang,
And it comes to my heart with a twang.

I am rock to the handsome, and pretty,
Can only be touch'd by the witty;
And beauty will ogle in vain,
The way to my heart's through my brain.
Let all whining lovers go hang;
 We wits, you must know,
 Have two strings to our bow,
To return them their darts with a twang, twang,
And return them their darts with a twang.

PROLOGUE

from "The Clandestine Marriage"

Poets and painters, who from Nature draw
Their best and richest stores, have made this law:
That each should neighbourly assist his brother,
And steal with decency from one another.
To-night, your matchless Hogarth gives the thought,
Which from his canvas to the stage is brought.
And who so fit to warm the poet's mind,
As he who pictured morals and mankind?
But not the same their characters and scenes;
Both labour for one end, by different means:
Each, as it suits him, takes a separate road,
Their one great object, Marriage-à-la-mode!
Where titles deign with cits to have and hold,
And change rich blood for more substantial gold!

178

And honoured trade from interest turns aside,
To hazard happiness for titled pride.
The painter dead, yet still he charms the eye;
While England lives, his fame can never die:
But he who struts his hour upon the stage,
Can scarce extend his fame for half an age;
Nor pen nor pencil can the actor save,
The art, and artist, share one common grave.
    O let me drop one tributary tear
On poor Jack Falstaff's grave, and Juliet's bier!
You to their worth must testimony give;
'Tis in your hearts alone their fame can live.
Still as the scenes of life will shift away,
The strong impressions of their art decay.
Your children cannot feel what you have known;
They'll boast of Quins and Cibbers of their own:
The greatest glory of our happy few,
Is to be felt, and be approved by you.

A SONG

from "The Clandestine Marriage"

    I hate all their nonsense,
    Their Shakespeares and Johnsons,
Their plays, and their playhouse, and bards;
    'Tis singing, not saying:
    A fig for all playing,
But playing, as we do, at cards!

    I love to see Jonas,
    Am pleased too with Comus:
Each well the spectator rewards.
    So clever, so neat in
    Their tricks, and their cheating!
Like them we would fain deal our cards.

RICHARD OWEN CAMBRIDGE (1717-1802)

TOBACCO: A TALE

Addressed to J.H. Browne, Esq., author of
the "Pipe of Tobacco, in Imitation of Six Several Authors"

The folks of old were not so nice
But that they'd ask and take advice.
'Twas then the Phythian's prudent voice
Directed Tully in his choice.
Consult your genius, said the maid;
No more; the humble youth obey'd.
This rule so short, so just, so plain,
Our lively moderns all disdain;
And scorn to have their flights control'd
By any Pythians new or old;
Nor ask what may their genius fit,
But all, forsooth, must aim at wit.
　　When first that fragrant leaf came o'er
To bless our barren northern shore,
Which your immortal verses raise
A rival to the poet's bays,
A squire of Sussex gave command
To plant it in his marshy land:
His anxious friends and neighbours join
To drive him from this strange design.
"Tobacco," says a skilful farmer,
"Requires a dryer clime and warmer;
The wat'ry coldness of your soil
Will frustrate all the planter's toil;
Yet not ungrateful shall the clay
With beans a plenteous crop repay."
　　"Let peasant hinds," replies the squire,
"Whose grov'ling souls can rise no higher,
Drudge on, content with piddling gain
From vulgar means, and common grain;
But I will make this northern isle
With India's boasted harvest smile,
And show how needless 'tis to roam
For what we may produce at home."
　　He said, and wide as his command,
Tobacco filled the hungry land;
The restive marl obstructs the shoot,
And checks the plant, and kills the root.

Yearly his project he repeated,
Yearly he saw his hopes defeated,
Till all, at length, his fate deplore,
And find him begging at their door.
  Thus may'st thou see, discerning Browne,
A sauntering crowd infest the town;
Whom providential Nature made
To thrive in physic, law, or trade.
What she directs, perverse they quit,
And strive to force spontaneous wit;
Mispend their time, misplace their toil,
To cultivate a barren soil;
And find no art or force can breed,
What in your garden grows a weed.

HORACE WALPOLE, EARL OF ORFORD (1717-1797)

THE ENTAIL

A Fable

In a fair summer's radiant morn,
A butterfly divinely born,
Whose lineage dated from the mud
Of Noah's or Deucalion's flood,
Long hov'ring round a perfum'd lawn,
By various gusts of odours drawn,
At last establish'd his repose
On the rich bosom of a rose.
The palace pleas'd the lordly guest:
What insect own'd a prouder nest?
The dewy leaves luxurious shed
Their balmy odours o'er his head,
And with their silken tapestry fold
His limbs, enthron'd on central gold,
He thinks the thorns embattled round
To guard his castle's lovely mound,
And all the bush's wide domain
Subservient to his fancied reign.

Such Ample blessings swell'd the fly!
Yet in his mind's capricious eye
He roll'd the change of mortal things,
The common fate of flies and kings.
With grief he saw how lands and honours
Are apt to slide to various owners;
Where Mowbrays dwelt, now grocers dwell,
And now cits buy what barons sell.
"Great Phoebus, patriarch of my line,
Avert such shame from sons of thine!
To them confirm these roofs," he said;
And then he swore an oath so dread,
The stoutest wasp that wears a sword
Had trembled to have heard the word!
"If law can rivet down entails,
These manors ne'er shall pass to snails.
I swear,"—and then then he smote his ermine—
"These towers were never built for vermin."

A caterpillar grovell'd near,
A subtle slow conveyancer,
Who summon'd, waddles with his quill
To draw the haughty insect's will;

182

None but his heirs must own the spot,
Begotten, or to be begot:
Each leaf he binds, each bud he ties
To eggs of eggs of butterflies.
　　When lo! how fortune loves to teaze
Those who would dictate her decrees!
A wanton boy was passing by;
The wanton child beheld the fly,
And eager ran to seize the prey;
But too impetuous in his play,
Crush'd the proud tenant of an hour,
And swept away the mansion-flow'r.

JAMES CAWTHORN (1719-1761)

AN ELEGY TO THE MEMORY OF CAPTAIN HUGHES

A Particular Friend of the Author's

Vain were the task to give the soul to glow,
The nerve to kindle, and the verse to flow;
When the fond mourner, hid from every eye,
Bleeds in the anguish of too keen a sigh;
And, lost to glory, lost to all his fire,
Forgets the poet ere he grasps the lyre.
    Nature! 'tis thine with manly warmth to mourn
Expiring Virtue, and the closing urn;
To teach, dear seraph! o'er the good and wise
The dirge to murmur, and the bust to rise.
Come then, O guiltless of the tear of art!
Sprung from the sky, and thron'd within the heart!
O come, in all the pomp of grief array'd,
And weep the warrior, whilst I grace the shade.
    'Tis o'er——the bright delusive scene is o'er,
And War's proud visions mock the soul no more;
The laurel fades, th' imperial car retires,
All youth ennobles, and all worth admires.
    Alas! my HUGHES! and must this mourning verse
Resign thy triumph to attend thy hearse!
Was it for this that Friendship's genial flame
Woke all my wishes from the trance of Fame?
Was it for this I left the hallow'd page,
Where every science beams of every age;
On thought's strong pinion rang'd the martial scene,
From Rome's first Caesar to the great Eugene;
Explor'd th' embattled van, the deep'ning line,
Th' enambush'd phalanx, and the springing mine;
Then, pale with horrour, bent the suppliant knee,
And heav'd the sigh, and dropp'd the tear for thee!
    What boots it now, that when, with hideous roar,
The gath'ring tempest howl'd from ev'ry shore,
Some pitying angel, vigilant to save,
Spread all his plumes, and snatch'd thee from the wave!
Preserv'd thee sacred from the fell disease,
When the blue plague had fir'd th' autumnal breeze?
Ah! when my hero panted to engage
Where all the battle burst in all its rage;
Where dreadful flew the missive deaths around,
And the mad falchion blush'd from wound to wound;

184

Was he deny'd the privilege to bleed,
Sav'd on the main to fall upon the Tweed?
　Ye Graces! tell with what address he stole
The listening ear, and open'd all the soul.
What though rough Winter bade his whirlwinds rise,
Hid his pale suns, and frown'd along his skies,
Pour'd the big deluge on the face of day,
My HUGHES was here to smile the gloom away,
With all the luxuries of sound to move
The pulse of glory, or the sigh of love;
And, spite of winter, lassitude, or pain,
Taught life and joy to throb in ev'ry vein.
Fancy! dear artist of the mental pow'r!
Fly, ——fetch my genius to the social hour;
Give me again his glowing sense to warm,
His song to warble, and his wit to charm.
Alas! alas! how impotently true
Th' aerial pencil forms the scene anew!
　E'en now, when all the vision beams around,
And my ear kindles with th' ideal sound——
Just as the smiles, the graces live imprest,
And all his image takes up all my breast——
Some gloomy phantom brings the awful bier,
And the short rapture melts into a tear.
　Thus in the lake's clear crystal we descry
The bright diffusion of a radiant sky——
Reflected Nature sheds a milder green;
While half her forests float into the scene.
Ah! as we gaze the luckless zephyr flies,
The surface trembles, and the picture dies.
　O blest with all that youth can give to please,
The form majestic, and the mien of ease,
Alike empower'd by Nature, and by Art,
To storm the rampart, and to win the heart;
Correct of manners, delicate of mind,
With spirit humble, and with truth refin'd;
For public life's meridian sunshine made,
Yet known to ev'ry virtue of the shade;
In war, while all the trumps of Fame inspire,
Each passion raving, and each wish on fire;
At home, without or vanity, or rage;
　As soft as pity, and as cool as age.
　These were thy virtues——these will still be just,
Light all their beams, and blaze upon thy dust,
While Pride in vain solemnity bequeaths
To Pow'r her statues, and to Guilt her wreaths:
Or, warm'd by faction, impudently flings
The price of nations on the urns of kings.

JAMES MERRICK (1720-1769)

THE IGNORANCE OF MAN

Behold yon new-born infant, griev'd
  With hunger, thirst, and pain;
That asks to have the wants reliev'd,
  It knows not to explain.

Aloud the speechless suppliant cries,
  And utters, as it can,
The woes that in its bosom rise,
  And speaks its nature man.

That infant, whose advancing hour
  Life's various sorrows try,
(Sad proof of sin's transmissive pow'r)
  That infant, Lord, am I.

A childhood yet my thoughts confess,
  Tho' long in years mature;
Unknowing whence I feel distress,
  And where, or what its cure.

Author of good, to thee I turn;
  Thy ever-wakeful eye
Alone can all my wants discern,
  Thy hand alone supply.

O let thy fear within me dwell,
  Thy love my footsteps guide,
That love shall vainer loves expell,
  That fear all fears beside.

And O, by error's force subdu'd,
  Since oft my stubborn will
Prepost'rous shuns the latent good,
  And grasps the specious ill;

Not to my wish, but to my want,
  Do Thou thy gifts apply:
Unask'd, what good thou knoweth, grant;
  What ill, though ask'd, deny.

THE CHAMELEON

Oft has it been my lot to mark
A proud, conceited, talking spark,
With eyes that hardly served at most
To guard their master 'gainst a post;
Yet round the world the blade has been,
To see whatever could be seen.
Returning from his finished tour,
Grown ten times perter than before;
Whatever word you chance to drop,
The travelled fool your mouth will stop:
"Sir, if my judgment you'll allow——
I've seen——and sure I ought to know."
So begs you'd pay a due submission,
And acquiesce in his decision.
　　Two travellers of such a cast,
As o'er Arabia's wilds they passed,
And on their way, in friendly chat,
Now talked of this, and then of that,
Discoursed awhile, 'mongst other matter,
Of the chameleon's form and nature.
"A stranger animal," cries one,
"Sure never lived beneath the sun:
A lizard's body, lean and long,
A fish's head, a serpent's tongue,
Its foot with triple claw disjoined;
And what a length of tail behind!
How slow its pace! and then its hue——
Who ever saw so fine a blue?"
　　"Hold there," the other quick replies;
"'T is green, I saw it with these eyes,
As late with open mouth it lay,
And warmed it in the sunny ray;
Stretched at its ease the beast I viewed,
And saw it eat the air for food."
　　"I've seen it, sir, as well as you,
And must again affirm it blue;
At leisure I the beast surveyed
Extended in the cooling shade."
　　"'T is green, 't is green, sir, I assure ye."
"Green!" cries the other in a fury;
"Why, sir, d'ye think I've lost my eyes?"
"'T were no great loss," the friend replies;
"For if they always serve you thus,
You'll find them but of little use."

187

So high at last the contest rose,
From words they almost came to blows:
When luckily came by a third;
To him the question they referred,
And begged he'd tell them, if he knew,
Whether the thing was green or blue.
  "Sirs," cries the umpire, "cease your pother;
The creature's neither one nor t'other.
I caught the animal last night,
And viewed it o'er by candlelight;
I marked it well, 't was black as jet——
You stare——but, sirs, I've got it yet,
And can produce it."——"Pray, sir, do;
I'll lay my life the thing is blue."
"And I'll be sworn, that when you've seen
The reptile, you'll pronounce him green."
"Well, then, at once to ease the doubt,"
Replies the man, "I'll turn him out;
And when before your eyes I've set him,
If you don't find him black, I'll eat him."
  He said; and full before their sight
Produced the beast, and lo!——'t was white.
Both stared; the man looked wondrous wise——
"My children," the chameleon cries
(Then first the creature found a tongue),
"You all are right, and all are wrong:
When next you talk of what you view,
Think others see as well as you;
Nor wonder if you find that none
Prefers your eyesight to his own."

FRANCIS FAWKES (1720-1777)

THE BROWN JUG: A SONG

Imitated from the Latin of Hieronymus Amaltheus

Dear Tom, this brown jug that now foams with mild ale,
(In which I will drink to sweet Nan of the Vale)
Was once Toby Fillpot, a thirsty old soul
As e'er drank a bottle, or fathom'd a bowl;
In boosing about 'twas his praise to excel,
And among jolly topers he bore off the bell.

It chanc'd as in dog-days he sat at his ease
In his flow'r-woven arbour as gay as you please,
With a friend and a pipe puffing sorrows away,
And with honest old stingo was soaking his clay,
His breath-doors of life on a sudden were shut,
And he died full as big as a Dorchester butt.

His body, when long in the ground it had lain,
And time into clay had resolv'd it again,
A potter found out in its covert so snug,
And with part of fat Toby he form'd this brown jug,
Now sacred to friendship, and mirth, and mild ale,
So here's to my lovely sweet Nan of the Vale.

THE DEATH OF THE LARK

1738

The golden Sun, emerging from the main,
Beams a blue lustre on the dewy plain;
Elate with joy all creatures hail his rise,
That haunt the forest, or that skim the skies.
Gay-blooming flow'rs their various charms renew,
A breathing fragrance, or a lovely hue:
Sweet pipes the shepherd, the fair morn to greet,
To his stout team the ploughman whistles sweet.
All nature smiles around. On airy wing
The lark, harmonious herald of the spring,
Rises aloft to breathe his mattins loud
On the bright bosom of some fleecy cloud.
Ah! little conscious that he dies to day,

189

He sports his hour in innocence away,
And from the treble of his tuneful throat
Pours the soft strain, or trills the sprightly note;
Or calls his mate, and as he sweetly sings,
Soars in the sun-beam, wavering on his wings.
The ruthless fowler, with unerring aim,
Points the dire tube——forth streams the sudden flame:
Swift in hoarse thunder flies the leaden wound,
The rigid rocks return the murdering sound;
The strains unfinish'd with the warbler die,
Float into air, and vanish in the sky.
  Thus oft, fond man, rejoicing in his might,
Sports in the sunshine of serene delight;
Fate comes unseen, and snaps the thin spun thread,
He dies, and sleeps forgotten with the dead.

ON THE DEATH OF A YOUNG GENTLEMAN

September, 1739

Man cometh forth like a flower, and is cut down.
                                        ——JOB, xiv. 2

Short and precarious is the life of man;
The line seems fathomless, but proves a span;
A youth of follies, and old-age of sorrow;
Like flowers to day we bloom, we die to morrow.
Say then, what specious reasons can we give,
And why this longing, fond desire to live?
Blind as we are to what the Lord ordains,
We stretch our troubles, and prolong our pains.
  But you, blest genius, dear departed shade,
Now wear a chaplet that shall never fade;
Now sit exalted in those realms of rest
Where virtue reigns, and innocence is blest,
Relentless death's inevitable doom
Untimely wrapt you in the silent tomb,
Ere the first tender down o'erspread your chin,
A stranger yet to sorrow, and to sin.
  As some sweet rose-bud, that has just begun
To ope its damask beauties in the sun,
Cropt by a virgin's hand, remains confest
A sweeter rose-bud in her balmy breast:
  Thus the fair youth, when Heav'n requir'd his breath,
Sunk, sweetly smiling, in the arms of death;

For endless joys exchanging endless strife,
And bloom'd renew'd in everlasting life.

TOBIAS SMOLLETT (1721-1771)

THE TEARS OF SCOTLAND

1746

Mourn, hapless Caledonia, mourn
Thy banish'd peace, thy laurels torn!
Thy sons, for valour long renown'd,
Lie slaughter'd on their native ground;
Thy hospitable roofs no more,
Invite the stranger to the door;
In smoky ruins sunk they lie,
The monuments of cruelty.

The wretched owner sees afar
His all become the prey of war;
Bethinks him of his babes and wife,
Then smites his breast, and curses life.
Thy swains are famish'd on the rocks,
Where once they fed their wanton flocks:
Thy ravish'd virgins shriek in vain;
Thy infants perish on the plain.

What boots it then, in every clime,
Thro' the wide-spreading waste of time,
Thy martial glory, crown'd with praise,
Still shone with undiminish'd blaze?
Thy tow'ring spirit now is broke,
Thy neck is bended to the yoke.
What foreign arms could never quell,
By civil rage and rancour fell.

The rural pipe and merry lay
No more shall cheer the happy day:
No social scenes of gay delight
Beguile the dreary winter night:
No strains but those of sorrow flow,
And nought be heard but sounds of woe,
While the pale phantoms of the slain
Glide nightly o'er the silent plain.

O baneful cause, oh, fatal morn,
Accurs'd to ages yet unborn!
The sons against their fathers stood,

The parent shed his children's blood.
Yet, when the rage of battle ceas'd,
The victor's soul was not appeas'd:
The naked and forlorn must feel
Devouring flames, and murd'ring steel!

The pious mother doom'd to death,
Forsaken wanders o'er the heath,
The bleak wind whistles round her head,
Her helpless orphans cry for bread;
Bereft of shelter, food, and friend,
She views the shades of night descend,
And, stretch'd beneath th' inclement skies,
Weeps o'er her tender babes and dies.

While the warm blood bedews my veins,
And unimpair'd remembrance reigns,
Resentment of my country's fate
Within my filial breast shall beat;
And, spite of her insulting foe,
My sympathizing verse shall flow:
"Mourn, hapless Caledonia, mourn
Thy banish'd peace, thy laurels torn."

VERSES

On a Young Lady Playing on a Harpsichord and Singing

When Sappho struck the quiv'ring wire,
The throbbing breast was all on fire:
And when she rais'd the vocal lay,
The captive soul was charm'd away!

But had the nymph, possest with these,
Thy softer, chaster, pow'r to please;
Thy beauteous air of sprightly youth,
Thy native smiles of artless truth;

The worm of grief had never prey'd
On the forsaken love-sick maid:
Nor had she mourn'd a hapless flame,
Nor dash'd on rocks her tender frame.

193

ODE TO BLUE-EY'D ANN

When the rough North forgets to howl,
And Ocean's billows cease to roll;
When Lybian sands are bound in frost,
And cold to Nova Zembla's lost!
When heav'nly bodies cease to move,
My blue'ey'd Ann I'll cease to love.

No more shall flowers the meads adorn;
Nor sweetness deck the rosy thorn;
Nor swelling buds proclaim the spring;
Nor parching heats the dog-star bring;
Nor laughing lilies paint the grove,
When blue-ey'd Ann I cease to love.

No more shall joy in hope be found;
Nor pleasures dance their frolic round;
Nor love's light god inhabit Earth;
Nor beauty give the passion birth;
Nor heat to summer sunshine cleave,
When blue-ey'd Nanny I deceive.

When rolling seasons cease to change,
Inconstancy forgets to range;
When lavish May no more shall bloom;
Nor gardens yield a rich perfume;
When Nature from her sphere shall start,
I'll tear my Nanny from my heart.

ODE TO LEVEN-WATER

On Leven's banks, while free to rove,
And tune the rural pipe to love;
I envied not the happiest swain
That ever trod th' Arcadian plain.
    Pure stream! in whose transparent wave
My youthful limbs I wont to lave;
No torrents stain thy limpid source,
No rocks impede thy dimpling course,
That sweetly warbles o'er its bed,
With white, round, polish'd pebbles spread;
While, lightly pois'd, the scaly brood
In myriads cleave thy crystal flood;
The springing trout in speckled pride;

194

The salmon, monarch of the tide,
The ruthless pike, intent on war;
The silver eel and motled par.
Devolving from thy parent lake,
A charming maze thy waters make,
By bow'rs of birch, and groves of pine,
And hedges flow'r'd with eglantine.
    Still on thy banks so gayly green,
May numerous herds and flocks be seen;
And lasses chanting o'er the pail,
And shepherds piping in the dale,
And antient faith that knows no guile,
And industry imbrown'd with toil,
And hearts resolv'd, and hands prepar'd
The blessings they enjoy to guard.

DR. THOMAS BLACKLOCK (1721-1791)

ODE, WRITTEN WHEN SICK

O prime of life! O taste of joy!
Whither so early do you fly?
Scarce half your transient sweetness known,
Why are you vanish'd ere full-blown?
  The beauteous progeny of spring,
That tinge the zephyr's fragrant wing,
Each tender bloom, each short-liv'd flow'r,
Still flourish till their destin'd hour:
Your winter too, too soon will come,
And chill in death your vernal bloom.
  On my wan cheek the colour dies,
Suffus'd and languid roll mine eyes;
Cold horrours thrill each sick'ning vein;
Deep broken sighs my bosom strain;
The salient pulse of health gives o'er,
And life and pleasure are no more.

A PASTORAL SONG

Sandy, the gay, the blooming swain,
  Had lang frae love been free;
Lang made ilk heart that fill'd the plain
  Dance quick with harmless glee.

As blythsome lambs that scour the green,
  His mind was unconstrain'd;
Nae face could ever fix his een,
  Nae sang his ear detain'd.

Ah! luckless youth! a short-liv'd joy
  Thy cruel fates decree;
Fell tods shall on thy lambkins prey,
  And love mair fell on thee.

Twas e'er the Sun exhal'd the dew,
  As morn of cheerful May,
Forth Girzy walk'd, the flow'rs to view,
  A flow'r mair sweet than they!

Like sunbeams sheen her waving locks;

Her een like stars were bright;
The rose lent blushes to her cheek;
The lily purest white.

Jimp was her waist, like some tall pine
That keeps the woods in awe;
Her limbs like iv'ry columns turn'd,
Her breasts like hills of snaw.

Her robe around her loosely thrown,
Gave to the shepherd's een
What fearless innocence would show;
The rest was all unseen.

He fix'd his look, he sigh'd, he quak'd,
His colour went and came;
Dark grew his een, his ears resound,
His breast was all on flame.

Nae mair yon glen repeats his sang,
He jokes and smiles nae mair;
Unplaited now his cravat hung,
Undrest his chesnut hair.

To him how lang the shortest night!
How dark the brightest day!
Till, with the slow consuming fire,
His life was worn away.

Far, far frae shepherds and their flocks,
Opprest with care, he lean'd;
And, in a mirky, beachen shade,
To hills and dales thus plean'd:

"At length, my wayward heart, return,
Too far, alas! astray:
Say, whence you caught that bitter smart,
Which works me such decay.

"Ay me! 'twas Love, 'twas Girzy's charms,
That first began my woes;
Could he sae saft, or she sae fair,
Prove such relentless foes?

"Fierce winter nips the sweetest flower;
Keen lightning rives the tree;
Bleak mildew taints the fairest crop,
And love has blasted me.

197

"Sagacious hounds the foxes chase;
　　The tender lambkins they;
Lambs follow close their mother ewes,
　　And ewes the blooms of May.

"Sith a' that live, with a' their might,
　　Some dear delight pursue;
Cease, ruthless maid! to scorn the heart
　　That only pants for you.

"Alas! for griefs, to her unken'd,
　　What pity can I gain?
And should she ken, yet love refuse,
　　Could that redress my pain?

"Come, Death, my wan, my frozen bride,
　　Ah! close those wearied eyes:
But Death the happy still pursues,
　　Still from the wretched flies.

"Could wealth avail; what wealth is mine
　　Her high-born mind to bend?
Her's are those wide delightful plains,
　　And her's the flocks I tend.

"What tho', whene'er I tun'd my pipe,
　　Glad fairies heard the sound,
And, clad in freshest April green,
　　Aft tript the circle round:

"Break, landward clown, thy dinsome reed,
　　And brag thy skill nae mair:
Can aught that gies na Girzy joy,
　　Be worth thy lightest care?

"Adieu! ye harmless, sportive flocks!
　　Who now your lives shall guard?
Adieu! my faithful dog, who oft,
　　The pleasing vigil shar'd:

"Adieu! ye plains, and light, anes sweet,
　　Now painful to my view:
Adieu to life; and thou, mair dear,
　　Who caus'd my death; adieu!"

AN EPITAPH, ON A FAVOURITE LAP-DOG

I never bark'd when out of season;
I never bit without a reason;
I ne'er insulted weaker brother;
Nor wrong'd by force nor fraud another.
Though brutes are plac'd a rank below,
Happy for man, could he say so!

JOHN SKINNER (1721-1807)

TULLOCHGORUM

Come gie's a sang, Montgomery cry'd,
And lay your disputes all aside,
What signifies't for folks to chide
        For what was done before them:
Let Whig and Tory all agree,
    Whig and Tory, Whig and Tory,
    Whig and Tory all agree,
        To drop their Whig-mig-morum;
Let Whig and Tory all agree
To spend the night wi' mirth and glee,
And cheerful sing alang wi' me
        The Reel o' Tullochgorum.

O' Tullochgorum's my delight,
It gars us a' in ane unite,
And ony sumph that keeps a spite,
        In conscience I abhor him:
For blythe and cheerie we'll be a',
    Blythe and cheerie, blythe and cheerie,
    Blythe and cheerie we'll be a',
        And make a happy quorum,
For blythe and cheerie we'll be a'
As lang as we hae breath to draw,
And dance till we be like to fa'
        The Reel o' Tullochgorum.

What needs there be sae great a fraise
Wi' dringing dull Italian lays,
I wadna gie our ain Strathspeys
        For half a hunder score o' them;
They're dowf and dowie at the best,
    Dowf and dowie, dowf and dowie,
    Dowf and dowie at the best,
        Wi' a' their variorum;
They're dowf and dowie at the best,
Their allegros and a' the rest,
They canna' please a Scottish taste
        Compar'd wi' Tullochgorum.

Let warldly worms their minds oppress
Wi' fears o' want and double cess,
And sullen sots themsells distress

200

Wi' keeping up decorum:
Shall we sae sour and sulky sit,
  Sour and sulky, sour and sulky,
  Sour and sulky shall we sit
    Like old philosophorum!
Shall we sae sour and sulky sit,
Wi' neither sense, nor mirth, nor wit,
Nor ever try to shake a fit
    To th' Reel o' Tullochgorum?

May choicest blessings ay attend
Each honest, open hearted friend,
And calm and quiet be his end,
    And a' that's good watch o'er him;
May peace and plenty be his lot,
  Peace and plenty, peace and plenty,
  Peace and plenty be his lot,
    And dainties a great store o' them;
May peace and plenty be his lot,
Unstain'd by any vicious spot,
And may he never want a groat,
    That's fond o' Tullochgorum!

But for the sullen frumpish fool,
That loves to be oppression's tool,
May envy gnaw his rotten soul,
    And discontent devour him;
May dool and sorrow be his chance,
  Dool and sorrow, dool and sorrow,
  Dool and sorrow be his chance,
    And nane say, wae's me for him!
May dool and sorrow be his chance,
Wi' a' the ills that come frae France,
Wha e'er he be that winna dance
    The Reel o' Tullochgorum.

WILLIAM WILKIE (1721-1772)

THE YOUNG LADY AND THE LOOKING-GLASS

A Fable

Ye deep philosophers who can
Explain that various creature, man,
Say, is there any point so nice,
As that of offering an advice?
To bid your friend his errours mend,
Is almost certain to offend:
Though you in softest terms advise,
Confess him good; admit him wise;
In vain you sweeten the discourse,
He thinks you call him fool, or worse;
You paint his character, and try
If he will own it, and apply.
Without a name reprove and warn:
Here none are hurt, and all may learn.
This too must fail, the picture shown,
No man will take it for his own.
In moral lectures treat the case,
Say this is honest, that is base;
In conversation none will bear it;
And for the pulpit, few come near it.
And is there then no other way
A moral lesson to convey?
Must all that shall attempt to teach,
Admonish, satyrize, or preach?
Yes, there is one, an ancient art,
By sages found to reach the heart,
Ere science with distinctions nice
Had fixt what virtue is, and vice,
Inventing all the various names
On which the moralist declaims:
They wou'd by simple tales advise,
Which took the hearer by surprise;
Alarm'd his conscience, unprepar'd,
Ere pride had put it on its guard;
And made him from himself receive
The lessons which they meant to give.
That this device will oft prevail,
And gain its end, when others fail,
If any shall pretend to doubt,
The tale which follows makes it out.

There was a little stubborn dame
Whom no authority could tame,
Restive by long indulgence grown,
No will she minded but her own:
At trifles oft she'd scold and fret,
Then in a corner take a seat,
And sourly moping all the day,
Disdain alike to work or play.
Papa all softer arts had try'd,
And sharper remedies apply'd;
But both were vain, for every course
He took still made her worse and worse,
'Tis strange to think how female wit,
So oft shou'd make a lucky hit,
When man with all his high pretence
To deeper judgment, sounder sense,
Will err, and measures false pursue—
'Tis very strange I own, but true.
Mama observ'd the rising lass,
By stealth retiring to the glass,
To practise little airs unseen,
In the true genius of thirteen:
On this a deep design she laid
To tame the humour of the maid;
Contriving like a prudent mother
To make one folly cure another.
Upon the wall against the seat
Which Jessy us'd for her retreat,
Whene'er by accident offended,
A looking-glass was straight suspended,
That it might show her how deform'd
She look'd, and frightful when she storm'd;
And warn her, as she priz'd her beauty,
To bend her humour to her duty.
All this the looking glass achiev'd,
Its threats were minded and believ'd.

The maid, who spurn'd at all advice,
Grew tame and gentle in a trice.
So when all other means had fail'd,
The silent monitor prevail'd.

Thus, fable to the human-kind
Presents an image of the mind;
It is a mirror where we spy
At large our own deformity,
And learn of course those faults to mend,
Which but to mention would offend.

WILLIAM COLLINS (1721-1759)

AN ODE

1746

How sleep the brave, who sink to rest,
By all their Country's wishes blest!
When Spring, with dewy fingers cold,
Returns to deck their hallow'd mold,
She there shall dress a sweeter sod,
Than Fancy's feet have ever trod.

By fairy hands their knell is rung,
By forms unseen their dirge is sung;
There Honour comes, a pilgrim grey,
To bless the turf that wraps their clay,
And Freedom shall a-while repair,
To dwell a weeping Hermit there!

DR. JOSEPH WARTON (1722-1800)

VERSES ON A BUTTERFLY

Fair child of Sun and Summer! we behold
With eager eyes thy wings bedropp'd with gold;
The purple spots that o'er thy mantle spread,
The sapphire's lively blue, the ruby's red,
Ten thousand various blended tints surprise,
Beyond the rainbow's hues or peacock's eyes:
Not Judah's king in eastern pomp array'd,
Whose charms allur'd from far the Sheban maid,
High on his glitt'ring throne, like you could shine
(Nature's completest miniature divine):
For thee the rose her balmy buds renews,
And silver lillies fill their cups with dews;
Flora for thee the laughing fields perfumes,
For thee Pomona sheds her choicest blooms,
Soft Zephyr wafts thee on his gentlest gales
O'er Hackwood's sunny hill and verdant vales;
For thee, gay queen of insects! do we rove
From walk to walk, from beauteous grove to grove;
And let the critics know, whose pedant pride
And awkward jests our sprightly sport deride:
That all who honours, fame, or wealth pursue,
Change but the name of things——they hunt for you.

ODE TO THE NIGHTINGALE

O thou, that to the moon-light vale
Warblest oft thy plaintive tale,
What time the village-murmurs cease,
And the still eye is hush'd to peace,
When now no busy sound is heard,
Contemplation's favourite bird!

Chauntress of night, whose amorous song
(First heard the tufted groves among)
Warns wanton Mabba to begin
Her revels on the circled green,
Whene'er by meditation led
I nightly seek some distant mead,

A short repose of cares to find,

And sooth my love-distracted mind,
O fail not then, sweet Philomel;
Thy sadly-warbled woes to tell;
In sympathetic numbers join
Thy pangs of luckless love with mine!

So may no swain's rude hand infest
Thy tender young, and rob thy nest;
Nor ruthless fowler's guileful snare
Lure thee to leave the fields of air,
No more to visit vale or shade,
Some barbarous virgin's captive made.

ODE TO A LADY ON THE SPRING

Lo! Spring, array'd in primrose-colour'd robe,
Fresh beauties sheds on each enliven'd scene,
With show'rs and sunshine cheers the smiling globe,
And mantles hill and vale in glowing green.

All nature feels her vital heat around,
The pregnant glebe now bursts with foodful grain,
With kindly warmth she opes the frozen ground,
And with new life informs the teeming plain.

She calls the fish from out their ouzy beds,
And animates the deep with genial love,
She bids the herds bound sportive o'er the meads,
And with glad songs awakes the joyous grove,

No more the glaring tiger roams for prey,
All-powerful love subdues his savage soul,
To find his spotted mate he darts away,
While gentler thoughts the thirst of blood controul.

But ah! while all is warmth and soft desire,
While all around Spring's cheerful spirit own,
You feel not, Amoret, her quickening fire,
To Spring's kind influence you a foe alone!

ODE TO MUSIC

Queen of every moving measure,
Sweetest source of purest pleasure,

Music; why thy powers employ
Only for the sons of joy?
Only for the smiling guests
At natal or at nuptial feasts?
Rather thy lenient numbers pour
On those whom secret griefs devour;
Bid be still the throbbing hearts
Of those, whom death, or absence parts,
And, with some softly whisper'd air,
Smooth the brow of dumb despair.

AN ODE

O gentle, feather-footed Sleep,
In downy dews her temples steep,
Softly waving o'er her head
Thy care-beguiling rod of lead;
Let Hymen in her dreams appear
And mildly whisper in her ear,
That constant hearts can never prove
True transports, but in wedded love.

VERSES

Written on Passing Through Hackwood Park,
August 7th, 1779

O much lov'd haunts! O beech-embower'd vales!
O lonely lawns! where oft at pensive eve
I met in former hours the Muse, and sought
Far from the busy world your deepest shades,
Receive my lovely Delia; to her eye,
Well skill'd to judge of Nature's various charms,
Display your inmost beauties, lead her steps
To each inspiring avenue, but chief
O guide her to that airy hill, where Health
Sits on the verdant turf enthron'd, and smiles
Around the joyous villages; O breathe
Into her tender breast your balmiest gales;
O ease her languid head! that she who feels
For other pains, may ne'er lament her own.

CHRISTOPHER SMART (1722-1771)

ODE XII

A Morning Piece, or an Hym for the Hay-Makers

Quinetiam Gallum noctem explaudentibus alis
Auroram clara consuetum voce vocare.   —LUCRETIUS

Brisk Chanticleer his matins had begun,
    And broke the silence of the night.
And thrice he call'd aloud the tardy Sun,
    And thrice he hail'd the dawn's ambiguous light;
Back to their graves the fear-begotten phantoms run.
    Strong Labour got up. — With his pipe in his mouth,
        He stoutly strode over the dale,
    He lent new perfumes to the breath of the south,
        On his back hung his wallet and flail.
Behind him came Health from her cottage of thatch,
Where never physician had lifted the latch.

First of the village Collin was awake,
And thus he sung reclining on his rake.
        Now the rural graces three
        Dance beneath yon maple tree;
        First the vestal Virtue, known
        By her adamantine zone;
        Next to her in rosy pride,
        Sweet Society the bride;
        Last Honesty, full seemly drest
        In her cleanly home-spun vest.
    The abbey bells in wak'ning rounds
        The warning peal have giv'n;
    And pious Gratitude resounds
        Her morning hymn to Heav'n.

All nature wakes—the birds unlock their throats,
And mock the shepherd's rustic notes.
        All alive o'er the lawn,
        Full glad of the dawn,
        The little lambkins play,
Sylvia and Sol arise, and all is day—
        Come, my mates, let us work
        And all hands to the fork,
While the Sun shines, our hay-cocks to make,
        So fine is the day,

And so fragrant the hay,
That the meadow's as blith as the wake.

Our voices let's raise
In Phoebus's praise,
Inspir'd by so glorious a theme,
Our musical words
Shall be join'd by the birds,
And we'll dance to the tune of the stream.

WHERE'S THE POKER?

A Fable

The poker lost, poor Susan storm'd,
And all the rites of rage perform'd;
As scolding, crying, swearing, sweating,
Abusing, fidgetting, and fretting.
"Nothing but villainy, and thieving;
Good Heavens! what a world we live in?
If I don't find it in the morning,
I'll surely give my master warning,
He'd better far shut up his doors,
Than keep such good for nothing whores;
For wheresoe'er their trade they drive,
We vartuous bodies cannot thrive."
Well may poor Susan grunt and groan;
Misfortunes never come alone,
But tread each other's heels in throngs,
For the next day she lost the tongs:
The salt box, cullender, and pot,
Soon shar'd the same untimely lot.
In vain she vails and wages spent
On new ones——for the new ones went.
There'd been, (she swore) some dev'l or witch in,
To rob or plunder all the kitchen.
One night she to her chamber crept;
(Where for a month she had not slept;
Her master being, to her seeming,
A better playfellow than dreaming.)
Curse on the author of these wrongs,
In her own bed she found the tongs,
(Hang Thomas for an idle joker!)
In her own bed she found the poker;
With salt box, pepper box, and kettle,
With all the culinary metal. ——

Be warn'd, ye fair, by Susan's crosses,
Keep chaste, and guard yourselves from losses;
For if young girls delight in kissing,
No wonder, that the poker's missing.

SWEET WILLIAM

A Ballad

By a prattling stream, on a Midsummer's eve,
Where the woodbine and jess'mine their boughs interweave,
"Fair Flora," I cry'd, "to my harbour repair,
For I must have a chaplet for sweet William's hair."

She brought me the vi'let that grows on the hill,
The vale-dwelling lily, and gilded jonquill:
But such languid odours how cou'd I approve,
Just warm from the lips of the lad that I love.

She brought me, his faith and his truth to display,
The undying myrtle, and ever-green bay:
But why these to me, who've his constancy known?
And Billy has laurels enough of his own.

The next was the gift that I could not contemn,
For she brought me two roses that grew on a stem:
Of the dear nuptial tie they stood emblems confest,
So I kiss'd 'em, and press'd 'em quite close to my breast.

She brought me a sun-flow'r——"This, fair one's your due;
For it once was a maiden, and love-sick like you:"
Oh! give it me quick, to my shepherd I'll run,
As true to his flame, as this flow'r to the Sun.

TO MISS KITTY BENNET, AND HER CAT CROP

A Ballad

Full many a heart, that now is free,
May shortly, fair one, beat for thee,
    And court thy pleasing chain;
Then prudent hear a friend's advice,
And learn to guard, by conduct nice,
    The conquests you shall gain.

210

When Tabby Tom your Crop pursues,
How many a bite, and many a bruise
    The amorous swain endures?
E'er yet one favouring glance he catch,
What frequent squalls, how many a scratch
    His tenderness procures?

Tho' this, 'tis own'd, be somewhat rude,
And Puss by nature be a prude,
    Yet hence you may improve,
By decent pride, and dint of scoff,
Keep caterwauling coxcombs off,
    And ward th' attacks of love.

Your Crop a mousing when you see,
She teaches you economy,
    Which makes the pot to boil:
And when she plays with what she gains,
She shows you pleasure springs from pains,
    And mirth's the fruit of toil.

SIR GILBERT ELLIOT (1722-1777)

AMYNTA

My sheep I neglected, I broke my sheep-hook,
And all the gay haunts of my youth I forsook;
No more for Amynta fresh garlands I wove;
For ambition, I said, would soon cure me of love.
Oh, what had my youth with ambition to do?
Why left I Amynta? Why broke I my vow?
Oh, give me my sheep, and my sheep-hook restore,
And I'll wander from love and Amynta no more.

Through regions remote in vain do I rove,
And bid the wide ocean secure me from love!
O fool! to imagine that aught could subdue
A love so well-founded, a passion so true!

Alas! 'tis too late at thy fate to repine;
Poor shepherd, Amynta can never be thine:
Thy tears are all fruitless, thy wishes are vain,
The moments neglected return not again.

GEN. JOHN BURGOYNE (1722-1792)

A SONG

from "Richard Coeur de Lion"

Oh! would the night my blushes hide,
The truth to thee I would confide.
   Yes, yes, I own 'tis true,
     Whene'er his eyes I meet,
     I feel my heart begins to beat,
   It beats, and trembles too.

For when my hand he gently presses,
A struggling sigh I fear confesses,
Ah! more than blushes could impart,
And more than words betrays my heart.

Oh! would the night, &tc.

A SONG

from "The Maid of the Oaks"

   Come, rouse from your trances,
     The sly morn advances,
  To catch sluggish mortals in bed!
    Let the horn's jocund note
    In the wind sweetly float,
While the fox from the brake lifts his head!
      Now creeping,
       Now peeping,
  The fox from the brake lifts his head:
    Each away to his steed,
    Your goddess shall lead,
  Come follow, my worshippers, follow;
    For the chace all prepare,
    See the hounds snuff the air,
Hark, hark, to the huntsman's sweet hollo!

    Hark Jowler, hark Rover,
    See reynard breaks cover,
  The hunters fly over the ground;

213

Now they skim o'er the plain,
Now they dart down the lane,
And the hills, woods, and vallies resound;
With dashing,
And splashing,
The hills, woods, and vallies resound!
Then away with full speed,
Your goddess shall lead,
Come follow, my worshippers, follow;
O'er hedge, ditch, and gate,
If you stop you're too late,
Hark, hark, to the huntsman's sweet hollo!

JOSEPH REED (1723-1787)

A SONG

from "The Register Office"

My sweet pretty Mog, you're as soft as a bog,
And as wild as a kitten, as wild as a kitten:
Those eyes in your face—(O! pity my case)
Poor Paddy hath smitten, poor Paddy hath smitten.
Far softer than silk, and as fair as new milk,
Your lily-white hand is, your lily-white hand is:
Your shape's like a pail; from your head to your tail,
You're straight as a wand is, you're straight as a wand is.

Your lips red as cherries, and your curling hair is
As black as the devil, as black as the devil;
Your breath is as sweet too as any potatoe,
Or orange from Seville, or orange from Seville.
When dress'd in your boddice, you trip like a goddess,
So nimble, so frisky! so nimble, so frisky!
A kiss on your cheek ('tis so soft and so sleek),
Would warm me like whisky, would warm me like whisky.

I grunt and I pine, like a pig or a swine,
Because you're so cruel, because you're so cruel;
No rest I can take, and asleep or awake,
I dream of my jewel, I dream of my jewel.
Your hate then give over, nor Paddy your lover
So cruelly handle, so cruelly handle;
Or Paddy must die, like a pig in a sty,
Or snuff of a candle, or snuff of a candle.

JOHN GILBERT COOPER (1723-1769)

A SONG

The nymph that I lov'd was as cheerful as day,
And as sweet as the blossoming hawthorn in May;
Her temper was smooth as the down on the dove,
And her face was as fair as the mother's of love.

Tho' mild as the pleasantest zephyr that sheds,
And receives gentle odours from violet beds,
Yet warm in affection as Phoebus at noon,
And as chaste as the silver-white beams of the Moon.

Her mind was unsullied as new-fallen snow,
Yet as lively as tints of young Iris's bow,
As firm as the rock, and as calm as the flood,
Where the peace-loving halcyon deposits her brood.

The sweets that each virtue or grace had in store,
She cull'd as the bee would the bloom of each flow'r;
Which treasur'd for me, O! how happy was I,
For tho' her's to collect, it was mine to enjoy.

WILLIAM MASON (1724-1797)

ODE TO MEMORY

Mother of Wisdom! thou, whose sway
The throng'd ideal hosts obey;
Who bid'st their ranks, now vanish, now appear,
Flame in the van, or darken in the rear;
    Accept this votive verse. Thy reign
    Nor place can fix, nor power restrain.
All, all is thine. For thee the ear, and eye
Rove thro' the realms of grace, and harmony:
    The senses thee spontaneous serve,
    That wake, and thrill thro' ev'ry nerve.
Else vainly soft, lov'd Philomel! would flow
The soothing sadness of thy warbled woe:
    Else vainly sweet yon woodbine shade
    With clouds of fragrance fill the glade;
Vainly, the cygnet spread her downy plume,
The vine gush nectar, and the virgin bloom.
    But swift to thee, alive and warm,
    Devolves each tributary charm:
See modest Nature bring her simple stores,
Luxuriant Art exhaust her plastic powers;
    While every flower in fancy's clime,
    Each gem of old heroic time,
Cull'd by the hand of the industrious Muse,
Around thy shrine their blended beams diffuse.
    Hail, Mem'ry! hail. Behold, I lead
    To that high shrine the sacred maid:
Thy daughter she, the empress of the lyre,
The first, the fairest, of Aonia's quire.
    She comes, and lo, thy realms expand!
    She takes her delegated stand
Full in the midst, and o'er thy num'rous train
Displays the awful wonders of her reign.
    There thron'd supreme in native state,
    If Sirius flame with fainting heat,
She calls; ideal groves their shade extend,
The cool gale breathes, the silent show'rs descend.
    Or, if bleak winter, frowning round,
    Disrobe the trees, and chill the ground,
She, mild magician, waves her potent wand,
And ready summers wake at her command.
    See, visionary suns arise,
    Thro' silver clouds and azure skies;

217

See, sportive zephyrs fan the crisped streams;
Thro' shadowy brakes light glance the sparkling beams:
    While, near the secret moss-grown cave,
    That stands beside the crystal wave,
Sweet Echo, rising from her rocky bed,
Mimics the feather'd chorus o'er her head.
    Rise, hallow'd Milton! rise, and say,
    How, at thy gloomy close of day,
How, when "deprest by age, beset with wrongs:"
When "fall'n on evil days and evil tongues;"
    When darkness, brooding on thy sight,
    Exil'd the sov'reign lamp of light;
Say, what could then one cheering hope diffuse?
What friends were thine, save Mem'ry and the Muse?
    Hence the rich spoils, thy studious youth
    Caught from the stores of antient truth:
Hence all thy classic wand'rings could explore,
When rapture led thee to the Latian shore;
    Each scene, that Tiber's bank supply'd;
    Each grace, that play'd on Arno's side;
The tepid gales, thro' Tuscan glades that fly:
The blue serene, that spreads Hesperia's sky;
    Were still thine own: thy ample mind
    Each charm receiv'd, retain'd, combin'd.
And thence "the nightly visitant," that came
To touch thy bosom with her sacred flame,
    Recall'd the long-lost beams of grace,
    That whilom shot from Nature's face,
When God, in Eden, o'er her youthful breast
Spread with his own right hand perfection's gorgeous vest.

EDWARD LOVIBOND (1724-1775)

HITCHIN CONVENT

A Tale

Where Hitch's gentle current glides,
    An ancient convent stands,
Sacred to prayer and holy rites
    Ordain'd by pious hands.

Here monks of saintly Benedict
    Their nightly vigils kept,
And lofty anthems shook the choir
    At hours when mortals slept.

But Harry's wide reforming hand
    That sacred order wounded;
He spoke——from forth their hallow'd walls
    The friars fled confounded.

Then wicked laymen ent'ring in,
    Those cloisters fair prophan'd;
Now riot loud usurps the seat
    Where bright devotion reign'd.

Ev'n to the chapel's sacred roof,
    Its echoing vaults along,
Resounds the flute, and sprightly dance,
    And hymeneal song.

Yet fame reports, that monkish shades
    At midnight never fail
To haunt the mansions once their own,
    And tread its cloisters pale.

One night, more prying than the rest,
    It chanc'd a friar came,
And enter'd where on beds of down
    Repos'd each gentle dame.

Here, softening midnight's raven gloom,
    Lay R———e, blushing maid;
There, wrapt in folds of cypress lawn,
    Her virtuous aunt was laid.

He stopp'd, he gaz'd, to wild conceits
    His roving fancy run,
He took the aunt for prioress,
    And R———e for a nun.

It hap'd that R———'s capuchin,
    Across the couch display'd,
To deem her sister of the veil,
    The holy sire betray'd.

Accosting then the youthful fair,
    His raptur'd accents broke;
Amazement chill'd the waking nymph;
    She trembled as he spoke.

"Hail halcyon days! Hail holy nun!
    This wondrous change explain:
Again religion lights her lamp,
    Reviews these walls again.

"For ever blest the power that checkt
    Reformists' wild disorders,
Restor'd again the church's lands,
    Reviv'd our sacred orders.

"To monks indeed, from Edward's days,
    Belong'd this chaste foundation;
Yet sister nuns may answer too
    The founder's good donation.

"Ah! well thy virgin vows are heard:
    For man were never given
Those charms, reserv'd to nobler ends,
    Thou spotless spouse of Heaven!

"Yet speak what cause from morning mass
    Thy ling'ring steps delays:
Haste to the deep-mouth'd organ's peal
    To join thy vocal praise.

"Awake thy abbess sisters all;
    At Mary's holy shrine,
With bended knees and suppliant eyes
    Approach, thou nun divine!"

"No Nun am I," recov'ring cried
    The nymph; "No nun, I say,

Nor nun will be, unless this fright
   Should turn my locks to grey.

"'Tis true, at church I seldom fail
   When aunt or uncle leads;
Yet never rise by four o'clock
   To tell my morning beads.

"No mortal lover yet, I vow,
   My virgin heart has fixt,
But yet I bear the creatures talk
   Without a grate betwixt.

"To Heav'n my eyes are often cast
   (From Heav'n their light began)
Yet deign sometimes to view on Earth
   Its image stampt on man.

"Ah me! I fear in borrow'd shape
   Thou com'st, a base deceiver;
Perhaps the devil, to tempt the faith
   Of orthodox believer.

"For once my hand, at masquerade,
   A reverend friar prest;
His form as thine, but holier sounds
   The ravish'd saint addrest.

"He told me vows no more were made
   To senseless stone and wood,
But adoration paid alone
   To saints of flesh and blood,

"That rosy cheeks, and radiant eyes,
   And tresses like the morn,
Were given to bless the present age,
   And light the age unborn:

"That maids, by whose obdurate pride
   The hapless lover fell,
Were doom'd to never-dying toils
   Of leading apes in Hell.

"'Respect the first command,' (he cried,)
   'Its sacred laws fulfil,
And well observe the precept given
   To Moses, — Do not kill.'

"Thus spoke, ah yet I hear him speak!
   My soul's sublime physician;
Then get thee hence, thy doctrines vile
   Would sink me to perdition."

She ceas'd—the monk in shades of night
   Confus'dly fled away,
And superstition's clouds dissolv'd
   In sense, and beauty's ray.

A DREAM

With bridal cake beneath her head,
   As Jenny prest her pillow,
She dreamt that lovers, thick as hops,
   Hung pendent from the willow.

Around her spectres shook their chains,
   And goblins kept their station;
They pull'd, they pinch'd her, till she swore
   To spare the male creation.

Before her now the buck, the beau,
   The squire, the captain trips;
The modest seiz'd her hand to kiss,
   The forward seiz'd her lips.

For some she felt her bosom pant,
   For some she felt it smart;
To all she gave enchanting smiles,
   To one she gave her heart.

She dreamt (for magic charms prevail'd,
   And fancy play'd her farce on)
That, soft reclin'd in elbow-chair,
   She kist a sleeping parson.

She dreamt—but, O rash Muse! forbear,
   Nor virgins dreams pursue;
Yet blest above the gods is he
   Who proves such visions true.

A SONG

Hang my lyre upon the willow,
  Sigh to winds thy notes forlorn;
Or, along the foamy billow
  Float the wrecking tempest's scorn.

Sprightly sounds no more it raises,
  Such as Laura's smiles approve;
Laura scorns her poet's praises,
  Calls his artless friendship love:

Calls it love, that spurning duty,
  Spurning Nature's chastest ties,
Mocks thy tears, dejected beauty,
  Sports with fallen virtue's sighs.

Call it love, no more profaning
  Truth with dark suspicion's wound;
Or, my fair, the term retaining,
  Change the sense, preserve the sound.

Yes, 'tis love——that name is given,
  Angels, to your purest flames:
Such a love as merits Heaven,
  Heaven's divinest image claims.

INSCRIPTION FOR A FOUNTAIN

O you, who mark what flowrets gay,
  What gales, what odours breathing near,
What sheltering shades from summer's ray
  Allure my spring to linger here:

Yet see me quit this margin green,
  Yet see me deaf to pleasure's call,
Explore the thirsty haunts of men,
  Yet see my bounty flow for all.

O learn of me——no partial rill,
  No slumbering selfish pool be you;
But social laws alike fulfil;
  O flow for all creation too!

FRANCES BROOKE (1724-1789)

AN AIR

from "Rosina"

When William at eve meets me down at the stile,
　　How sweet is the nightingale's song!
Of the day I forget the labour and toil,
　　Whilst the moon plays yon branches among.

By her beams, without blushing, I hear him complain,
　　And believe every word of his song:
You know not how sweet 'tis to love the dear swain,
　　Whilst the moon plays yon branches among.

RICHARD GIFFORD (1725-1807)

from CONTEMPLATION

Dropt is the sable mantle of the night;
The early lark salutes the rising day,
And, while she hails the glad return of light,
Provokes each bard to join the raptur'd lay.

The music spreads through nature: while the flocks
Scatter their silver fleeces o'er the mead,
The jolly shepherd, 'mid the vocal rocks,
Pipes many a strain upon his oaten reed:

And sweetest Phoebe, she, whose rosy cheeks
Outglow the blushes of the ruddy morn,
All as her cows with eager step she seeks,
Vies with the tuneful thrush on yonder thorn.

Unknown to these each fair Aonian maid,
Their bosoms glow with Nature's truer fire;
Little, ye Sister-Nine, they need your aid
Whose artless breasts these living scenes inspire.

Even from the straw-roofed cot the note of joy
Flows full and frequent as the village fair,
Whose little wants the busy hours employ,
Chanting some rural ditty soothes her care.

Verse sweetens toil, however rude the sound,
She feels no biting pang the while she sings;
Nor, as she turns the giddy wheel around,
Revolves the sad vicissitude of things.

JEAN ELLIOT (1727-1805)

THE FLOWERS OF THE FOREST

I've heard them lilting, at the ewe milking,
　Lasses a' lilting, before dawn of day;
But now they are moaning, on ilka green loaning;
　The flowers of the forest are a' wede away.

At bughts, in the morning, nae blithe lads are scorning;
　Lasses are lonely, and dowie, and wae;
Nae daffing, nae gabbing, but sighing and sabbing;
　Ilk ane lifts her leglin, and hies her away.

At har'st, at the shearing, nae youths now are jearing;
　Bandsters are runkled, and lyart or gray;
At fair, or at preaching, nae wooing, nae fleeching;
　The flowers of the forest are a' wede away.

At e'en, in the gloaming, nae younkers are roaming
　'Bout stacks, with the lasses at bogle to play;
But ilk maid sits dreary, lamenting her deary——
　The flowers of the forest are weded away.

Dool and wae for the order, sent our lads to the Border!
　The English, for ance, by guile wan the day;
The flowers of the forest, that fought aye the foremost,
　The prime of our land, are cauld in the clay.

We'll hear nae mair lilting, at the ewe milking;
　Women and bairns are heartless and wae:
Sighing and moaning, on ilka green loaning——
　The flowers of the forest are a' wede away.

ARTHUR MURPHY (1727-1805)

A SONG

from "The Way to Keep Him"

Attend all ye fair, and I'll tell ye the art,
    To bind every fancy with ease in your chains,
To hold in soft fetters the conjugal heart,
    And banish from Hymen his doubts and his pains.

When Juno accepted the cestus of love,
    At first she was handsome; she charming became;
With skill the soft passions it taught her to move,
    To kindle at once, and to keep up the flame.

'Tis this gives the eyes all their magic and fire;
    The voice melting accents; impassions the kiss;
Confers the sweet smiles, that awaken desire,
    And plants round the fair, each incentive to bliss.

Thence flows the gay chat, more than reason that charms;
    The eloquent blush, that can beauty improve;
The fond sigh, the fond vow, the soft touch that alarms,
    The tender disdain, the renewal of love.

Ye fair, take the cestus, and practise its art;
    The mind unaccomplish'd, mere features are vain,
Exert your sweet pow'r, you will conquer each heart,
    And the loves, joys, and graces, shall walk in your train.

THOMAS WARTON (1728-1790)

ODE I: TO SLEEP

On this my pensive pillow, gentle Sleep!
Descend, in all thy downy plumage drest:
Wipe with thy wing these eyes that wake to weep,
And place thy crown of poppies on my breast.

O steep my senses in oblivion's balm,
And sooth my throbbing pulse with lenient hand;
This tempest of my boiling blood becalm!
Despair grows mild at thy supreme command.

Yet ah! in vain, familiar with the gloom,
And sadly toiling through the tedious night,
I seek sweet slumber, while that virgin bloom,
For ever hovering, haunts my wretched sight.

Nor would the dawning day my sorrows charm:
Black midnight and the blaze of noon alike
To me appear, while with uplifted arm
Death stands prepar'd, but still delays, to strike.

ODE II: THE HAMLET

Written in Whichwood Forest

The hinds how blest, who ne'er beguil'd
To quit their hamlet's hawthorn wild;
Nor haunt the crowd, nor tempt the main,
For splendid care, and guilty gain!
    When morning's twilight-tinctur'd beam
Strikes their low thatch with slanting gleam,
They rove abroad in ether blue,
To dip the scythe in fragrant dew;
The sheaf to bind, the beech to fell,
That nodding shades a craggy dell.
    Midst gloomy glades, in warbles clear,
Wild nature's sweetest notes they hear:
On green untrodden banks they view
The hyacinth's neglected hue:
In their lone haunts, and woodland rounds,
They spy the squirrel's airy bounds:

228

And startle from her ashen spray,
Across the glen, the screaming jay:
Each native charm their steps explore
Of Solitude's sequestered store.
For them the Moon with cloudless ray
Mounts, to illume their homeward way:
Their weary spirits to relieve,
The meadows incense breathe at eve.
No riot mars the simple fare,
That o'er a glimmering hearth they share:
But when the curfeu's measur'd roar
Duly, the darkening valleys o'er,
Has echoed from the distant town,
They wish no beds of cygnet-down,
No trophied canopies, to close
Their drooping eyes in quick repose.
Their little sons, who spread the bloom
Of health around the clay-built room,
Or through the primros'd coppice stray,
Or gambol in the new-mown hay;
Or quaintly braid the cowslip-twine,
Or drive afield the tardy kine;
Or hasten from the sultry hill,
To loiter at the shady rill;
Or climb the tall pine's gloomy crest,
To rob the raven's ancient nest.
Their humble porch with honied flow'rs
The curling woodbine's shade imbow'rs:
From the small garden's thymy mound
Their bees in busy swarms resound:
Nor fell Disease, before his time,
Hastes to consume life's golden prime:
But when their temples long have wore
The silver crown of tresses hoar;
As studious still calm peace to keep,
Beneath a flowery turf they sleep.

ODE IV: SOLITUDE AT AN INN

May 15th, 1769

Oft upon the twilight plain,
Circled with thy shadowy train,
While the dove at distance coo'd,
Have I met thee, Solitude!

Then was loneliness to me
Best and true society,
But ah! how alter'd is thy mien
In this sad deserted scene!
Here all thy classic pleasures cease,
Musing mild, and thoughtful peace;
Here thou com'st in sullen mood,
Not with thy fantastic brood
Of magic shapes and visions airy
Beckon'd from the land of Fairy:
'Mid the melancholy void
Not a pensive charm enjoy'd!
No poetic being here
Strikes with airy sounds mine ear;
No converse here to fancy cold
With many a fleeting form I hold,
Here all inelegant and rude
Thy presence is, sweet Solitude.

ODE FOR THE NEW YEAR, 1788

Rude was the pile, and massy proof,
That first uprear'd its haughty roof
On Windsor's brow sublime, in warlike state:
The Norman tyrant's jealous hand
The giant fabric proudly plann'd:
With recent victory elate,
    "On this majestic steep," he cried,
    "A regal fortress, threatening wide,
Shall spread my terrours to the distant hills;
    Its formidable shade shall throw
    Far o'er the broad expanse below,
    Where winds yon mighty flood, and amply fills
    With flowery verdure, or with golden grain,
    The fairest fields that deck my new domain!
And London's towers that reach the watchman's eye,
Shall see with conscious awe my bulwark climb the sky."

Unchang'd, through many a hardy race,
Stood the rough dome in sullen grace;
Still on its angry front defiance frown'd:
Though monarchs kept their state within,
    Still murmur'd with the martial din
    The gloomy gateway's arch profound;
    And armed forms, in airy row,
    Bent o'er the battlements their bows,

And blood-stain'd banners crown'd its hostile head;
   And oft its hoary ramparts wore
   The rugg'd scars of conflict sore;
What time, pavilion'd on the neighbouring mead,
   Th' indignant barons rang'd in bright array
   Their feudal bands to curb despotic sway;
     And leagu'd a Briton's birthright to restore,
From John's reluctant grasp the roll of freedom bore.

   When lo, the king, that wreath'd his shield
   With lilies pluck'd on Cressy's field,
Heav'd from its base the mould'ring Norman frame!
   New glory cloth'd th' exulting steep,
   The portals tower'd with ampler sweep;
   And Valour's soften'd genius came,
   Here held his pomp, and trail'd the pall
   Of triumph through the trophied hall;
And War was clad awhile in gorgeous weeds:
     Amid the martial pageantries,
     While Beauty's glance adjudg'd the prize,
   And beam'd sweet influence on heroic deeds.
   Nor long, ere Henry's holy zeal, to breathe
   A milder charm upon the scenes beneath,
   Rear'd in the watery glade his classic shrine,
And call'd his stripling-quire, to woo the willing Nine.

   To this imperial seat to lend
   Its pride supreme, and nobly blend
British magnificence with Attic art;
   Proud castle, to thy banner'd bowers,
   Lo! Picture bids her glowing powers
   Their bold historic groups impart;
   She bids th' illuminated pane,
   Along thy lofty-vaulted fane,
Shed the dim blaze of radiance richly clear.
   Still may such arts of Peace engage
   Their patron's care! But should the rage
Of war to battle rouse the new-born year,
Britain arise, and wake the slumbering fire,
Vindictive dart thy quick-rekindling ire!
   Or, arm'd to strike, in mercy spare the foe;
And lift thy thundering hand, and then withhold the blow!

SONNET IV

Written at Stonehenge

Thou noblest monument of Albion's isle!
Whether by Merlin's aid, from Scythia's shore,
To Amber's fatal plain Pendragon bore,
Huge frame of giant-hands, the mighty pile,
T' entomb his Britons slain by Hengist's guile:
Or Druid priests, sprinkled with human gore,
Taught 'mid thy massy maze their mystic lore:
Or Danish chiefs, enrich'd with savage spoil,
To Victory's idol vast, an unhewn shrine,
Rear'd the rude heap; or, in thy hallow'd round,
Repose the kings of Brutus' genuine line;
Or here those kings in solemn state were crown'd:
Studious to trace thy wondrous origine,
We muse on many an ancient tale renown'd.

SONNET IX

To the River Lodon

Ah! what a weary race my feet have run,
Since first I trod thy banks with alders crown'd,
And thought my way was all through fairy ground,
Beneath thy azure sky, and golden sun:
Where first my Muse to lisp her notes begun!
While pensive memory traces back the round,
Which fills the varied interval between;
Much pleasure, more of sorrow marks the scene.
Sweet native stream! whose skies and suns so pure
No more return, to chear my evening road!
Yet still one joy remains, that not obscure,
Nor useless, all my vacant days have flow'd,
From youth's gay dawn to manhood's prime mature;
Nor with the Muse's laurel unbestowed.

ODE TO A GRIZZLE WIG

By a Gentleman who had Just Left Off His Bob

All hail, ye curls, that, rang'd in reverend row,

232

With snowy pomp my conscious shoulders hide!
That fall beneath in venerable flow,
And crown my brows above with feathery pride!

High on your summit, Wisdom's mimick'd air
Sits thron'd, with Pedantry her solemn sire,
And in her net of awe-diffusing hair
Entangles fools, and bids the crowd admire.

O'er every lock, that floats in full display,
Sage Ignorance her gloom scholastic throws;
And stamps o'er all my visage, once so gay,
Unmeaning Gravity's serene repose.

Can thus large wigs our reverence engage?
Have barbers thus the pow'r to blind our eyes?
Is science thus conferr'd on every sage,
By Bayliss, Blenkinsop, and lofty Wise?

But thou, farewell, my Bob! whose thin-wove thatch
Was stor'd with quips and cranks, and wanton wiles,
That love to live within the one-curl'd scratch,
With Fun, and all the family of Smiles.

Safe in thy privilege, near Isis' brook,
Whole afternoons at Wolvercote I quaff'd;
At eve my careless round in High-street took,
And call'd at Jolly's for the casual draught.

No more the wherry feels my stroke so true;
At skittles, in a Grizzle, can I play?
Woodstock, farewell! and Wallingford, adieu!
Where many a scheme reliev'd the lingering day.

Such were the joys that once Hilario crown'd,
Ere grave Preferment came my peace to rob:
Such are the less ambitious pleasures found
Beneath the liceat of an humble Bob.

DR. THOMAS PERCY (1729-1811)

THE FRIAR OF ORDERS GRAY

Dispersed through Shakespeare's plays are innumerable little fragments of ancient ballads, the entire copies of which could not be recovered. Many of these being of the most beautiful and pathetic simplicity, the Editor was tempted to select some of them, and with a few supplemental stanzas to connect them together and form them into a little TALE, which is here submitted to the Reader's candour.

One small fragment was taken from Beaumont and Fletcher.

It was a friar of orders gray,
    Walkt forth to tell his beades;
And he met with a lady faire,
    Clad in a pilgrime's weedes.

Now Christ thee save, thou reverend friar,
    I pray thee tell to me,
If ever at yon holy shrine
    My true love thou didst see.

And how should I know your true love,
    From many another one?
O by his cockle hat, and staff,
    And by his sandal shoone.

But chiefly by his face and mien,
    That were so fair to view;
His flaxen locks that sweetly curl'd,
    And eyne of lovely blue.

O lady, he is dead and gone!
    Lady, he's dead and gone!
And at his head a green grass turfe,
    And at his heels a stone.

Within these holy cloysters long
    He languisht, and he dyed,
Lamenting of a ladyes love,
    And 'playning of her pride.

Here bore him barefac'd on his bier

Six proper youths and tall,
And many a tear bedew'd his grave
    Within yon kirk-yard wall.

And art thou dead, thou gentle youth!
    And art thou dead and gone!
And didst thou dye for love of me!
    Break, cruel heart of stone!

O weep not, lady, weep not soe;
    Some ghostly comfort seek:
Let not vain sorrow rive thy heart
    Ne teares bedew thy cheek.

O do not, do not, holy friar,
    My sorrow now reprove;
For I have lost the sweetest youth,
    That e'er wan ladyes love.

And nowe, alas! for thy sad losse,
    I'll evermore weep and sigh;
For thee I only wisht to live,
    For thee I wish to dye.

Weep no more, lady, weep no more,
    Thy sorrowe is in vaine:
For, violets pluckt the sweetest showers
    Will ne'er make grow againe.

Our joys as winged dreams doe flye,
    Why then should sorrow last?
Since grief but aggravates thy losse,
    Grieve not for what is past.

O say not soe, thou holy friar;
    I pray thee, say not soe:
For since my true-love dyed for mee,
    'Tis meet my tears should flow.

And will he ne'er come again!
    Will he ne'er come again?
Ah! no, he is dead and laid in his grave,
    For ever to remain.

His cheek was redder than the rose,
    The comliest youth was he:—
But he is dead and laid in his grave:
    Alas, and woe is me!

235

Sigh no more, lady, sigh no more,
    Men were deceivers ever:
One foot on sea and one on land,
    To one thing constant never.

Hadst thou been fond, he had been false,
    And left thee sad and heavy;
For young men ever were fickle found,
    Since summer trees were leafy.

Now say not so, thou holy friar,
    I pray thee say not soe:
My love he had the truest heart:
    O he was ever true!

And art thou dead, thou much-lov'd youth,
    And didst thou dye for mee?
Then farewell home; for, ever-more
    A pilgrim I will bee.

But first upon my true-love's grave
    My weary limbs I'll lay,
And thrice I'll kiss the green-grass turf,
    That wraps his breathless clay.

Yet stay, fair lady; rest awhile
    Beneath this cloyster wall:
See through the hawthorn blows the cold wind,
    And drizzly rain doth fall.

O stay me not, thou holy friar;
    O stay me not I pray:
No drizzly rain that falls on me,
    Can wash my fault away.

Yet stay, fair lady, turn again,
    And dry those pearly tears;
For see beneath this gown of gray
    Thy owne true-love appears.

Here forc'd by grief, and hopeless love,
    These holy weeds I sought;
And here amid these lonely walls
    To end my days I thought.

But haply for my year of grace
    Is not yet past away,

Might I still hope to win thy love,
   No longer would I stay.

Now farewell grief, and welcome joy
   Once more unto my heart:
For since I have found thee, lovely youth,
   We never more will part.

JOHN CUNNINGHAM (1729-1773)

THE THRUSH AND PIE

A Tale

Conceal'd within an hawthorn bush,
We're told, that an experienc'd Thrush
Instructed, in the prime of spring,
Many a neighbouring bird to sing.
She caroll'd, and her various song
Gave lessons to the list'ning throng:
But (the entangling boughs between)
'Twas her delight to teach unseen.
    At length, the little wond'ring race
Would see their fav'rite face to face;
They thought it hard to be deny'd
And begg'd that she'd no longer hide.
O'er-modest, worth's peculiar fault,
Another shade the tut'ress sought;
And loth to be too much admir'd,
In secret from the bush retir'd.
    An impudent, presuming Pie,
Malicious, ignorant, and sly,
Stole to the matron's vacant seat,
And in her arrogance elate,
Rush'd forward with——"My friends, you see
The mistress of the choir in me:
Here, be your due devotion paid,
I am the songstress of the shade."
    A Linnet, that sat list'ning nigh,
Made the impostor thus reply:
"I fancy, friend, that vulgar throats
Were never form'd for warbling notes:
But if these lessons came from you,
Repeat them in the public view;
That your assertions may be clear,
Let us behold as well as hear."
    The length'ning song, the soft'ning strain,
Our chatt'ring Pie attempts in vain,
For to the fool's eternal shame,
All she could compass was a scream.
    The birds, enrag'd, around her fly,
Nor shelter nor defence is nigh.
    The caitiff wretch, distress'd——forlorn!
On every side is peck'd and torn;

Till for her vile, atrocious lies,
Under their angry beaks she dies.
    Such be his fate, whose scoundrel claim
Obtrudes upon a neighbour's fame.
    Friend E——n, the tale apply,
You are——yourself——the chatt'ring Pie;
Repent, and with a conscious blush,
Go make atonement to the Thrush.

THE HAWTHORN BOWER

A Song

Palemon, in the hawthorn bower,
    With fond impatience lay,
He counted every anxious hour
    That stretch'd the tedious day.

The rosy dawn, Pastora nam'd,
    And vow'd that she'd be kind;
But ah! the setting sun proclaim'd
    That woman's vows are——wind.

The fickle sex, the boy defy'd!
    And swore, in terms profane,
That Beauty in her brightest pride
    Might sue to him in vain.

When Delia from the neighb'ring glade
    Appear'd in all her charms,
Each angry vow Palemon made
    Was lost in Delia's arms.

The lovers had not long reclin'd
    Before Pastora came;
Inconstancy, she cry'd, I find
    In every heart's the same.

For young Alexis sigh'd and prest,
    With such bewitching power,
I quite forgot the wishing guest
    That waited in the bower.

MAY-EVE; OR, KATE OF ABERDEEN

The silver Moon's enamour'd beam
 Steals softly through the night,
To wanton with the winding stream,
 And kiss reflected light.
To beds of state go, balmy Sleep,
 ('Tis where you've seldom been)
May's vigil while the shepherds keep
 With Kate of Aberdeen.

Upon the green the virgins wait,
 In rosy chaplets gay,
Till Morn unbar her golden gate,
 And give the promis'd May.
Methinks I hear the maids declare,
 The promis'd May, when seen,
Not half so fragrant, half so fair,
 As Kate of Aberdeen.

Strike up the tabor's boldest notes,
 We'll rouse the nodding grove;
The nested birds shall raise their throats,
 And hail the maid I love:
And see——the matin lark mistakes,
 He quits the tufted green:
Fond bird! 'tis not the morning breaks,
 'Tis Kate of Aberdeen.

Now lightsome o'er the level mead,
 Where midnight Fairies rove,
Like them, the jocund dance we'll lead,
 Or tune the reed to love:
For see the rosy May draws nigh:
 She claims a virgin queen;
And hark, the happy shepherds cry,
 'Tis Kate of Aberdeen.

THE VIOLET

Shelter'd from the blight, ambition,
 Fatal to the pride of rank,
See me in my low condition,
 Laughing on the tufted bank.

240

On my robes (for emulation)
  No variety's imprest:
Suited to an humble station,
  Mine's an unembroider'd vest.

Modest though the maids declare me,
  May in her fantastic train,
When Pastora deigns to wear me,
  Ha'n't a flow'ret half so vain.

THE MILLER

A Ballad

In a plain pleasant cottage, conveniently neat,
With a mill and some meadows——a freehold estate,
A well-meaning miller by labour supplies
Those blessings, that grandeur to great ones denies:
No passions to plague him, no cares to torment,
His constant companions are Health and Content;
Their lordships in lace may remark, if they will,
He's honest, though daub'd with the dust of his mill.

Ere the lark's early carols salute the new day,
He springs from his cottage as jocund as May;
He cheerfully whistles, regardless of care,
Or sings the last ballad he bought at the fair:
While courtiers are toil'd in the cobwebs of state,
Or bribing elections, in hopes to be great,
No fraud or ambition his bosom e'er fill,
Contented he works, if there's grist for his mill.

On Sunday, bedeck'd in his homespun array,
At church he's the loudest to chant or to pray;
He sits to a dinner of plain English food,
Though simple the pudding, his appetite's good.
At night, when the priest and exciseman are gone,
He quaffs at the alehouse with Roger and John,
Then reels to his pillow, and dreams of no ill;
No monarch more blest than the man of the mill.

A LANDSCAPE

Rura mihi et irrigui placeant in vallibus omnes.
                                        ——VIRGIL

Now that summer's ripen'd bloom
Frolics where the winter frown'd,
Stretch'd upon these banks of broom,
We command the landscape round.

Nature in the prospect yields
Humble dales and mountains bold,
Meadows, woodlands, heaths——and fields
Yellow'd o'er with waving gold.

Goats upon that frowning steep
Fearless with their kidlings browse;
Here a flock of snowy sheep,
There an herd of motley cows.

On the uplands ev'ry glade
Brightens in the blaze of day;
O'er the vales the sober shade
Softens to an ev'ning gray.

Where the rill by slow degrees
Swells into a crystal pool,
Shaggy rocks and shelving trees
Shoot to keep the waters cool.

Shiver'd by a thunderstroke
From the mountain's misty ridge,
O'er the brook a ruin'd oak
Near the farmhouse forms a bridge.

On her breast the sunny beam
Glitters in meridian pride,
Yonder as the virgin stream
Hastens to the restless tide.

Where the ships by wanton gales
Wafted o'er the green waves run,
Sweet to see their swelling sails
Whiten'd by the laughing sun.

High upon the daisy'd hill,
Rising from the slope of trees,
How the wings of yonder mill
Labour in the busy breeze! ——

Cheerful as a summer's morn,
Bouncing from her loaded pad,
Where the maid presents her corn,

242

Smirking to the miller's lad.

O'er the green a festal throng
Gambols in fantastic trim
As the full cart moves along:
Hearken! — 'tis the harvest hymn.

Linnets on the crowded sprays
Chorus—and the woodlarks rise,
Soaring with a song of praise
Till the sweet notes reach the skies.

Torrents in extended sheets
Down the cliffs dividing break;
'Twixt the hills the water meets,
Settling in a silver lake.

From his languid flocks the swain,
By the sunbeams sore opprest,
Plunging on the wat'ry plain,
Ploughs it with his glowing breast.

Where the mantling willows nod
From the green bank's slopy side,
Patient, with his well-thrown rod,
Many an angler breaks the tide.

On the isles, with osiers drest,
Many a fair-plum'd halcyon breeds;
Many a wild bird hides her nest,
Cover'd in yon crackling reeds.

Fork-tail'd prattlers, as they pass
To their nestlings in the rock,
Darting on the liquid glass,
Seem to kiss the mimic'd flock.

Where the stone cross lifts its head,
Many a saint and pilgrim hoar
Up the hill was wont to tread
Barefoot in the days of yore.

Guardian of a sacred well,
Arch'd beneath yon rev'rend shades,
Whilome in that shatter'd cell
Many an hermit told his beads.

Sultry mists surround the heath

Where the Gothic dome appears,
O'er the trembling groves beneath
Tott'ring with a load of years.

Turn to the contrasted scene,
Where, beyond these hoary piles,
Gay upon the rising green,
Many an Attic building smiles.

Painted gardens—grots—and groves,
Intermingling shade and light,
Lengthen'd vistas, green alcoves,
Join to give the eye delight.

Hamlets—villages, and spires,
Scatter'd on the landscape lie,
Till the distant view retires,
Closing in an azure sky.

CONTENT

A Pastoral

O'er moorlands and mountains, rude, barren and bare,
    As wilder'd and weary'd I roam,
A gentle young shepherdess sees my despair,
    And leads me—o'er lawns—to her home,
Yellow sheaves from rich Ceres her cottage had crown'd,
    Green rushes were strew'd on her floor,
Her casement sweet woodbines crept wantonly round,
    And deck'd the sod seats at her door.

We sat ourselves down to a cooling repast:
    Fresh fruits! and she cull'd me the best:
While, thrown from my guard by some glances she cast,
    Love slily stole into my breast!
I told my soft wishes; she sweetly reply'd,
    (Ye virgins, her voice was divine!)
I've rich ones rejected, and great ones deny'd,
    But take me, fond shepherd—I'm thine.

Her air was so modest, her aspect so meek!
    So simple, yet sweet, were her charms!
I kiss'd the ripe roses that glow'd on her cheek,
    And lock'd the lov'd maid in my arms.
Now jocund together we tend a few sheep,

And if, by yon prattler, the stream,
Reclin'd on her bosom, I sink into sleep,
  Her image still softens my dream.

Together we range o'er the slow rising hills,
    Delighted with pastoral views,
Or rest on the rock whence the streamlet distils,
    And point out new themes for my muse.
To pomp or proud titles she ne'er did aspire,
    The damsel's of humble descent;
The cottager, Peace, is well known for her fire,
    And shepherds have nam'd her Content.

A SONG

He that Love hath never try'd,
Nor had Cupid for his guide,
Cannot hit the passage right
To the palace of delight.

What are honours, regal wealth,
Florid youth, and rosy health?
Without Love his tribute brings,
Impotent, unmeaning things!

Gentle shepherds, persevere,
Still be tender, still sincere;
Love and Time, united, do,
Wonders, if the heart be true.

THE SHEEP AND THE BRAMBLE-BUSH

A Thick-twisted brake, in the time of a storm,
    Seem'd kindly to cover a sheep:
So snug, for a while, he lay shelter'd and warm,
    It quietly sooth'd him asleep.

The clouds are now scatter'd—the winds are at peace,
    The sheep to his pasture inclin'd;
But ah! the fell thicket lays hold of his fleece,
    His coat is left forfeit behind.

My friend, who the thicket of law never try'd,
    Consider before you get in;

245

Tho' judgment and sentence are pass'd on your side,
   By Jove, you'll be fleec'd to your skin.

THE WITHERED ROSE

Sweet object of the zephyr's kiss,
   Come, rose, come courted to my bower:
Queen of the banks! the garden's bliss!
   Come and abash yon' tawdry flower.

Why call us to revokeless doom?
   With grief the opening buds reply;
Not suffered to extend our bloom,
   Scarce born, alas! before we die!

Man having pass'd appointed years,
   Our are but days—the scene must close:
And when Fate's messenger appears,
   What is he but a WITHERED ROSE?

JOHN SCOTT (1730-1783)

VERSES, OCCASIONED BY A DESCRIPTION
OF THE AEOLIAN HARP

1754

Untaught o'er strings to draw the rosin'd bow,
Or melting strains on the soft flute to blow,
With others long I mourn'd the want of skill
Resounding roofs with harmony to fill.
Till happy now th' Aeolian lyre is known,
And all the powers of music are my own.
Swell all thy notes, delightful harp, O! swell!
Inflame thy poet to describe thee well,
When the full chorus rises with the breeze,
Or, slowly sinking, lessens by degrees,
To sounds more soft than amorous gales disclose,
At evening panting on the blushing rose;
More sweet than all the notes that organs breathe,
Or tuneful echoes, when they die, bequeathe;
Oft where some Sylvan temple decks the grove,
The slave of easy indolence I rove;
There the wing'd breeze the lifted sash pervades,
Each breath is music, vocal all the shades.
Charm'd with the soothing sound, at ease reclin'd,
To Fancy's pleasing pow'r I yield my mind:
And now enchanted scenes around me rise,
And some kind Ariel the soft air supplies:
Now lofty Pindus through the shades I view,
Where all the Nine their tuneful art pursue;
To me the sound the panting gale conveys,
And all my heart is ecstasy and praise.
Now to Arcadian plains at once convey'd,
Some shepherd's pipe delights his favourite maid;
Mix'd with the murmurs of a neighbouring stream,
I hear soft notes that suit an amorous theme!
Ah! then a victim to the fond deceit,
My heart begins with fierce desires to beat;
To fancy'd sighs I real sighs return,
By turns I languish, and by turns I burn.
Ah! Delia, haste! and here attentive prove,
Like me, that "music is the voice of love:"
So shall I mourn my rustic strains no more,
While pleas'd you listen, who could frown before.

ELEGY WRITTEN IN THE HOT WEATHER

July 1757

Three hours from noon the passing shadow shows,
    The sultry breeze glides faintly o'er the plains,
The dazzling ether fierce and fiercer grows,
    And human nature scarce its rage sustains.

Now still and vacant is the dusty street,
    And still and vacant all yon fields extend,
Save where those swains, oppress'd with toil and heat,
    The grassy harvest of the mead attend.

Lost is the lively aspect of the ground,
    Low are the springs, the reedy ditches dry;
No verdant spot in all the vale is found,
    Save what yon stream's unfailing stores supply.

Where are the flow'rs, the garden's rich array?
    Where is their beauty, where their fragrance fled?
Their stems relax, fast fall their leaves away,
    They fade and mingle with their dusty bed:

All but the natives of the torrid zone,
    What Afric's wilds, or Peru's fields display,
Pleas'd with a clime that imitates their own,
    They lovelier bloom beneath the parching ray.

Where is wild Nature's heart-reviving song,
    That fill'd in genial spring the verdant bow'rs?
Silent in gloomy woods the feather'd throng
    Pine through this long, long course of sultry hours.

Where is the dream of bliss by summer brought?
    The walk along the riv'let-water'd vale?
The field with verdure clad, with fragrance fraught?
    The Sun mild-beaming, and the fanning gale?

The weary soul Imagination cheers,
    Her pleasing colours paint the future gay:
Time passes on, the truth itself appears,
    The pleasing colours instant fade away.

In diff'rent seasons diff'rent joys we place,
    And these will spring supply, and summer these;

Yet frequent storms the bloom of spring deface,
    And summer scarcely brings a day to please.

O for some secret shady cool recess,
    Some Gothic dome o'erhung with darksome trees,
Where thick damp walls this raging heat repress,
    Where the long aisle invites the lazy breeze!

But why these plaints?——reflect, nor murmur more——
    Far worse their fate in many a foreign land,
The Indian tribes on Darien's swampy shore,
    The Arabs wand'ring over Mecca's sand.

Far worse, alas! the feeling mind sustains,
    Rack'd with the poignant pangs of fear or shame;
The hopeless lover bound in Beauty's chains,
    The bard whom Envy robs of hard-earn'd fame;

He, who a father or a mother mourns,
    Or lovely consort lost in early bloom;
He, whom fell Febris, rapid fury! burns,
    Or Phthisis slow leads ling'ring to the tomb——

Lest man should sink beneath the present pain;
    Lest man should triumph in the present joy;
For him th' unvarying laws of Heav'n ordain,
    Hope in his ills, and to his bliss alloy.

Fierce and oppressive is the heat we bear,
    Yet not unuseful to our humid soil;
Thence shall our fruits a richer flavour share,
    Thence shall our plains with riper harvests smile.

Reflect, nor murmur more——for, good in all,
    Heav'n gives the due degrees of drought or rain;
Perhaps ere morn refreshing show'rs may fall,
    Nor soon yon Sun rise blazing fierce again:

Ev'n now behold the grateful change at hand!
    Hark, in the east loud blust'ring gales arise;
Wide and more wide the dark'ning clouds expand,
    And distant lightnings flash along the skies!

O, in the awful concert of the storm,
    While hail, and rain, and wind, and thunder join;
May deep-felt gratitude my soul inform,
    May joyful songs of rev'rent praise be mine.

ODE ON HEARING THE DRUM

I hate that drum's discordant sound,
Parading round, and round, and round:
To thoughtless youth it pleasure yields,
And lures from cities and from fields,
To sell their liberty for charms
Of tawdry lace and glitt'ring arms;
And when Ambition's voice commands,
To march, and fight, and fall, in foreign lands.

I hate that drum's discordant sound,
Parading round, and round, and round:
To me it talks of ravag'd plains,
And burning towns, and ruin'd swains,
And mangled limbs, and dying groans,
And widows tears, and orphans' moans;
And all that Misery's hand bestows,
To fill the catalogue of human woes.

A LANDSCAPE

An Ode

On the eastern hill's steep side
Spreads the rural hamlet wide;
Cross the vale, where willows rise,
Further still another lies;
And, beneath a steeper hill,
Lies another further still:
Near them many a field and grove—
Scenes where Health and Labour rove!
Northward swelling slopes are seen,
Clad with corn-fields neat and green;
There, through grassy plains below,
Broad and smooth the waters flow;
While the town, their banks along,
Bids its clust'ring houses throng,
In the sunshine glitt'ring fair;
Haunts of business, haunts of care!
Westward o'er the yellow meads
Wind the rills through waving reeds;
From dark elms a shadow falls
On the abbey's whiten'd walls:
Wide the park's green lawns expand;

250

Thick its tufted lindens stand:
Fair retreat! that well might please
Wealth, and Elegance, and Ease.
  Hark! amidst the distant shades
Murm'ring drop the deep cascades;
Hark! amidst the rustling trees
Softly sighs the gentle breeze;
And the Eolian harp, reclin'd
Obvious to the stream of wind,
Pours its wildly-warbled strain,
Rising now, now sunk again.
  How the view detains the sight!
How the sounds the ear delight!
Sweet the scene! but think not there
Happiness sincere to share:
Reason still regrets the day
Passing rapidly away;
Less'ning life's too little store;
Passing, to return no more!

ODE ON VIEWING THE RUINS OF AN ABBEY

To a Friend

How steep yon mountains rise around,
How bold yon gloomy woods ascend!
How loud the rushing torrents sound
That midst these heaps of ruin bend,
Where one arch'd gateway yet remains,
And one long aisle its roof retains,
And one tall turret's walls impend!

Here once a self-sequester'd train
Renounc'd life's tempting pomp and glare;
Rejected pow'r, relinquish'd gain,
And shun'd the great, and shun'd the fair:
The voluntary slaves of toil,
By day they till'd their little soil,
By night they woke, and rose to prayer.

Though Superstition much we blame,
That bade them thus consume their years;
Their motive still our praise must claim,
Their constancy our thought reveres:
And sure their solitary scheme

251

Must check each passion's wild extreme,
And save them cares, and save them fears.

Their convent's round contain'd their all;
Their minds no sad presage oppress'd,
What fate might absent wealth befall,
How absent friends might be distress'd:
Domestic ills ne'er hurt their ease;
They nought of pain could feel from these,
Who no domestic joys possess'd.

But imperfection haunts each place:
Would this kind calm atone to thee
For Fame's or Fortune's sprightly chase,
Whose prize in prospect still we see;
Or Hymen's happy moments bless'd,
With Beauty leaning on thy breast,
Or childhood prattling at thy knee?

APOLOGY FOR RETIREMENT

A Sonnet: 1766

Why asks my friend what cheers my passing day,
Where these lone fields my rural home enclose,
That all the pomp the crowded city shows
Ne'er from that home allures my steps away?
Now through the upland shade I musing stray,
And catch the gale that o'er the woodbine blows;
Now in the meads on river banks repose,
And breathe rich odour from the new-mown hay:
Now pleas'd I read the poet's lofty lay,
Where music fraught with useful knowledge flows;
Now Delia's converse makes the moments gay,
The maid for love and innocence I chose:
O friend! the man who joys like these can taste,
On vice and folly needs no hour to waste.

LEAVING BATH: AN ODE

1776

Bath! ere I quit thy pleasing scene,
Thy beachen cliff I'll climb again,

To view thy mountains' vivid green,
To view thy hill-surrounded plain:
　　To see distinct beneath the eye,
　　As in a pictur'd prospect nigh,
Those attic structures shining white,
That form thy sunny crescent's bend,
Or by thy dusty streets extend,
Or near thy winding rivers site.

Did Commerce these proud piles upraise?
For thee she ne'er unfurl'd her sails——
Hygeia gave thy fountains praise,
And Pain and Languor sought thy vales:
　　But these suffic'd an humble cell,
　　If they with Strength and Ease might dwell.
Then Fashion call'd; his potent voice
Proud Wealth with ready step obey'd,
And Pleasure all her arts essay'd,
To fix with thee the fickle choice.

Precarious gift!——Thy mansions gay,
Where peers and beauties lead the ball,
Neglected, soon may feel decay;
Forsaken, moulder to their fall.
　　Palmyra, once like thee renown'd,
　　Now lies a ruin on the ground.
But still thy environs so fair,
Thy waters' salutary aid,
Will surely always some persuade
To render thee their care.

JOHN COLLINS (?-1808)

A SONG

In the downhill of life, when I find I'm declining,
　　May my lot no less fortunate be
Than a snug elbow-chair can afford for reclining,
　　And a cot that o'erlooks the wide sea;
With an ambling pad-pony to pace o'er the lawn,
　　While I carol away idle sorrow,
And blithe as the lark that each day hails the dawn,
　　Look forward with hope for to-morrow.

With a porch at my door, both for shelter and shade too,
　　As the sunshine or rain may prevail;
And a small spot of ground for the use of the spade too,
　　With a barn for the use of the flail:
A cow for my dairy, a dog for my game,
　　And a purse when a friend wants to borrow;
I'll envy no nabob his riches or fame,
　　Nor what honours await him to-morrow.

From the bleak northern blast may my cot be completely
　　Secured by a neighbouring hill;
And at night may repose steal upon me more sweetly
　　By the sound of a murmuring rill:
And while peace and plenty I find at my board,
　　With a heart free from sickness and sorrow,
With my friends may I share what to-day may afford,
　　And let them spread the table to-morrow.

And when I at last must throw off this frail covering
　　Which I've worn for three-score years and ten,
On the brink of the grave I'll not seek to keep hovering,
　　Nor my thread wish to spin o'er again:
But my face in the glass I'll serenely survey,
　　And with smiles count each wrinkle and furrow;
As this old worn-out stuff which is threadbare to-day,
　　May become everlasting to-morrow.

ROBERT LLOYD (1733-1764)

A SONG

The beauty which the gods bestow,
Did they but give it for a show?
   No——'twas lent thee from above,
To shed its lustre o'er thy face,
And with its pure and native grace
   To charm the soul to love.

The flaunting Sun, whose western beams,
This evening drink of Oceans' streams,
   To morrow springs to light.
But when thy beauty sets, my fair,
No morrow shall its beam repair,
   'Tis all eternal night.

See too, my love, the virgin rose,
How sweet, how bashfully it blows
   Beneath the vernal skies!
How soon it blooms in full display,
Its bosom opening to the day,
   Then withers, shrinks, and dies.

Of mortal life's declining hour,
Such is the leaf, the bud, the flow'r;
   Then crop the rose in time.
Be blest and bless, and kind impart
The just return of heart for heart,
   Ere love becomes a crime.

To pleasure then, my charmer, haste,
And ere thy youth begins to waste,
   Ere beauty dims its ray,
The proffer'd gift of love employ,
Improve each moment into joy,
   Be happy, whilst you may.

WILLIAM JULIUS MICKLE (1735-1788)

THERE'S NAE LUCK ABOUT THE HOUSE

And are ye sure the news is true?
  And are ye sure he's weel?
Is this a time to think o' wark?
  Mak haste, lay by your wheel;
Is this the time to spin a thread
  When Colin's at the door?
Reach me my cloak, I'll to the quay
  And see him come ashore.
For there's nae luck about the house,
  There's nae luck at a',
There's little pleasure in the house
  When our gudeman's awa.

And gie to me my bigonet,
  My bishop's satin gown;
For I maun tell the bailie's wife
  That Colin's come to town.
My Turkey slippers maun gae on,
  My stockings pearly blue;
It's a' to pleasure my gudeman,
  For he's baith leel and true.

Rise, lass, and mak a clean fire side,
  Put on the muckle pot,
Gie little Kate her button gown,
  And Jock his Sunday coat;
And mak their shoon as black as slaes,
  Their hose as white as snaw,
It's a' to please my ain gudeman,
  For he's been lang awa.

There's twa fat hens upo' the bauk,
  Been fed this month and mair,
Mak haste and thraw their necks about,
  That Colin weel may fare;
And mak the table neat and clean,
  Gar ilka thing look braw,
For wha can tell how Colin fared
  When he was far awa?

Sae true his heart, sae smooth his speech,
  His breath like cauler air,

His very foot has music in't
    As he comes up the stair!
And will I see his face again,
    And will I hear him speak?
I'm downright dizzy wi' the thought,
    In troth I'm like to greet.

If Colin's weel, and weel content,
    I hae nae mair to crave—
And gin I live to keep him sae,
    I'm blest aboon the lave.
And will I see his face again,
    And will I hear him speak?
I'm downright dizzy wi' the thought,
    In troth I'm like to greet.

THE LINNETS

As bringing home the other day
    Two linnets I had ta'en,
The pretty warblers seem'd to pray
    For liberty again.
Unheedful of their plaintive notes
    I sprung across the mead,
In vain they tun'd their downy throats,
    And warbled to be freed.

As passing through the tufted grove
    In which my cottage stood,
I thought I saw the queen of love
    When Chlora's charms I view'd.
I gaz'd, I lov'd, I press'd her stay
    To hear my tender tale,
But all in vain, she fled away,
    Nor could my sighs prevail.

Soon through the wounds that love had made
    Came pity to my breast,
And thus I, as compassion bade,
    The feather'd pair address'd:
"Ye little warblers, cheerful be,
    Remember not ye flew;
For I, who thought myself so free,
    Am caught as well as you."

CUMNOR HALL

The dews of summer nighte did falle,
The moone (sweete regente of the skye)
Silver'd the walles of Cumnor Halle,
And manye an oake that grewe therebye.

Nowe noughte was hearde beneath the skies,
(The soundes of busye lyfe were stille,)
Save an unhappie ladie's sighes,
That issued from that lonelye pile.

"Leicester," shee cried, "is thys thy love
That thou so oft has sworne to mee,
To leave mee in thys lonelye grove,
Immurr'd in shameful privitie?

"No more thou com'st with lover's speede,
Thy once-beloved bryde to see;
But bee shee alive, or bee shee deade,
I feare (sterne earle's) the same to thee.

"Not so the usage I receiv'd,
When happye in my father's halle;
No faithlesse husbande then me griev'd,
No chilling feares did mee appall.

"I rose up with the chearful morne,
No lark more blith, no flow'r more gaye;
And, like the birde that hauntes the thorne,
So merrylie sung the live-long daye.

"If that my beautye is but smalle,
Among court ladies all despis'd;
Why didst thou rend it from that halle,
Where (scorneful earle) it well was priz'de?

"And when you first to mee made suite,
How fayre I was you oft would saye!
And, proude of conquest——pluck'd the fruite,
Then lefte the blossom to decaye.

"Yes, nowe neglected and despis'd,
The rose is pale——the lilly's deade——
But hee that once their charmes so priz'd,
Is sure the cause those charmes are fledde.

"For knowe, when sick'ning griefe doth preye
   And tender love's repay'd with scorne,
The sweetest beautye will decaye——
   What flow'ret can endure the storme?

"At court I'm tolde is beauty's throne,
   Where everye lady's passing rare;
That eastern flow'rs, that shame the sun,
   Are not so glowing, not soe fayre.

"Then, earle, why didst thou leave the bedds
   Where roses and where lillys vie,
To seek a primrose, whose pale shades
   Must sicken——when those gaudes are bye?

"'Mong rural beauties I was one,
   Among the fields wild flow'rs are faire;
Some countrye swayne might mee have won,
   And thoughte my beautie passing rare.

"But, Leicester, (or I much am wronge)
   Or tis not beautye lures thy vowes;
Rather ambition's gilded crowne
   Makes thee forget thy humble spouse.

"Then, Leicester, why, again I pleade
   (The injur'd surelye may repyne,)
Why didst thou wed a countrye mayde,
   When some fayre princesse might be thyne?

"Why didst thou praise my humble charmes,
   And, oh! then leave them to decaye?
Why didst thou win me to thy armes,
   Then leave me to mourne the live-long daye?

"The village maidens of the plaine
   Salute me lowly as they goe;
Envious they marke my silken trayne,
   Nor thinke a countesse can have woe.

"The simple nymphs! they little knowe,
   How farre more happy's their estate——
——To smile for joye——than sigh for woe——
   ——To be contente——than to be greate.

"Howe farre lesse bleste am I than them?
   Dailye to pyne and waste with care!

Like the poore plante, that from its stem
    Divided——feeles the chilling ayre.

"Nor (cruel earl!) can I enjoye
    The humble charmes of solitude;
Your minions proude my peace destroye,
    By sullen frownes or pratings rude.

"Laste nyghte, as said I chanc'd to straye,
    The village deathe-bell smote my eare;
They wink'd asyde, and seem'd to saye,
    Countesse, prepare——thy end is neare.

"And nowe, while happye peasantes sleepe,
    Here I set lonelye and forlorne;
No one to soothe mee as I weepe,
    Save phylomel on yonder thorne.

"My spirits flag——my hopes decaye——
    Still that dreade deathe-bell smites my eare,
And many a boding seems to saye,
    Countess, prepare——thy end is neare."

Thus sore and sad that ladie griev'd,
    In Cumnor Halle so lone and dreare;
And manye a heartefelte sighe shee heav'd,
    And let falle manye a bitter teare.

And ere the dawne of daye appear'd,
    In Cumnor Hall so lone and dreare,
Full manye a piercing screame was hearde,
    And manye a crye of mortal feare.

The death-belle thrice was hearde to ring,
    And aerial voyce was hearde to call,
And thrice the raven flapp'd its wyng
    Arounde the tow'rs of Cumnor Hall.

The mastiffe howl'd at village doore,
    The oaks were shatter'd on the greene;
Woe was the houre——for never more
    That haplesse countesse e'er was seene.

And in that manor now no more
    Is chearful feaste and sprightly balle;
For ever since that drearye houre
    Have spirits haunted Cumnor Hall.

The village maides, with fearful glance,
　Avoid the antient mossgrowne walle;
Nor ever leade the merrye dance,
　Among the groves of Cumnor Halle.

Full manye a travellor oft hath sigh'd,
　And pensive wepte the countess' falle,
As wand'ring onwards they've espied
　The haunted tow'rs of Cumnor Halle.

DR. JOHN LANGHORNE (1735-1779)

A FAREWELL HYMN TO THE VALLEY OF IRWAN

Farewell the fields of Irwan's vale,
   My infant years where fancy led;
And sooth'd me with the western gale,
   Her wild dreams waving round my head;
While the blythe blackbird told his tale.
Farewell, the fields of Irwan's vale!

The primrose on the valley's side,
   The green thyme on the mountain's head;
The wanton rose, the daisy pied,
   The wilding's blossom blushing red:
No longer I their sweets inhale.
Farewell, the fields of Irwan's vale!

How oft, within yon vacant shade,
   Has ev'ning clos'd my careless eyes!
How oft, along those banks, I've stray'd,
   And watch'd the wave that wander'd by!
Full long their loss shall I bewail.
Farewell, the fields of Irwan's vale!

Yet still within yon vacant grove,
   To mark the close of parting day;
Along yon flow'ry banks to rove,
   And watch the wave that winds away;
Fair fancy sure shall never fail,
Though far from these, and Irwan's vale!

WRITTEN IN A COTTAGE-GARDEN,
AT A VILLAGE IN LORRAIN

Occasioned by a Tradition Concerning a Tree of Rosemary

Arbustum loquitur.

O thou, whom love and fancy lead
   To wander near this woodland hill,
   If ever music smooth'd thy quill,
Or pity wak'd thy gentle reed,

Repose beneath my humble tree,
If thou lov'st simplicity.

Stranger, if thy lot has laid
   In toilsome scenes of busy life,
   Full sorely may'st thou rue the strife
Of weary passions ill repaid.
   In a garden live with me,
   If thou lov'st simplicity.

Flowers have sprung for many a year
   O'er the village maiden's grave,
   That, one memorial sprig to save,
Bore it from a sister's bier;
   And, homeward walking, wept o'er me
   The true tears of simplicity.

And soon, her cottage window near,
   With care my slender stem she plac'd;
   And fondly thus her grief embrac'd;
And cherish'd sad remembrance dear:
   For love sincere and friendship free
   Are children of simplicity.

When past was many a painful day,
   Slow-pacing o'er the village green,
   In white were all its maidens seen,
And bore my guardian friend away.
   Ah death! what sacrifice to thee,
   The ruins of simplicity.

One gen'rous swain her heart approv'd,
   A youth whose fond and faithful breast,
   With many an artless sigh confess'd,
In Nature's language, that he lov'd:
   But, stranger, 'tis no tale to thee,
   Unless thou lov'st simplicity.

He died—and soon her lip was cold,
   And soon her rosy cheek was pale;
   The village wept to hear the tale,
When for both the slow bell toll'd—
   Beneath yon flow'ry turf they lie,
   The lovers of simplicity.

Yet one boon have I to crave;
   Stranger, if thy pity bleed,

263

Wilt thou do one tender deed,
And strew my pale flowers o'er their grave?
So lightly lie the turf on thee,
Because thou lov'st simplicity.

TO A REDBREAST

Little bird, with bosom red,
Welcome to my humble shed!
Courtly domes of high degree
Have no room for thee and me;
Pride and pleasure's fickle throng
Nothing mind an idle song.
Daily near my table steal,
While I pick my scanty meal.
Doubt not, little though there be,
But I'll cast a crumb to thee;
Well rewarded, if I spy
Pleasure in thy glancing eye;
See thee, when thou'st eat thy fill,
Plume thy breast, and wipe thy bill.
Come, my feather'd friend, again,
Well thou know'st the broken pane.
Ask of me thy daily store;
Go not near Avaro's door;
Once within his iron hall,
Woeful end shall thee befall.
Savage! He would soon divest
Of its rosy plumes thy breast;
Then, with solitary joy,
Eat thee, bones and all, my boy!

JAMES BEATTIE (1735-1803)

RETIREMENT

1758

When in the crimson cloud of even,
The lingering light decays,
And Hesper on the front of Heaven
His glittering gem displays;
Deep in the silent vale, unseen,
Beside a lulling stream,
A pensive youth, of placid mien,
Indulg'd this tender theme.

"Ye cliffs, in hoary grandeur pil'd
High o'er the glimmering dale;
Ye woods, along whose windings wild
Murmurs the solemn gale:
Where Melancholy strays forlorn,
And Woe retires to weep,
What time the wan Moon's yellow horn
Gleams on the western deep:

"To you, ye wastes, whose artless charms
Ne'er drew Ambition's eye,
Scap'd a tumultuous world's alarms,
To your retreats I fly.
Deep in your most sequester'd bower
Let me at last recline,
Where Solitude, mild, modest power,
Leans on her ivy'd shrine.

"How shall I woo thee, matchless fair!
Thy heavenly smile how win!
Thy smile that smooths the brow of Care,
And stills the storm within.
O wilt thou to thy favourite grove
Thine ardent votary bring,
And bless his hours, and bid them move
Serene, on silent wing!

"Oft let Remembrance sooth his mind
With dreams of former days,
When in the lap of Peace reclin'd

265

He fram'd his infant lays;
When Fancy rov'd at large, nor Care
Nor cold Distrust alarm'd,
Nor Envy with malignant glare
His simple youth had harm'd.

"'Twas then, O Solitude! to thee
His early vows were paid,
From heart sincere, and warm, and free,
Devoted to the shade.
Ah why did Fate his steps decoy
In stormy paths to roam,
Remote from all congenial joy! ——
O take the wand'rer home.

"Thy shades, thy silence now be mine,
Thy charms my only theme;
My haunt the hollow cliff, whose pine
Waves o'er the gloomy stream.
Whence the scar'd owl on pinions gray
Breaks from the rustling boughs,
And down the lone vale sails away
To more profound repose.

"O, while to thee the woodland pours
Its wildly warbling song,
And balmy from the bank of flow'rs
The Zephyr breathes along;
Let no rude sound invade from far,
No vagrant foot be nigh,
No ray from Grandeur's gilded car,
Flash on the startled eye.

"But if some pilgrim through the glade
Thy hallow'd bowers explore,
O guard from harm his hoary head,
And listen to his lore;
For he of joys divine shall tell,
That wean from earthly wo,
And triumph o'er the mighty spell
That chains his heart below.

"For me, no more the path invites
Ambition loves to tread;
No more I climb those toilsome heights
By guileful Hope misled;
Leaps my fond flutt'ring heart no more
To Mirth's enliv'ning strain;

266

For present pleasure soon is o'er,
And all the past is vain."

ISAAC BICKERSTAFFE (1735?-1812?)

AIR XXXVI

from "Love in a Village"

A plague on those wenches, they make such a pother,
    When once they have let'n a man have his will;
They're always a whining for something or other,
    And cry he's unkind in his carriage.
What tho'f he speaks them ne'er so fairly,
    Still they keep teazing, teazing on:
            You cannot persuade 'em
            'Till promise you've made 'em;
            And after they've got it,
            They tell you——add rot it,
Their character's blasted, they're ruin'd, undone:
            And then to be sure, sir,
            There is but one cure, sir,
    And all their discourse is of marriage.

AN AIR

from "The Maid of the Mill"

When you meet a tender creature,
Neat in limb, and fair in feature,
Full of kindness and good nature,
    Prove as kind again to she;
Happy mortal! to possess her,
In your bosom, warm, to press her,
Morning, noon, and night, caress her,
    And be fond, as fond can be.

But if one you meet that's froward,
Saucy, jilting, and untoward,
Should you act the whining coward,
    'Tis to mend her ne'er the wit.

Nothing's tough enough to bind her;
Then agog, when once you find her,
Let her go, and never mind her;
    Heart alive, you're fairly quit.

ROBERT JEPHSON (1736-1803)

ANTONY AND CLEOPATRA

But not content with half the world's domain,
Caesar and Antony alone would reign;
The first, a steady sceptre born to wield,
O'er all his acts extends the public shield;
The last, abhorrent from the toils of state,
Rots on the Nile, a hoary profligate;
While subtle Caesar sapp'd his eastern throne,
He clasp'd his world in Cleopatra's zone.
Not she for whom Dardanian Troy was lost,
The pride of nature, and her country's boast;
Nor she, who bade the Macedonian's hand
Hurl at Persepolis the blazing brand,
Nor Phaedra, nor Ariadne, still more fair,
Could with the Sorceress of Nile compare;
In her, not face and shape alone could please,
(Though with unrival'd grace she charm'd by these),
But the whole store of Cytherea's wiles,
Sighs, gentlest blandishments, and ambush'd smiles;
The ready tear, the blush of well-feign'd truth,
And the ripe woman, fresh as new-sprung youth.
Beneath her roseat palms the lute, compress'd,
Chas'd thought and trouble from the anxious breast
In dulcet bonds the imprison'd soul she held,
While the sweet chords her warbling voice excell'd.
A thousand forms the Syren could put on,
And seem as many mistresses in one;
Serious or sportive, as the mood requir'd,
No whim grew irksome, and no frolic tir'd;
Enough of coyness to provoke desire,
Of warmth enough to share the amorous fire,
All, her delighted lovers could receive,
Seem'd but fond earnests she had more to give;
Nor with possession was the promise o'er,
Love's fruit and slower at once her bosom bore;
No languid pause of bliss near her was known,
But with new joys new hours came laughing on.
By arts like these was wiser Julius won,
And Antony, more fond, was more undone.
His soul, enamour'd, to the wanton clung,
Glow'd at her eyes, or melted from her tongue;
Lull'd in the dear Elysium of her arms,

269

Nor interest moves him, nor ambition warms:
Sometimes, with short remorse, he look'd within,
But kept at once the conscience and the sin:
In vain he saw the yawning ruin nigh;
Content with her, he bade the world go by;
He sought no covert of the friendly shade,
'Twas half the zest to have his shame display'd.
He deem'd it still his best exchange through life,
A melting mistress for a railing wife.
Perpetual orgies unabash'd they keep,
Wine fires their veins, and revels banish sleep:
Timbrels and songs, and feasts of deaf'ning joy,
By arts till then unknown, forbore to cloy,
See for one banquet a whole kingdom sink,
And gems dissolv'd, impearl her luscious drink,
Pleasure was hunted through each impious mode;
An Isis she, and he the vine-crown'd god.
Old Nile, astonish'd, on his bosom bore
Monsters more strange than e'er deform'd his shore;
For what so monstrous sight beneath the skies
As self-created human deities?—
But heaven, for vengeful retribution, means
The sword and asp should close these frantic scenes.
Spectators mute the sorrowing captains stand,
While empire shoulders from his palsied hand:
But rous'd at length, unwilling, to the fight,
His star at Actium sunk in endless night.
With equal pomp, as when down Cydnus' stream
Her burnish'd prow struck back the sun's bright beam,
The enchantress bade her bloated train prepare
To meet the horrors of the naval war;
But the first shouts her trembling spirits quail;
She flies, and he pursues her shameful sail:
His heart-strings to the harlot's rudder tied,
What lust began, his dotage ratified:
In Alexandria's towers he veil'd his head,
Where, self-expell'd, the vital spirit fled.
He tried all vices, and surpass'd in all,
Luxurious, cruel, wild, and prodigal;
Lavish of hours, of character, and gold,
But warlike, hardy, and in dangers bold;
His mind was suited to the boist'rous times,
A soldier's virtues, and a tyrant's crimes.

JAMES MACPHERSON (1736-1796)

THE CAVE

The wind is up, the field is bare,
  Some hermit lead me to his cell,
Where Contemplation, lonely fair,
  With blest Content has chose to dwell.

Behold! it opens to my sight,
  Dark in the rock, beside the flood;
Dry fern around obstructs the light;
  The winds above it move the wood.

Reflected in the lake, I see
  The downward mountains and the skies,
The flying bird, the waving tree,
  The goats that on the hill arise.

The gray-cloaked herd drives on the cow;
  The slow-paced fowler walks the heath;
A freckled pointer scours the brow;
  A musing shepherd stands beneath.

Curved o'er the ruin of an oak,
  The woodman lifts his axe on high;
The hills re-echo to the stroke;
  I see—I see the shivers fly!

Some rural maid, with apron full,
  Brings fuel to the homely flame;
I see the smoky columns roll,
  And, through the chinky hut, the beam.

Beside a stone o'ergrown with moss,
  Two well-met hunters talk at ease;
Three panting dogs beside repose;
  One bleeding deer is stretched on grass.

A lake at distance spreads to sight,
  Skirted with shady forests round;
In midst, an island's rocky height
  Sustains a ruin, once renowned.

One tree bends o'er the naked walls;
  Two broad-winged eagles hover nigh;

271

By intervals a fragment falls,
    As blows the blast along the sky.

The rough-spun hinds the pinnace guide
    With labouring oars along the flood;
An angler, bending o'er the tide,
    Hangs from the boat the insidious wood.

Beside the flood, beneath the rocks,
    On grassy bank, two lovers lean;
Bend on each other amorous looks,
    And seem to laugh and kiss between.

The wind is rustling in the oak;
    They seem to hear the tread of feet;
They start, they rise, look round the rock;
    Again they smile, again they meet.

But see! the gray mist from the lake
    Ascends upon the shady hills;
Dark storms the murmuring forests shake,
    Rain beats around a hundred rills.

To Damon's homely hut I fly;
    I see it smoking on the plain;
When storms are past, and fair the sky,
    I'll often seek my cave again.

DR. JOHN WOLCOT ("PETER PINDAR") (1738-1819)

ODE ON CAMBRIA, A MOUNTAIN IN CORNWALL

Near yonder solitary tower,
   'Lone glooming 'midst the moony light,
I roam at midnight's spectred hour,
   And climb the wild majestic height:
Low to the mountain let me rev'rence bow,
Where Wisdom, Virtue, taught their founts to flow.

Pale on a rock's aspiring steep,
   Behold a Druid sits forlorn,
I see the white-rob'd phantom weep,
   I hear his harp of sorrow mourn.
The vanish'd grove provokes his deepest sigh,
And altars open'd to the gazing eye.

Permit me, Druid, here to stray,
   And ponder 'mid thy drear retreat;
To wail the solitary way
   Where Wisdom held her hallow'd seat;
Here let me roam, in spite of Folly's smile,
A pensive pilgrim, o'er each pitied pile.

Poor ghost! no more the Druid race
   Shall here their sacred fires relume:
No more their show'rs of incense blaze;
   No more their tapers gild the gloom.
Lo! snakes obscene along the temples creep,
And foxes on the broken altars sleep.

No more beneath the golden brook,
   The treasure's of the grove shall fall;
Time triumphs o'er each blasted oak,
   Whose power at length shall crush the ball.
Led by the wrinkled Pow'r, with gladden'd mien,
Gigantic Ruin treads the weeping scene.

No more the bards in strains sublime
   The actions of the brave proclaim,
Thus rescuing from the rage of Time
   Each glorious deed approv'd by Fame.
Deep in the dust each lyre is laid unstrung,
While mute for ever stops each tuneful tongue.

273

Here Wisdom's, Virtue's awful voice
    Inspired the youths of Cornwall's plains:
With such no more these hills rejoice,
    But sullen, death-like, silence reigns,
While melancholy, in yon mould'ring tow'r
Sits list'ning to old ocean's distant roar.

Let others, heedless of the hill,
    With eye incurious pass along;
My muse with grief the scene shall fill,
    And swell with softest sighs her song.

THE PILGRIMS AND THE PEAS

A brace of sinners, for no good,
    Were ordered to the Virgin Mary's shrine,
Who at Loretto dwelt in wax, stone, wood,
    And in a curled white wig looked wondrous fine.

Fifty long miles had these sad rogues to travel,
With something in their shoes much worse than gravel;
In short, their toes so gentle to amuse,
The priest had ordered peas into their shoes.

A nostrum famous in old popish times
For purifying souls that stunk with crimes,
    A sort of apostolic salt,
    That popish parsons for its powers exalt,
For keeping souls of sinners sweet,
Just as our kitchen salt keeps meat.

The knaves set off on the same day,
Peas in their shoes, to go and pray;
    But very different was their speed, I wot:
One of the sinners galloped on,
Light as a bullet from a gun;
    The other limped as if he had been shot.

One saw the Virgin, soon peccavi cried;
    Had his soul whitewashed all so clever,
When home again he nimbly hied,
    Made fit with saints above to live for ever.

In coming back, however, let me say,
He met his brother rogue about half-way,

274

Hobbling with outstretched hams and bending knees,
Cursing the souls and bodies of the peas;
His eyes in tears, his cheeks and brow in sweat,
Deep sympathising with his groaning feet.

"How now!" the light-toed whitewashed pilgrim broke,
  "You lazy lubber!"
"Confound it!" cried the t'other, "'tis no joke;
My feet, once hard as any rock,
  Are now as soft as blubber.

"Excuse me, Virgin Mary, that I swear:
As for Loretto, I shall not get there;
No! to the Devil my sinful soul must go,
For hang me if I ha'n't lost every toe!

"But, brother sinner, do explain
How 'tis that you are not in pain——
  What power hath worked a wonder for your toes——
Whilst I, just like a snail, am crawling,
Now swearing, now on saints devoutly bawling,
  Whilst not a rascal comes to ease my woes?

"How is't that you can like a greyhound go,
  Merry as if nought had happened, burn ye?"
"Why," cried the other, grinning, "you must know
  That just before I ventured on my journey,
    To walk a little more at ease,
    I took the liberty to boil my peas."

APPLE DUMPLINGS AND A KING

Once on a time, a Monarch, tir'd with whooping,
        Whipping and spurring,
        Happy in worrying
    A poor, defenceless, harmless buck,
    The horse and rider wet as muck,
From his high consequence and wisdom stooping,
    Enter'd, through curiosity, a cot,
    Where sat a poor old woman and her pot.
        The wrinkl'd, blear-ey'd, good old granny,
        In this same cot illum'd by many a cranny,
          Had finish'd apple dumplings for her pot:
        In tempting row the naked dumplings lay,
          When, lo! the Monarch, in his usual way,
Like lightning spoke, "What's this? what's this? what? what?"

275

Then taking up a dumpling in his hand,
His eyes with admiration did expand——
    And oft did Majesty the dumpling grapple:
"'Tis monstrous, monstrous hard indeed," he cried:
"What makes it, pray, so hard?"——The Dame replied,
    Low curtsying, "Please Your Majesty, the apple."

"Very astonishing indeed!——strange thing!"
Turning the dumpling round, rejoined the King.
    "'Tis most extraordinary then, all this is——
    It beats Pinetti's conjuring all to pieces——
Strange I should never of a dumpling dream——
But, Goody, tell me where, where, where's the seam?"

"Sir, there's no seam (quoth she); I never knew
That folks did apple dumplings sew."——
"No! (cried the staring Monarch with a grin)
How, how the devil got the apple in?"

Reader, thou likest not my tale——look'st blue——
    Thou art a Courtier, ——roarest "Lies, Lies, Lies!"——
        Do, for a moment, stop thy cries——
I tell thee, roaring infidel, 'tis true.

Why should it not be true? The greatest men
May ask a foolish question now and then——
    This is the language of all ages:
Folly lays many a trap——we can't escape it:
Nemo (says some one) omnibus horis sapit:
    Then why not Kings, like me and other sages?

Far from despising Kings, I like the breed,
    Provided King-like they behave:
    Kings are an instrument we need,
        Just as we razors want——to shave;
To keep the State's face smooth——give it an air——
Like my Lord North's, so jolly, round, and fair.

My sense of Kings tho' freely I impart——
I hate not royalty, Heav'n knows my heart:
Princes and Princesses I like, so loyal——
    Great GEORGE's children are my great delight;
The sweet Augusta, and sweet Princess Royal,
    Obtain my love by day, and pray'rs by night.

Yes! I like Kings——and oft look back with pride
    Upon the Edwards, Harrys of our isle——

Great souls! in virtue as in valour try'd,
　Whose actions bid the cheek of Britons smile.

　　Muse! let us also forward look,
　　And take a peep into Fate's book.

Behold! the sceptre young AUGUSTUS sways;
　I hear the mingled voice of millions rise;
　I see uprais'd to Heav'n their ardent eyes;
That for their Monarch ask a length of days.

Bright in the brightest annals of renown,
Behold fair Fame his youthful temples crown
　With laurels of unfading bloom;
Behold DOMINION swell beneath his care,
And GENIUS, rising from a dark despair,
　His long-extinguish'd fires relume.

Such are the Kings that suit my taste, I own——
　Not those where all the littlenesses join——
Whose souls should start to find their lot a throne,
　And blush to show their noses on a coin.

LORD GREGORY

"Ah ope, Lord Gregory, thy door,
　A midnight wand'rer sighs;
Hard rush the rains, the tempests roar,
　And lightnings cleave the skies."

"Who comes with woe at this drear night,
　A pilgrim of the gloom?
If she whose love did once delight,
　My cot shall yield her room."

"Alas! thou heardst a pilgrim mourn
　That once was priz'd by thee:
Think of the ring by yonder burn
　Thou gav'st to love and me.

"But shouldst thou not poor Marion know,
　I'll turn my feet and part;
And think the storms that round me blow,
　Far kinder than thy heart."

277

ODE TO JURYMEN

Sirs, it may happen, by the grace of God,
    That I, Great Peter, one day come before ye,
To answer to the man of wig, for ode,
    Full of sublimity, and pleasant story.

Yes, it may so fall out that lofty men,
    Dundas, and Richmond, Hawksb'ry, Portland, Pitt,
May wish to cut the nib of Peter's pen,
    And, cruel, draw the holders of his wit;

Nay, Dame Injustice in their cause engage,
    To clap the gentle poet in a cage;
And should a grimly judge for death harangue,
    Don't let the poet of the people hang.

What are my crimes? A poor tame cur am I,
    Though some will swear I've snapp'd them by the heels;
A puppy's pinch, that's all, I don't deny;
    But Lord! how sensibly a great man feels!

A harmless joke, at times, on kings and queens;
    A little joke on lofty earls and lords;
Smiles at the splendid homage of court scenes,
    The modes, the manners, sentiments, and words:

A joke on Marg'ret Nicholson's mad knights;
    A joke upon the shave of cooks at court,
Charms the fair muse, and eke the world delights;
    A pretty piece of inoffensive sport.

Lo, in a little inoffensive smile,
    There lurks no lever to o'erturn the state,
And king, and parliament! intention vile!
    And hurl the queen of nations to her fate.

No gunpowder my modest garrets hold,
    Dark-lanterns, blunderbusses, masks, and matches;
Few words my simple furniture unfold;
    A bed, a stool, a rusty coat in patches.

Carpets, nor chandeliers so bright are mine;
    Nor mirrors, ogling vanity to please;
Spaniels, nor lap-dogs, with their furs so fine:
    Alas! my little live-stock are——my fleas!

AUGUSTUS MONTAGUE TOPLADY (1740-1778)

A PRAYER

Rock of ages, cleft for me,
Let me hide myself in Thee!
Let the Water and the Blood,
From thy riven Side which flow'd,
Be of sin the double cure;
Cleanse me from it's guilt and pow'r.

Not the labors of my hands
Can fulfill thy Law's demands:
Could my zeal no respite know,
Could my tears for ever flow,
All for sin could not atone:
Thou must save, and Thou alone.

Nothing in my hand I bring;
Simply to thy Cross I cling;
Naked, come to Thee for dress;
Helpless, look to Thee for grace;
Foul, I to the Fountain fly:
Wash me, SAVIOR, or I die!

While I draw this fleeting breath—
When my eye-strings break in death—
When I soar to worlds unknown—
See Thee on thy judgment-throne—
Rock of ages, cleft for me,
Let me hide myself in Thee.

ANNA LETITIA BARBAULD (1743-1825)

ODE TO SPRING

Sweet daughter of a rough and stormy sire,
Hoar Winter's blooming child, delightful Spring!
    Whose unshorn locks with leaves
    And swelling buds are crowned;

From the green islands of eternal youth—
Crowned with fresh blooms and ever-springing shade—
    Turn, hither turn thy step,
    O thou, whose powerful voice,

More sweet than softest touch of Doric reed
Or Lydian flute, can soothe the madding winds,
    And through the stormy deep
    Breathe thy own tender calm.

Thee, best beloved! the virgin train await
With songs and festal rites, and joy to rove
    Thy blooming wilds among,
    And vales and dewy lawns,

With untired feet; and cull thy earliest sweets
To weave fresh garlands for the glowing brow
    Of him, the favoured youth
    That prompts their whispered sigh.

Unlock thy copious stores; those tender showers
That drop their sweetness on the infant buds,
    And silent dews that swell
    The milky ear's green stem,

And feed the flow'ring osier's early shoots;
And call those winds, which through the whispering boughs
    With warm and pleasant breath
    Salute the blowing flowers.

Now let me sit beneath the whitening thorn,
And mark thy spreading tints steal o'er the dale;
    And watch with patient eye
    Thy fair unfolding charms.

O nymph, approach! while yet the temperate Sun
With bashful forehead, through the cool moist air

Throws his young maiden beams,
And with chaste kisses woos

The Earth's fair bosom; while the streaming veil
Of lucid clouds, with kind and frequent shade
      Protects thy modest blooms
      From his severer blaze.

Sweet is thy reign, but short: the red dog-star
Shall scorch thy tresses, and the mower's scythe
      Thy greens, thy flow'rets all,
      Remorseless shall destroy.

Reluctant shall I bid thee then farewell;
For oh! not all that Autumn's lap contains,
      Nor Summer's ruddiest fruits,
      Can aught for thee atone,

Fair spring! whose simplest promise more delights
Than all their largest wealth, and through the heart
      Each joy and new-born hope
      With softest influence breathes.

SIR BROOKE BOOTHBY (1743-1824)

SONNET SACRED TO THE MEMORY OF PENELOPE

Though since my date of woe long years have roll'd,
Darkness ne'er draws the curtains round my head,
Nor orient morning opes her eyes of gold,
But grief pursues my walks, or haunts my bed.
Visions, in sleep, their tristful shapes unfold;
Show Misery living, Hope and Pleasure dead,
Pale shrouded beauty, kisses faint and cold,
Or murmur words the parting angels said.
Thoughts, when awake, their wonted trains renew;
With all their stings my tortured breast assail;
Her faded form now glides before my view;
Her plaintive voice now floats upon the gale.
The hope now vain, that time should bring relief!
Time does but deeper root a real grief.

HENRY JAMES PYE (1745-1813)

ODE FOR THE NEW YEAR, 1793

Not with more joy from desert shades,
    Where prowl untam'd the savage train,
From pathless moors and barren glades,
    Sad desolation's gloomy reign
Averted, bends the weary eye
To seats of rural industry,
Where harvests wave in yellow pride,
Where spreads the fertile champaign wide,
The lucid stream while Commerce leads
Through peopled towns and laughing meads;
Than turns the mind from scenes of woe,
Where ceaseless tears of anguish flow,
Where Anarchy's insatiate brood
Their horrid footsteps mark with blood,
To shores where temperate Freedom reigns,
Where Peace and Order bless the plains,
Where men the Sovereign of their choice obey,
Where Britain's grateful Sons exult in George's sway.

Yet Albion ne'er with selfish aim
    To her own race her care confines,
On all, the sacred gift who claim,
    The golden beam of Freedom shines.
Sad out-cast from his native shore,
The wretched Exile wafted o'er,
Feels Pity's lenient hand assuage
The wounds of Faction's cruel rage;
Her laws, to all protective, yield
Security's impartial shield;
Who breathes her air, breathes purest liberty,
Gaunt Slavery flies the coast; who treads her soil is free.

Ambition's clarion has not charm'd
    Her dauntless legions to the war,
Nor have her Sons, by fury arm'd,
    Follow'd Oppression's iron car;
Tho' prompt at honour's call to brave
The hostile clime, the adverse wave,
Their thunder 'neath the burning zone
Shook the proud Despot on his throne;
Yet while aloft in orient skies

Conquest's triumphant banner flies,
The generous Victor bids the conflict cease,
And 'midst his laurels twines the nobler wreaths of peace.

Blest Peace! O may thy radiance mild
   Beam kindly on the op'ning year!
Yet, should with frantic vengeance wild
   The fiends of Discord urge their rash career,
Not cold in Freedom's sacred cause,
Nor slow to guard her holy laws,
Faithful to him their hearts approve,
The Monarch they revere, the man they love;
Britannia's sons shall arm with patriot zeal,
Their Prince's cause their own, his rights the general weal.

CHARLES DIBDIN (1745-1814)

TOM BOWLING

Here, a sheer hulk, lies poor Tom Bowling,
    The darling of our crew;
No more he'll hear the tempest howling,
    For Death has broached him to.
His form was of the manliest beauty,
    His heart was kind and soft;
Faithful below he did his duty,
    But now he's gone aloft.

Tom never from his word departed,
    His virtues were so rare;
His friends were many and true-hearted,
    His Poll was kind and fair:
And then he'd sing so blithe and jolly;
    Ah, many's the time and oft!
But mirth is turned to melancholy,
    For Tom is gone aloft.

Yet shall poor Tom find pleasant weather,
    When He, who all commands,
Shall give, to call life's crew together,
    The word to pipe all hands.
Thus Death, who kings and tars despatches,
    In vain Tom's life has doffed;
For though his body's under hatches,
    His soul is gone aloft.

POOR JACK

Go, patter to lubbers and swabs, do you see,
    'Bout danger, and fear, and the like;
A tight-water boat and good sea-room give me,
    And it a'nt to a little I'll strike.
Though the tempest top-gallant mast smack smooth should smite,
    And shiver each splinter of wood,
Clear the deck, stow the yards, and bouse everything tight,
    And under reefed foresail we'll scud:
Avast! nor don't think me a milksop so soft,
    To be taken for trifles aback;

For they say there's a Providence sits up aloft,
    To keep watch for the life of poor Jack!

I heard our good chaplain palaver one day
    About souls, heaven, mercy, and such;
And, my timbers! what lingo he'd coil and belay;
    Why, 'twas just all as one as High Dutch;
For he said how a sparrow can't founder, d'ye see,
    Without orders that come down below;
And a many fine things that proved clearly to me
    That Providence takes us in tow:
For, says he, do you mind me, let storms e'er so oft
    Take the top-sails of sailors aback,
There's a sweet little cherub that sits up aloft,
    To keep watch for the life of poor Jack!

SIR HENRY BATE DUDLEY (1745-1824)

AN AIR

from "The Woodman"

When first I slipp'd my leading strings, to please her little Poll,
My mother bought me, at the fair, a pretty waxen doll;
Such sloe-black eyes and cherry cheeks the smiling dear
   possess'd,
How could I kiss it oft enough, or hug it to my breast?

No sooner I could prattle it, as forward misses do,
Than how I long'd and sigh'd to hear my Dolly prattle too!
I curl'd her hair in ringlets neat, and dress'd her very gay,
And yet the sulky hussey not a syllable would say.

My head, on this, I bridled up, and threw the plaything by,
Altho' my sister snubb'd me for't, I know the reason why:
I fancy she would wish to keep the sweethearts all her own;
But that she sha'n't, depend upon't, when I'm a woman grown.

THOMAS HOLCROFT (1745-1809)

GAFFER GRAY

Ho! why dost thou shiver and shake,
    Gaffer Gray?
And why doth thy nose look so blue?
    "'Tis the weather that's cold;
    'Tis I'm grown very old,
And my doublet is not very new,
    Well-a-day!"

Then, line thy worn doublet with ale,
    Gaffer Gray;
And warm thy old heart with a glass.
    "Nay, but credit I've none,
    And my money's all gone;
Then say how may that come to pass?
    Well-a-day!"

Hie away to the house on the brow,
    Gaffer Gray;
And knock at the jolly priest's door.
    "The priest often preaches
    Against worldly riches;
But ne'er gives a mite to the poor,
    Well-a-day!"

The lawyer lives under the hill,
    Gaffer Gray;
Warmly fenc'd both in back and in front.
    "He will fasten his locks,
    And will threaten the stocks,
Should he ever more find me in want,
    Well-a-day!"

The 'squire has fat beeves and brown ale,
    Gaffer Gray;
And the season will welcome you there.
    "The fat beeves and the beer,
    And his merry new year,
And all for the flush and the fair,
    Well-a-day!"

My keg is but low, I confess,
    Gaffer Gray;

What, then, while it lasts, man, we'll live.
     The poor man alone,
     When he hears the poor moan,
Of his morsel a morsel will give,
     Well-a-day!

MICHAEL BRUCE (1746-1767)

ODE TO THE CUCKOO

Hail, beauteous stranger of the wood,
   Attendant on the spring!
Now heav'n repairs thy rural seat,
   And woods thy welcome sing.

Soon as the daisie decks the green,
   Thy certain voice we hear:
Hast thou a star to guide thy path,
   Or mark the rolling year?

Delightful visitant! with thee
   I hail the time of flow'rs,
When heav'n is fill'd with music sweet
   Of birds among the bow'rs.

The schoolboy, wand'ring in the wood
   To pull the flow'rs so gay,
Starts, thy curious voice to hear,
   And imitates thy lay.

Soon as the pea puts on the bloom,
   Thou fly'st thy vocal vale,
An annual guest, in other lands,
   Another spring to hail.

Sweet bird! thy bow'r is ever green,
   Thy sky is ever clear;
Thou hast no sorrow in thy song,
   No winter in thy year!

Alas, sweet bird! not so my fate,
   Dark scowling skies I see
Fast gathering round, and fraught with woe
   And wintry years to me.

O could I fly, I'd fly with thee:
   We'd make, with social wing,
Our annual visit o'er the globe,
   Companions of the spring.

THEOPHILUS SWIFT (1746-1815)

THE VIOLET

Thee, Flora's first and favourite child,
By Zephyr nurst on green bank wild,
    And chear'd by vernal showers!——
Thy fragrant beauties let me sing,
Cerulean harbinger of Spring,
    Chaste Vi'let, Queen of flowers!

Thy velvet birth, in golden groves,
The rosy hours and laughing loves
    With genial kisses fed:
And o'er thee, Peace, as on a day
In early innocence you lay,
    Her sylvan mantle spread.

When you in azure state appear,
Thy presence speaks the purple year,
    And promis'd Summer nigh.
Thus kisses blow the lover's fire,
Till the warm season of desire
    Mature the Spring of joy.

Blue skirts the Rain-bow's arch in air,
Blue melts the mass of colours there,
    The Heavens are hung with blue——
And she, the nymph that charms my soul,
Her eyes celestial azure roll,
    And best resemble you.

What though in humble shades you dwell,
And lurk in thicket, brake, or dell,
    Wasting your sweets away?
Yet shalt thou live embalm'd in song,
And there shalt reign, distinguish'd long,
    The blooming Queen of May.

Then quit the wild, lest some rude thorn
Invade they beauty's tender morn,
    All lovely as thou art!
So shall thy Poet lift his voice,
And to confirm his annual choice,
    Still lodge thee next his heart.

TO A LADY

Who Said the Author flattered her in his Verses

When Phoebus shoots his radiant beams
 Where silver Avon strays,
Less glorious in reflecting streams
 We mark the solar blaze.

The bordering flowers, that lovely blow
 Along yon fountain's side,
Less graceful in that mirror show,
 And half their beauties hide.

Thus in my rhymes thy graces shone
 With less attractive power. ——
Verse gives not glory to the fun,
 Nor beauty to the flower.

A SONG

When clouds that angel face deform,
Anxious I view the growing storm;
When angry lightnings arm thine eye,
And tell the gathering tempest nigh;
I curse the sex, and bid adieu
To female friendship, love, and you.

But when soft passions rule your breast,
And each kind look some love has drest;
When cloudless smiles around you play,
And give the world a holiday;
I bless the hour when first I knew
Dear female friendship, love, and you.

DR. JOHN AIKIN (1747-1822)

THE SEA SHORE

Frequent along the pebbly beach I pace,
And gaze intent on Ocean's varying face.
Now from the main rolls-in the swelling tide,
And waves on waves in long procession ride:
Gath'ring they come, 'till, gain'd the ridgy height,
No more the liquid mound sustains its weight;
It curls, it falls, it breaks, with hideous roar,
And pours a foamy deluge on the shore.
From the bleak pole now driving tempests sweep,
Tear the light clouds, and vex the ruffled deep:
White on the shoals the spouting breakers rise,
And mix the waste of waters with the skies:
The anch'ring vessels, stretch'd in long array,
Shake from their bounding sides the dashing spray;
Lab'ring they heave, the tighten'd cables strain,
And danger adds new horror to the main:
Then shifts the scene, as to the western gales
Delighted Commerce spreads her crowded sails.
A cluster'd groupe the distant fleet appear,
That, scatt'ring, breaks in varied figures near.
Now, all-illumin'd by the kindling ray,
Swan-like, the stately vessel cuts her way:
The full-wing'd barks now meet, now swiftly pass,
And leave long traces in the liquid glass:
Light boats, all sail, athwart the currents bound,
And dot with shining specks the surface round.
Nor with the day the sea-born splendours cease:
When ev'ning lulls each ruder gale to peace,
The rising moon with silv'ry lustre gleams,
And shoots across the flood her quiv'ring beams.
Or, if deep gloom succeed the sultry day,
On Ocean's bosom native meteors play,
Flash from the wave, pursue the dipping oar,
And roll in flaming billows to the shore.

SUSANNA BLAMIRE (1747-1794)

AULD ROBIN FORBES

And auld Robin Forbes hes gien tem a dance,
I pat on my speckets to see them aw prance;
I thout o' the days when I was but fifteen,
And skipped wi' the best upon Forbes's green.
Of aw things that is I think thout is meast queer,
It brings that that's bypast and sets it down here;
I see Willy as plain as I dui this bit leace,
When he tuik his cwoat lappet and deeghted his feace.

The lasses aw wondered what Willy cud see
In yen that was dark and hard-featured leyke me;
And they wondered ay mair when they talked o' my wit,
And slily telt Willy that cudn't be it.
But Willy he laughed, and he meade me his weyfe,
And whea was mair happy thro' aw his lang leyfe?
It's e'en my great comfort, now Willy is geane,
That he offen said——nea pleace was leyke his awn heame!

I mind when I carried my wark to yon steyle,
Where Willy was deyken, the time to beguile,
He wad fling me a daisy to put i' my breast,
And I hammered my noddle to mek out a jest.
But merry or grave, Willy often wad tell
There was nin o' the leave that was leyke my awn sel;
And he spak what he thout, for I'd hardly a plack
When we married, and nobbet ae gown to my back.

When the clock had struck eight, I expected him heame,
And wheyles went to meet him as far as Dumleane;
Of aw hours it telt, eight was dearest to me,
But now when it streykes there's a tear i' my ee.
O Willy! dear Willy! it never can be
That age, time, or death can divide thee and me!
For that spot on earth that's aye dearest to me,
Is the turf that has covered my Willie frae me.

THE NABOB

When silent time, wi' lightly foot,
   Had trod on thirty years,

I sought again my native land
   Wi' mony hopes and fears.
Wha kens gin the dear friends I left
   May still continue mine?
Or gin I e'er again shall taste
   The joys I left langsyne?

As I drew near my ancient pile
   My heart beat a' the way;
Ilk place I passed seemed yet to speak
   O' some dear former day;
Those days that followed me afar,
   Those happy days o' mine,
Whilk made me think the present joys
   A' naething to langsyne!

The ivied tower now met my eye,
   Where minstrels used to blaw;
Nae friend stepped forth wi' open hand,
   Nae weel-kenned face I saw;
Till Donald tottered to the door,
   Wham I left in his prime,
And grat to see the lad return
   He bore about langsyne.

I ran to ilka dear friend's room,
   As if to find them there,
I knew where ilk ane used to sit,
   And hang o'er mony a chair;
Till soft remembrance threw a veil
   Across these een o' mine,
I closed the door, and sobbed aloud,
   To think on auld langsyne.

Some pensy chiels, a new-sprung race
   Wad next their welcome pay,
Wha shuddered at my Gothic wa's,
   And wished my groves away.
"Cut, cut," they cried, "those aged elms;
   Lay low yon mournful' pine."
Na! na! our fathers' names grow there,
   Memorials o' langsyne.

To wean me frae these waefu' thoughts,
   They took me to the town;
But sair on ilka weel-kenned face
   I missed the youthfu' bloom.

At balls they pointed to a nymph
   Wham a' declared divine;
But sure her mother's blushing cheeks
   Were fairer far langsyne!

In vain I sought in music's sound
   To find that magic art,
Which oft in Scotland's ancient lays
   Has thrilled through a' my heart.
The song had mony an artfu' turn;
   My ear confess'd 'twas fine;
But miss'd the simple melody
   I listen'd to langsyne.

Ye sons to comrades o' my youth,
   Forgie an auld man's spleen,
Wha 'midst your gayest scenes still mourns
   The days he ance has seen.
When time has passed and seasons fled,
   Your hearts will feel like mine;
And aye the sang will maist delight
   That minds ye o' langsyne!

JOHN O'KEEFFE (1747-1833)

AN AIR

from "The Farmer"

Gad-a mercy! devil's in me,
  All the damsels wish to win me;
Like a maypole round me cluster,
Hanging garlands fuss and fluster.

Jilting, capering, grinning, smirking,
Pouting, bobbing, winking, jerking,
Cocking bills up, chins up perking.
      Kates and Betties,
      Polls and Letties,
All were doating, gentle creatures,
    On these features;
      Pretty damsels,
      Ugly damsels,
      Black hair'd damsels,
      Red hair'd damsels,
      Six feet damsels,
      Three feet damsels,
      Pale-faced damsels,
      Plump-faced damsels,
      Small-leg'd damsels,
      Thick-leg'd damsels,
      Dainty damsels,
      Dowdy damsels,
Pretty, ugly, black-hair'd, red-hair'd,
Six feet, three feet, pale-faced, plump-faced,
Small-leg'd, thick-leg'd, dainty, dowdy,
  All run after me, sir, me;
  For when pretty fellows we,
  Pretty Maids are frank and free.

Gad-a-mercy! devil's in me,
  All the ladies wish to win me:
For their stays, taking measure
Of the ladies, oh the pleasure!

Oh, such tempting looks they gi'me,
Wishing of my heart to nim me!
Pat, and cry, you devil Jemmy!
    Pretty ladies,

297

Ugly ladies,
Black-hair'd ladies,
Red-hair'd ladies,
Six feet ladies,
Three feet ladies,
Pale-faced ladies,
Plump-faced ladies,
Small-legg'd ladies,
Thick-legg'd ladies,
Dainty ladies,
Dowdy ladies,
Pretty, ugly, black-hair'd, red-hair'd,
Six feet, three feet, pale-faced, plump-faced,
Small-legg'd, thick-legg'd, dainty, dowdy,
All run after me, sir, me:
For when pretty fellows we,
Ladies all are frank and free.

AN AIR

from "The Highland Reel"

Oh, had I Allan Ramsay's art
To sing my passion tender!
In every verse she'd read my heart,
Such soothing strains I'd send her:
Nor his, nor gentle Rizio's aid
To shew is all a folly,
How much I love the charming maid,
Sweet Jane of Grisipoly.

She makes me know what all desire
With such bewitching glances;
Her modest air then checks my fire,
And stops my bold advances:
Meek as the lamb on yonder lawn,
Yet by her conquered wholly;
For sometimes sprightly as the fawn,
Sweet Jane of Grisipoly.

My senses she's bewilder'd quite,
I seem an amorous ninny;
A letter to a friend I write,
For Sandy I sign Jenny:
Last Sunday, when from church I came,
With looks demure and holy,

I cried, when asked the text to name,
'Twas Jane of Grisipoly.

My Jenny is no fortune great,
    And I am poor and lowly;
A straw for power and grand estate,
    Her person I love solely:
From every sordid, selfish view,
    So free my heart is wholly;
And she is kind as I am true,
    Sweet Jane of Grisipoly.

A SONG

from "The Highland Reel"

Boys, when I play, cry, oh crimini,
Shelty's chaunter, squeakerimini;
I love tunes, I'm so emphatical,
Fingers shaking, quiveratical,
        With agility,
        Grace, gentility,
        Girls shake heel and toe;
        Pipes I tickle so,
           My jiggs fill a pate,
        Tittilate
        Pretty mate,
My hops love mirth, young blood circulate.

Oh my chaunters sound so prettily,
Sweeter far than pipes from Italy;
Cross the Tweed I'll bring my tweedle dum,
Striking foreign flute and fiddle dumb!
        Modern Rizzi's so,
        Pleases ma'ams, misses though,
        Peers can marry strum,
        Act plays, very rum,
           I'll puff at Square Hanover,
        Can over,
        Man over,
All the puny pipes from Italy.

I'm in talk a pedant musical,
In fine terms I lug intrusical,
Slap bravuras, alt, the rage about,
Haydn, Mara, Opera, stage about;

Oratorios,
Cramers, Florios:
Things at Jubilee,
Neither he nor she
Dye at syren's note,
Tiny throat,
Petticoat,
This is amateur high musical.

ANNA SEWARD (1747-1809)

DECEMBER MORNING

I love to rise ere gleams the tardy light,
Winter's pale dawn; and as warm fires illume,
And cheerful tapers shine around the room,
Through misty windows bend my musing sight,
Where, round the dusky lawn, the mansions white,
With shutters closed, peer faintly through the gloom
That slow recedes; while yon grey spires assume,
Rising from their dark pile, an added height
By indistinctness given. ——Then to decree
The grateful thoughts to God, ere they unfold
To friendship or the Muse, or seek with glee
Wisdom's rich page. O hours more worth than gold,
By whose blest use we lengthen life, and, free
From drear decays of age, outlive the old!

JOHN LOGAN (1748-1788)

ODE TO THE CUCKOO

Hail, beauteous stranger of the grove!
   Thou messenger of Spring!
Now Heaven repairs thy rural seat,
   And woods thy welcome sing.

What time the daisy decks the green,
   Thy certain voice we hear;
Hast thou a star to guide thy path,
   Or mark the rolling year?

Delightful visitant! with thee
   I hail the time of flowers,
And hear the sound of music sweet
   From birds among the bowers.

The school-boy, wandering thro' the wood
   To pull the primrose gay,
Starts, the new voice of Spring to hear,
   And imitates thy lay.

What time the pea puts on the bloom
   Thou fliest thy vocal vale,
An annual guest in other lands,
   Another Spring to hail.

Sweet bird! thy bower is ever green,
   Thy sky is ever clear;
Thou hast no sorrow in thy song,
   No winter in thy year!

O could I fly, I'd fly with thee!
   We'd make, with joyful wing,
Our annual visit o'er the globe,
   Companions of the Spring.

THE BRAES OF YARROW

"Thy braes were bonny, Yarrow stream!
   When first on them I met my lover;
Thy braes how dreary, Yarrow stream!

302

When now thy waves his body cover!
For ever now, O Yarrow stream!
Thou art to me a stream of sorrow;
For never on thy banks shall I
Behold my love, the flower of Yarrow.

"He promised me a milk-white steed,
To bear me to his father's bowers;
He promised me a little page,
To 'squire me to his father's towers;
He promised me a wedding-ring, ——
The wedding-day was fix'd to-morrow;——
Now he is wedded to his grave,
Alas, his watery grave, in Yarrow!

"Sweet were his words when last we met;
My passion I as freely told him!
Clasp'd in his arms, I little thought
That I should never more behold him!
Scarce was he gone, I saw his ghost;
It vanish'd with a shriek of sorrow;
Thrice did the water-wraith ascend,
And gave a doleful groan thro' Yarrow.

"His mother from the window look'd,
With all the longing of a mother;
His little sister weeping walk'd
The green-wood path to meet her brother:
They sought him east, they sought him west,
They sought him all the forest thorough;
They only saw the cloud of night,
They only heard the roar of Yarrow!

"No longer from thy window look,
Thou hast no son, thou tender mother!
No longer walk, thou lovely maid!
Alas, thou hast no more a brother!
No longer seek him east or west,
And search no more the forest thorough;
For, wandering in the night so dark,
He fell a lifeless corse in Yarrow.

"The tear shall never leave my cheek,
No other youth shall be my marrow;
I'll seek thy body in the stream,
And then with thee I'll sleep in Yarrow."
The tear did never leave her cheek,
No other youth became her marrow;

She found his body in the stream,
And now with him she sleeps in Yarrow.

CHARLOTTE SMITH (1749-1806)

SONNET WRITTEN AT THE CLOSE OF SPRING

The garlands fade that Spring so lately wove,
    Each simple flower, which she had nurs'd in dew,
Anemonies that spangled every grove,
    The primrose wan, and hare-bell, mildly blue.
No more shall violets linger in the dell,
    Or purple orchis variegate the plain,
Till spring again shall call forth every bell,
    And dress with humid hands, her wreaths again.
Ah! poor humanity! so frail, so fair,
    Are the fond visions of thy early day,
Till tyrant passion, and corrosive care,
    Bid all thy fairy colours fade away!
Another May new buds and flowers shall bring;
Ah! why has happiness——no second spring?

SONNET TO A NIGHTINGALE

Poor melancholy bird, that all night long
    Tell'st to the moon thy tale of tender woe;
    From what sad cause can such sweet sorrow flow,
And whence this mournful melody of song?

Thy poet's musing fancy would translate
    What mean the sounds that swell thy little breast,
    When still at dewy eve thou leav'st thy nest,
Thus to the listening night to sing thy fate.

Pale Sorrow's victims wert thou once among,
    Tho' now releas'd in woodlands wild to rove,
    Or hast thou felt from friends some cruel wrong,
Or diedst thou martyr of disastrous love?
Ah! songstress sad! that such my lot might be,
To sigh and sing at liberty——like thee!

SONNET TO THE SOUTH DOWNS

Ah, hills belov'd! where once, an happy child,
    Your beechen shades, "your turf, your flowers among,"

I wove your blue-bells into garlands wild,
    And woke your echoes with my artless song.
Ah, hills belov'd! your turf, your flowers remain;
    But can they peace to this sad breast restore,
For one poor moment soothe the sense of pain,
    And teach a breaking heart to throb no more?
And you, Aruna! in the vale below,
    As to the sea your limpid waves you bear,
Can you one kind Lethean cup bestow,
    To drink a long oblivion to my care?
Ah, no!——when all, e'en hope's last ray is gone,
There's no oblivion——but in death alone!

SIR WILLIAM YOUNG (1749-1815)

THE BELLMAN'S VERSES

To Lady Melbourne, Brocket Hall, Christmas, 1800

Wide waves the oak its torn and shattered head,
Torn by the gale; and far the fragments spread;
The hail-storm beats upon the swollen lake,
And its surrounding rocks seem all to shake!

Beneath that nodding mountain's chalky scoop,
Colin and Phillis with their gipsey troop
In the lone caverns, on a heap of reeds
Listen, as blast to blast in storm succeeds;
And as each chilling gust the valley sweeps,
Phillis to Colin only closer creeps.
The batt'ling hurricane's impetuous roar,
Seems but to whisper, "love your Phillis more."

Thus, in the dreary chill of winter's gloom,
When, (save in Melbourne's cheek) no roses bloom;
The frost, which binds the stream and blasts the tree,
Serves but to melt the mind to social glee;
Warm grows the heart, as colder grows the day,
And Christmas boasts a smile, as sweet as May.

Spring has its roses and its lovely green;
Autumn its crops, which rural damsels glean;
And Christmas, too, its season hath of wealth,
Reaped with the work of joy, and glow of health.
When the hall fire and the lustres' blaze,
Rival the light and heat of summer's days;
And 'midst the dance and song, and jovial din;
"The sweet affections," get their harvest in.

Life, too, its seasons hath; its spring and fall,
Its buds, its glowing bloom, its changes all.
And oh! whene'er its cold and wintry snows
Shower on thy head, and furrow o'er thy brows,
May peace and virtue act in ages spite,
And give a cheerful heat, and cheerful light;
And leave——when chills and frosts of age set in, ——
A mind, to warm the mansion well within.

307

JOHN LOWE (1750-1798)

MARY'S DREAM

The moon had climbed the highest hill
  Which rises o'er the source of Dee,
And from the eastern summit shed
  Her silver light on tower and tree;
When Mary laid her down to sleep,
  Her thoughts on Sandy far at sea,
When, soft and low, a voice was heard,
  Saying: "Mary, weep no more for me!"

She from her pillow gently raised
  Her head, to ask who there might be,
And saw young Sandy shivering stand,
  With visage pale, and hollow ee.
"O Mary dear, cold is my clay;
  It lies beneath a stormy sea.
Far, far from thee I sleep in death;
  So, Mary, weep no more for me!

"Three stormy nights and stormy days
  We tossed upon the raging main;
And long we strove our bark to save,
  But all our striving was in vain.
Even then, when horror chilled my blood,
  My heart was fill'd with love for thee:
The storm is past, and I at rest;
  So, Mary, weep no more for me!

"O maiden dear, thyself prepare;
  We soon shall meet upon that shore,
Where love is free from doubt and care,
  And thou and I shall part no more!"
Loud crowed the cock, the shadow fled,
  No more of Sandy could she see;
But soft the passing spirit said:
  "Sweet Mary, weep no more for me!"

ROBERT FERGUSSON (1750-1774)

CAULER WATER

When father Adie first pat spade in
The bony yard o' ancient Eden,
His amry had nae liquor laid in
    To fire his mou;
Nor did he thole his wife's upbraidin',
    For bein' fou.

A cauler burn o' siller sheen,
Ran cannily out-owre the green;
And when our gutcher's drouth had been
    To bide right sair,
He loutit down, and drank bedeen
    A dainty skair.

His bairns had a', before the flood,
A langer tack o' flesh and blood,
And on mair pithy shanks they stood
    Than Noah's line,
Wha still hae been a feckless brood,
    Wi' drinkin' wine.

The fuddlin' bardies, now-a-days,
Rin maukin-mad in Bacchus' praise;
And limp and stoiter through their lays
    Anacreontic,
While each his sea of wine displays
    As big's the Pontic.

My Muse will no gang far frae hame,
Or scour a' airths to hound for fame;
In troth, the jillet ye might blame
    For thinkin' on't,
When eithly she can find the theme
    O' aquafont.

This is the name that doctors use,
Their patients' noddles to confuse;
Wi' simples clad in terms abstruse,
    They labour still
In kittle words to gar you roose
    Their want o' skill.

But we'll hae nae sic clitter-clatter;
And, briefly to expound the matter,
It shall be ca'd guid cauler water;
          Than whilk, I trow,
Few drugs in doctors' shops are better
          For me or you.

Though joints be stiff as ony rung,
Your pith wi' pain be sairly dung,
Be you in cauler water flung
          Out-owre the lugs,
'Twill mak you souple, swack, and young,
          Withouten drugs.

Though colic or the heart-scad tease us;
Or ony inward dwaam should seize us;
It masters a' sic fell diseases
          That would ye spulzie,
And brings them to a canny crisis
          Wi' little tulzie.

Were't no for it, the bonny lasses
Wad glower nae mair in keekin'-glasses;
And soon tyne dint o' a' the graces
          That aft conveen
In gleefu' looks, and bonny faces,
          To catch our een.

The fairest, then, might die a maid,
And Cupid quit his shootin' trade;
For wha, through clarty masquerade,
          Could then discover
Whether the features under shade
          Were worth a lover?

As simmer rains brings simmer flowers,
And leaves to cleed the birken bowers,
Sae beauty gets by cauler showers
          Sae rich a bloom,
As for estate, or heavy dowers,
          Aft stands in room.

What maks Auld Reekie's dames sae fair?
It canna be the halesome air;
But cauler burn, beyond compare,
          The best o' ony,
That gars them a' sic graces skair,
          And blink sae bonny.

On May-day, in a fairy ring,
We've seen them round St. Anthon's spring,
Frae grass the cauler dew-draps wring
    To weet their een,
And water, clear as crystal spring,
    To synd them clean.

O may they still pursue the way
To look sae feat, sae clean, sae gae!
Then shall their beauties glance like May;
    And, like her, be
The goddess of the vocal spray,
    The Muse and me.

BRAID CLAITH

Ye wha are fain to hae your name
Wrote i' the bonny book o' Fame,
Let Merit nae pretension claim
    To laurel'd wreath,
But hap ye weel, baith back and wame,
    In gude Braid Claith.

He that some ells o' this may fa',
An' slae-black hat on pow like snaw,
Bids bauld to bear the gree awa',
    Wi' a' this graith,
Whan beinly clad wi' shell fu' braw
    O' gude Braid Claith.

Waesuck for him wha has nae feck o't!
For he's a gowk they're sure to geck at,
A chiel that ne'er will be respekit,
    While he draws breath,
Till his four quarters are bedeckit
    Wi' gude Braid Claith.

On Sabbath-days the barber spark,
Whan he has done wi' scrapin wark,
Wi' siller broachie in his sark,
    Gangs trigly, faith!
Or to the Meadow, or the Park,
    In gude Braid Claith.

Weel might ye trow, to see them there,
That they to shave your haffits bare,

311

Or curl an' sleek a pickle hair,
      Would be right laith,
Whan pacing wi' a gawsy air
      In gude Braid Claith.

If ony mettl'd stirrah green
For favour frae a lady's een,
He maunna care for bein' seen
      Before he sheath
His body in a scabbard clean
      O' gude Braid Claith.

For, gin he come wi' coat thread-bare,
A feg for him she winna care,
But crook her bonny mou' fu' sair,
      And scald him baith:
Wooers shou'd ay their travel spare,
      Without Braid Claith.

Braid Claith lends fock an unco heese;
Makes mony kail-worms butterflies;
Gies mony a doctor his degrees
      For little skaith:
In short, you may be what you please
      Wi' gude Braid Claith.

For tho' ye had as wise a snout on
As Shakespeare or Sir Isaac Newton,
Your judgment fock would hae a doubt on,
      I'll tak my aith,
Till they cou'd see ye wi' a suit on
      O' gude Braid Claith.

ODE TO THE GOWDSPINK

Frae fields whare Spring her sweets has blawn
Wi' caller verdure o'er the lawn,
The gowdspink, comes in new attire,
The brawest 'mang the whistling choir,
That, ere the sun can clear his een,
Wi' glib notes sane the simmer's green.
   Sure Nature herried mony a tree,
For spraings and bonny spats to thee;
Nae mair the rainbow can impart
Sic glowing ferlies o' her art,
Whase pencil wrought its freaks at will

On thee, the sey-piece o' her skill.
Nae mair through straths in simmer dight
We seek the rose to bless our sight,
Or bid the bonny wa'-flowers blaw
Whare yonder ruins crumblin' fa';
Thy shining garments far outstrip
The cherries upo' Hebe's lip,
And fool the tints that Nature chose
To busk and paint the crimson rose.
    'Mang men, wae's-heart! we aften find
The brawest drest want peace of mind,
While he that gangs wi' ragged coat,
Is weel contentit wi' his lot.
Whan wand wi' glewy birdlime's set,
To steal far aff your dauntit mate,
Blyth wad ye change your cleething gay
In lieu of lav'rock's sober grey.
In vain thro' woods you sair may ban
Th' envious treachery of man,
That, wi' your gowden glister ta'en,
Still haunts you on the simmer's plain,
And traps you 'mang the sudden fa's
O' winter's dreary dreepin' snaws.
Now steekit frae the gowany field,
Frae ilka fav'rite houff and bield,
But mergh, alas! to disengage
Your bonny bouck frae fettering cage,
Your free-born bosom beats in vain
For darling liberty again.
In window hung, how aft we see
Thee keek around at warblers free,
That carol saft, and sweetly sing
Wi' a' the blythness of the spring!
Like Tantalus they hing you here
To spy the glories o' the year;
And tho' you're at the burnie's brink,
They douna suffer you to drink.
    Ah, Liberty! thou bonny dame,
How wildly wanton is thy stream,
Round whilk the birdies a' rejoice,
An' hail you wi' a gratefu' voice.
The gowdspink chatters joyous here,
And courts wi' gleesome sangs his peer;
The mavis frae the new-bloomed thorn
Begins his lauds at earest morn;
And herd-lowns, louping o'er the grass,
Need far less fleetching till their lass
Than paughty damsels bred at courts,

313

Wha thraw their mou's and take the dorts:
But, reft of thee, fient flee we care
For a' that life ahint can spare.
The gowdspink, that sae lang has kenned
Thy happy sweets (his wonted friend),
Her sad confinement ill can brook
In some dark chamber's dowy nook;
Tho' Mary's hand his nebb supplies,
Unkend to hunger's painfu' cries,
Ev'n beauty canna chear the heart
Frae life, frae liberty apart,
For now we tyne its wonted lay,
Sae lightsome sweet, sae blythely gay.
   Thus Fortune aft a curse can gie,
To wyle us far frae liberty:
Then tent her syren smiles wha list,
I'll ne'er envy your girnal's grist;
For whan fair Freedom smiles nae mair,
Care I for life? Shame fa' the hair:
A field o'ergrown wi' rankest stubble,
The essence of a paltry bubble.

THOMAS CHATTERTON (1752-1770)

SENTIMENT

1769

Since we can die but once, what matters it,
If rope or garter, poison, pistol, sword,
Slow-wasting sickness, or the sudden burst
Of valve arterial in the noble parts,
Curtail the miseries of human life?
Tho' varied is the cause, the effect's the same;
All to one common dissolution tends.

ELEGY

Written at Bristol, November 17th, 1769

Joyless I seek the solitary shade,
  Where dusky contemplation veils the scene,
The dark retreat (of leafless branches made)
  Where sick'ning sorrow wets the yellow'd green.

The darksome ruins of some sacred cell,
  Where erst the sons of superstition trod,
Tott'ring upon the mossy meadow, tell
  We better know, but less adore our God.

Now, as I mournful tread the gloomy cave,
  Thro' the wide window (once with mysteries dight)
The distant forest, and the dark'ned wave
  Of the swoln Avon ravishes my sight.

But see the thick'ning veil of evening's drawn,
  The azure changes to a sable blue;
The rapt'ring prospects fly the less'ning lawn,
  And nature seems to mourn the dying view.

Self-sprighted fear creeps silent thro' the gloom,
  Starts at the rustling leaf, and rolls his eyes;
Aghast with horrour, when he views the tomb,
  With every torment of a hell he flies.

The bubbling brooks in plaintive murmers roll,
  The bird of omen, with incessant scream,
To melancholy thoughts awakes the soul,
  And lulls the mind to contemplation's dream.

A dreary stillness broods o'er all the vale,
  The clouded Moon emits a feeble glare;
Joyless I seek the darkling hill and dale;
  Where'er I wander sorrow still is there.

MYNSTRELLES SONGE

O! Synge untoe mie roundelaie,
O! droppe the brynie teare wythe mee,
Daunce ne moe atte hallie daie,
Lycke a reynynge ryver bee;
        Mie love ys dedde,
        Gon to hys death-bedde,
        Al under the wyllowe tree.

Blacke hys cryne as the wyntere nyghte,
Whyte hys rode as the sommer snowe,
Rodde hys face as the mornynge lyghte,
Cale he lyes ynne the grave belowe;
        Mie love ys dedde,
        Gon to hys deathe-bedde,
        Al under the wyllowe tree.

Swote hys tyngue as the throstles note,
Quycke ynn daunce as thoughte canne bee,
Defte hys taboure, codgelle stote,
O! hee lyes bie the wyllowe tree:
        Mie love ys dedde,
        Gonne to hys deathe-bedde,
        Alle underre the wyllowe tree.

Harke! the ravenne flappes hys wynge,
In the briered delle belowe;
Harke! the dethe-owle loude dothe synge,
To the nyghte-mares as heie goe;
        Mie love ys dedde,
        Gone to hys deathe-bedde,
        Al under the wyllowe tree.

See! the whyte moone sheenes onne hie;

Whyterre ys mie true loves shroude;
Whyterre yanne the mornynge skie,
Whyterre yanne the evenynge cloude;
  Mie love ys dedde,
  Gon to hys deathe-bedde,
  Al under the wyllowe tree.

Heere, uponne mie true loves grave,
Schalle the baren fleurs be layde,
Nee one hallie Seyncte to save
Al the celness of a mayde.
  Mie love ys dedde,
  Gonne to hys death-bedde,
  Alle under the wyllowe tree.

Wythe mie hondes I'lle dente the brieres
Rounde his hallie corse to gre,
Ouphante fairie, lyghte youre fyres,
Heere mie boddie stylle schalle bee.
  Mie love ys dedde,
  Gon to hys death-bedde,
  Al under the wyllowe tree.

Comme, wythe acorne-coppe & thorne,
Drayne mie hartys blodde awaie;
Lyfe and all yttes goode I scorne,
Daunce bie nete, or feaste by daie.
  Mie love ys dedde,
  Gon to hys death-bedde,
  Al under the wyllowe tree.

Waterre wytches, crownede wythe reytes,
Bere mee to yer leathalle tyde.
I die; I comme; mie true love waytes.
Thos the damselle spake, and dyed.

THE METHODIST

May, 1770

Says Tom to Jack, "'Tis very odd,
These representatives of God,
In colour, way of life and evil,
Should be so very like the Devil."

317

Jack, understand, was one of those,
Who mould religion in the nose,
A red hot Methodist; his face
Was full of puritanic grace,
His loose lank hair, his low gradation,
Declar'd a late regeneration;
Among the daughters long renown'd,
For standing upon holy ground;
Never in carnal battle beat,
Tho' sometimes forc'd to a retreat.
But C———t, hero as he is,
Knight of incomparable phiz,
When pliant Doxy seems to yield,
Courageously forsakes the field.
Jack, or to write more gravely, John,
Thro' hills of Wesley's works had gone;
Could sing one hundred hymns by rote;
Hymns which will sanctify the throte:
But some indeed compos'd so oddly,
You'd swear 'twas bawdy songs made godly.

THE VIRGIN'S CHOICE

Young Strephon is as fair a swain,
As e'er a shepherd of the plain
   In all the hundred round;
But Ralph has tempting shoulders, true,
And will as quickly buckle to
   As any to be found.

Young Colin has a comely face,
And cudgels with an active grace,
   In every thing complete;
But Hobbinol can dance divine,
Gods! how his manly beauties shine,
   When jigging with his feet.

Roger is very stout and strong,
And Thyrsis sings a heavenly song,
   Soft Giles is brisk and small.
Who shall I choose? who shall I shun?
Why must I be confin'd to one?
   Why can't I have them all?

318

FANNY OF THE HILL

1770

If gentle love's immortal fire
    Could animate the quill,
Soon should the rapture-speaking lyre
    Sing Fanny of the Hill.

My panting heart incessant moves,
    No interval 'tis still;
And all my ravish'd nature loves
    Sweet Fanny of the Hill.

Her dying soft expressive eye,
    Her elegance must kill,
Ye gods! how many thousands die
    For Fanny of the Hill.

A love-taught tongue, angelic air,
    A sentiment, a skill
In all the graces of the fair,
    Mark Fanny of the Hill.

Thou mighty power, eternal fate,
    My happiness to fill,
O! bless a wretched lover's fate,
    With Fanny of the Hill.

WILLIAM ROSCOE (1753-1831)

THE HAPPINESS OF A COUNTRY LIFE

Thy splendid halls, thy palaces forgot,
   Can paths o'erspread with thorns a charm supply;
Or, dost thou seek, from our severer lot,
   To give to wealth and pow'r a keener joy?

Thus I replied——"I know no happier life,
   No better riches than you shepherds boast:
Freed from the hated jars of civil strife,
   Alike to treach'ry and to envy lost.

"The weed ambition 'midst your furrow'd field
   Springs not, and av'rice little root can find:
Content with what the changing seasons yield,
   You rest in cheerful poverty resign'd.

"What the heart thinks the tongue may here disclose,
   Nor inward grief with outward smiles is drest;
Not like the world, where wisest he who knows
   To hide the secret closest in his breast."

ELIZABETH INCHBALD (1753-1821)

from "LOVERS' VOWS"

Oh Muse, ascend the forked mount,
    And lofty strains prepare,
About a Baron and a Count,
    Who went to hunt the hare.

The hare she ran with utmost speed,
    And sad and anxious looks,
Because the furious hounds indeed
    Were near to her, gadzooks.

At length the Count and Baron bold
    Their footsteps homeward bended;
For why, because, as you were told,
    The hunting it was ended.

Before them strait a youth appears,
    Who made a piteous pother,
And told a tale with many tears,
    About his dying mother.

The youth was in severe distress,
    And seem'd as he had spent all,
He look'd a soldier by his dress,
    For that was regimental.

The Baron's heart was full of ruth,
    And from his eye fell brine o!
And soon he gave the mournful youth
    A little ready rino.

He gave a shilling, as I live,
    Which sure, was mighty well;
But to some people if you give
    An inch——they'll take an ell.

The youth then drew his martial knife,
    And seiz'd the Baron's collar,
He swore he'd have the Baron's life,
    Or else another dollar.

Then did the Baron, in a fume,
    Soon raise a mighty din,

Whereon came butler, huntsman, groom,
    And eke the whipper-in.

Maugre this young man's warlike coat,
    They bore him off to prison;
And held so strongly by his throat,
    And almost stopp'd his whizzen.

Soon may a neckcloth, call'd a rope,
    Of robbing cure this elf;
If so, I'll write, without a trope,
    His dying speech myself.

And had the Baron chanc'd to die,
    Oh! grief to all the nation,
I must have made an elegy,
    And not this fine narration.

MORAL

Henceforth let those who all have spent,
    And would by begging live,
Take warning here, and be content
    With what folks chuse to give.

A SONG

from "The Wedding Day"

In the dead of the night, when with labour opprest,
All mortals enjoy the calm blessing of ease,
Cupid knock'd at my window, disturbing my rest,
Who's there? I demanded—begone, if you please.

He answered so meekly, so modest, and mild,
Dear ma'am, it is I, an unfortunate child;
'Tis a cold rainy night, I am wet to the skin;
I have lost my way, ma'am, so pray let me in.

No sooner from wet and from cold he got ease,
When, taking his bow, he said, ma'am, if you please—
If you please, ma'am, I would by experiment know,
If the rain has not damaged the string of my bow.

Then away skipped the urchin, as brisk as a bee,

And, laughing, I wish you much joy, ma'am, said he;
My bow is undamaged, for true went the dart,
But you will have trouble enough with your heart.

JOHN CODRINGTON BAMPFYLDE (1754-1796)

SONNET ON A WET SUMMER

All ye who far from town in rural hall,
Like me, were wont to dwell near pleasant field,
Enjoying all the sunny day did yield,
With me the change lament, in irksome thrall,
By rains incessant held; for now no call
From early swain invites my hand to wield
The scythe. In parlour dim I sit concealed,
And mark the lessening sand from hour-glass fall;
Or 'neath my window view the wistful train
Of dripping poultry, whom the vine's broad leaves
Shelter no more. Mute is the mournful plain;
Silent the swallow sits beneath the thatch,
And vacant hind hangs pensive o'er his hatch,
Counting the frequent drips from reeded eaves.

SONNET TO THE REDBREAST

When that the fields put on their gay attire,
Thou silent sitt'st near brake or river's brim,
Whilst the gay thrush sings loud from covert dim;
But when pale Winter lights the social fire,
And meads with slime are sprent, and ways with mire,
Thou charm'st us with thy soft and solemn hymn
From battlement, or barn, or haystack trim;
And now not seldom tunest, as if for hire,
Thy thrilling pipe to me, waiting to catch
The pittance due to thy well-warbled song:
Sweet bird! sing on; for oft near lonely hatch,
Like thee, myself have pleased the rustic throng,
And oft for entrance, 'neath the peaceful thatch,
Full many a tale have told, a ditty long.

PRINCE HOARE (1755-1834)

AN AIR

from "Lock and Key"

A woman is like to—but stay,
What a woman is like, who can say?
  There's no living with, or without one.
    Love stings like a fly,
    Now an ear, now an eye,
   Buz, buz, always buzzing about one.
    But when she's tender and kind,
    She is like to my mind,
  (And Fanny was so I remember.)
    She is like to—O dear!
    She's as good very near
As a ripe melting peach in September.
    If she laugh, and she chat,
    Play, and joke, and all that,
  And with smiles and good humour she meet me,
    She is like a rich dish
    Of ven'son or fish,
  That cries from the table, "Come eat me:"
    But she'll plague you, and vex you,
    Distract and perplex you;
    False-hearted and ranging,
    Unsettled and changing, —
  What then do you think she is like?
    Like a sand! Like a rock!
    Like a wheel! Like a clock!
  Like a clock that is always at strike,
Her head's like the island, folks tell one,
Which nothing but monkies can dwell on;
Her heart's like a lemon, so nice,
She carves for each lover a slice;
    In short, she's to me
    Like the wind, like the sea,
Whose raging will hearken to no man,
    Like a mill,
    Like a pill,
    Like a flail,
    Like a whale,
    Like an ass,
    Like a glass,

Whose image is constant to no man:
        Like a flower,
        Like a shower,
        Like a fly,
        Like a pye,
        Like a witch,
        Like the itch,
        Like a thief,
        Like—in brief,
She's like nothing on earth but a woman.

ANN YEARSLEY (1756-1806)

A SONG

What ails my heart when thou art nigh?
Why heaves the tender rising sigh?
      Ah, Delia, is it love?
My breath in shorten'd pauses fly;
I tremble, languish, burn, and die;
      Dost thou those tremors prove?

Does thy fond bosom beat for me?
Dost thou my form in absence see,
      Still wishing to be near?
Does melting languor fill thy breast?
That something, which was ne'er express'd,
      Ah! tell me——if you dare.

But tho' my soul, soft, fond, and kind,
Could in thy arms a refuge find,
      Secur'd from ev'ry woe;
Yet, strict to Honour's louder strains,
A last adieu alone remains,
      'Tis all the Fates bestow.

Then blame me not, if doom'd to prove
The endless pangs of hopeless love,
      And live by thee unblest:
My joyless hours fly fast away;
Let them fly on, I chide their stay,
      For sure 'tis Heav'n to rest.

JOHN PHILIP KEMBLE (1757-1823)

AN AIR

from "Lodoiska"

Sweet bird, that cheer'st the heavy hours
　　Of winter's dreary reign,
O, still exert thy tuneful pow'rs,
　　And pour the vocal strain!

Go not to seek a scanty fare
　　From nature's frozen hand,
Whilst I, with gratitude, prepare
　　The food thy wants demand.

Domestic bird, with me remain,
　　Until next verdant spring
Again shall bring the woodland train,
　　Their grateful tribute bring.

Sweet Robin, then thou may'st explore
　　And join the feather'd throng,
And every vocal bush shall pour
　　The energy of song.

SAMUEL BIRCH (1757-1841)

A SONG

from "The Adopted Child"

At evening, when my work is done,
And the breeze at setting sun
Scarcely breathes upon the tide,
Then alone I love to glide—
Unheard, unseen, my silent oar
Steals along the shaded shore:
    All is dark, and all is mute,
    Save the moon, and lover's lute;
    Tang, Ting, Tang, it seems to say,
    Lovers dread return of day.

Toward the abbey wall I steer,
There the choral hymn I hear:
While the organ's lengthened note
Seems in distant woods to float:
Returning then my silent oar,
Steals along the shaded shore:
    All is dark, and all is mute,
    Save the moon, and lover's lute;
    Tang, Ting, Tang, it seems to say,
    Lovers dread return of day.

THOMAS KNIGHT (?-1820)

A SONG

from "The Turnpike Gate"

Pray, young man, your suit give over,
   Heaven design'd you not for me;
Cease to be a whining lover,
   Sour and sweet can ne'er agree:
Clownish in each limb and feature,
   You've no skill to dance or sing;
At best, you're but an awkward creature,
   I, you know, am quite the thing.

As I soon may roll in pleasure,
   Bumpkins I must bid adieu;
Can you think that such a treasure
   E'er was destined, man, for you?
No——mayhap, when I am carry'd,
   'Mongst the great to dance and sing,
To some great lord I may be marry'd:
   All allow—I'm quite the thing.

WILLIAM LISLE BOWLES (1762-1850)

BAMBOROUGH CASTLE

Ye holy towers that shade the wave-worn steep,
Long may ye rear your aged brows sublime,
Though hurrying silent by, relentless time
Assail you, and the wintry whirlwind sweep.
For, far from blazing grandeur's crowded halls,
Here Charity has fix'd her chosen seat;
Oft list'ning tearful when the wild winds beat
With hollow bodings round your ancient walls;
And Pity, at the dark and stormy hour
Of midnight, when the moon is hid on high,
Keeps her lone watch upon the topmost tower,
And turns her ear to each expiring cry,
Blest if her aid some fainting wretch might save,
And snatch him cold and speechless from the grave.

A WINTER EVENING AT HOME

Fair Moon! that at the chilly day's decline
Of sharp December, through my cottage pane
Dost lovely look, smiling, though in thy wane;
In thought, to scenes serene and still as thine,
Wanders my heart, whilst I by turns survey
Thee slowly wheeling on thy evening way;
And this my fire, whose dim, unequal light,
Just glimmering, bids each shadowy image fall
Sombrous and strange upon the darkening wall,
Ere the clear tapers chase the deepening night!
Yet thy still orb, seen through the freezing haze,
Shines calm and clear without; and whilst I gaze,
I think around me in this twilight gloom,
I but remark mortality's sad doom;
Whilst hope and joy, cloudless and soft, appear
In the sweet beam that lights thy distant sphere.

AT DOVER CLIFFS

July 20th, 1787

On these white cliffs, that calm above the flood
Uplift their shadowing heads, and, at their feet,
Scarce hear the surge that has for ages beat,
Sure many a lonely wanderer has stood;
And, whilst the lifted murmur met his ear,
And o'er the distant billows the still Eve
Sail'd slow, has thought of all his heart must leave
To-morrow, —of the friends he lov'd most dear, —
Of social scenes, from which he wept to part:—
But if, like me, he knew how fruitless all
The thoughts that would full fain the past recall,
Soon would he quell the risings of his heart,
And brave the wild winds and unhearing tide,
The world his country, and his GOD his guide.

GEORGE COLMAN, THE YOUNGER (1762-1836)

A SONG

from "Inkle and Yarico"

A clerk I was in London gay,
    Jemmy linkum feedle,
And went in boots to see the play,
    Merry fiddlem tweedle.
I march'd the lobby, twirled my stick,
    Diddle, daddle, deedle;
The girls all cry'd, "He's quite the kick."
    Oh, Jemmy linkum feedle.

Hey! for America I sail,
    Yankee doodle, deedle;
The sailor-boys cry'd, "Smoke his tail!"
    Jemmy linkum feedle.
On English belles I turned by back,
    Diddle, daddle, deedle;
And got a foreign fair quite black,
    O twaddle, twaddle, tweedle!

Your London girls, with roguish trip,
    Wheedle, wheedle, wheedle,
May boast their pouting under lip,
    Fiddle, faddle, feedle.
My Wows would beat a hundred such,
    Diddle, daddle, deedle,
Whose upper lip pouts twice as much,
    O, pretty double wheedle!

Rings I'll buy to deck her toes;
    Jemmy linkum feedle;
A feather fine shall grace her nose,
    Waving siddle seedle.
With jealousy I ne'er shall burst;
    Who'd steal my bone of bone-a?
A white Othello, I can trust
    A dingy Desdemona.

A SONG

from "The Surrender of Calais"

When I was at home, I was merry and frisky;
My dad kept a pig, and my mother sold whisky:
My uncle was rich, but would never be asy,
Till I was enlisted by Corporal Casey.
Oh! rub a dub, row de dow, Corporal Casey!
My dear little Sheelah I thought would run crazy,
When I trudged away with tough Corporal Casey.

I march'd from Kilkenny, and as I was thinking
On Sheelah, my heart in my bosom was sinking;
But soon I was forced to look fresh as a daisy,
For fear of a drubbing from Corporal Casey.
Och! rub a dub, row de dow, Corporal Casey!
The devil go with him, I ne'er could be lazy,
He stuck in my skirts so, ould Corporal Casey.

We went into battle; I took the blows fairly,
That fell on my pate, but they bother'd me rarely:
And who should the first be that dropp'd? why, an plase ye,
It was my good friend, honest Corporal Casey.
Och! rub a dub, row de dow, Corporal Casey!
Thinks I, you are quiet, and I shall be asy;
So eight years I fought, without Corporal Casey.

JAMES HURDIS (1763-1801)

THE DEATH OF THE BLACKBIRD

The sable bird melodious from the bough
No longer springs alert and clamorous,
Short flight and sudden with transparent wing
Along the ditch performing, fit by fit.
Shuddering he sits, in horrent coat out-swollen,
Despair has made him silent, and he falls
From his loved hawthorn, of its berry spoiled,
A wasted skeleton, shot through and through
By the near-aiming sportsman. Lovely bird,
So end thy sorrows and so ends thy song.
Never again in the still summer's eve,
Or early dawn of purple-vested morn
Shalt thou be heard, or solitary song
Whistle contented from the watery bough,
What time the sun flings o'er the dewy earth
An unexpected beam, fringing with flame
The cloud immense, whose shower-shedding folds
Have all day dwelt upon a deluged world.
No, thy sweet pipe is mute, it sings no more.

JOSEPH GEORGE HOLMAN (1764-1817)

A SONG

from "Abroad and at Home"

When to my pretty Poll I went,
   And I to travel sought her,
"Ah! stay at home, dear Jack," says she,
   "I cannot cross the water."
What could I do? Away I flew,
   A curricle I bought her;
Six smoking bays, all Hyde Park's gaze,
   From Tattersall's I brought her.
"Dear Jack," says she, "how kind you be!
   (She'd coax like Eve's own daughter,)
With you I will both live and die,
   Do all but cross the water."
Then splashing, dashing, through the town,
   She drove, the stare of all;
The echo of her rattling wheels
   Was, "There goes pretty Poll!
Oh! pretty, pretty Poll!"
From ev'ry tongue the echo rung
   "See, there goes pretty Poll!"

     What a lad then was I!
     All to dress at me try,
And my praise to withhold none so currish,
     With a girl so divine!
     Such dinners! such wine!
What a d——d clever dog was Jack Flourish!
     But an end to my cash,
     And my fame goes to smash,
No friends my good qualities nourish;
     For they, once so kind,
     Now agree in one mind,
What a d——d stupid flat was Jack Flourish!

Thus cut by my friends, by bailiffs seiz'd,
   And this vile limbo near,
Yet with one hope I still was pleas'd,
   That Poll my cage would cheer.
To Poll I told where I must go,
   And not to leave me sought her;

She, laughing, cried, "Dear Jack, you know
  I cannot cross the water."

ROBERT BLOOMFIELD (1766-1823)

ROSY HANNAH

A spring, o'erhung with many a flower,
   The gray sand dancing in its bed,
Embank'd beneath a hawthorn bower,
   Sent forth its waters near my head.
A rosy lass approached my view;
   I caught her blue eyes' modest beam;
The stranger nodded "How-d'ye-do?"
   And leaped across the infant stream.

The water heedless passed away;
   With me her glowing image stayed;
I strove, from that auspicious day,
   To meet and bless the lovely maid.
I met her where beneath our feet
   Through downy moss the wild thyme grew;
Nor moss elastic, flowers though sweet,
   Matched Hannah's cheek of rosy hue.

I met her where the dark woods wave,
   And shaded verdure skirts the plain;
And when the pale moon rising gave
   New glories to her rising train.
From her sweet cot upon the moor,
   Our plighted vows to heaven are flown;
Truth made me welcome at her door,
   And rosy Hannah is my own.

JOHN TOBIN (1770-1804)

A SONG

from "The Honey Moon"

At the front of a cottage, with woodbine grown o'er,
    Fair Lucy sat turning her wheel,
Unconscious that William was just at the door,
    And heard her her passion reveal.
        The bells rung,
        And she sung,
        Ding, dong, dell,
        It were well
If they rung for dear William and me.

But when she look'd up, and her lover espy'd,
    Ah! what was the maiden's surprise!
She blush'd as he woo'd her and called her his bride,
    And answered him only with sighs.
        The bells rung,
        And she sung,
        Ding, dong, dell,
        It is well!
They shall ring for dear William and me!

339

ROBERT TANNAHILL (1774-1810)

THE BRAES OF BALQUHITHER

Let us go, lassie, go,
  To the braes o' Balquhither,
Where the blae-berries grow
  'Mang the bonnie Highland heather;
Where the deer and the roe,
  Lightly bounding together,
Sport the lang summer day
  On the braes o' Balquhither.

I will twine thee a bower
  By the clear siller fountain,
And I'll cover it o'er
  Wi' the flowers of the mountain;
I will range through the wilds,
  And the deep glens sae drearie,
And return wi' the spoils
  To the bower o' my dearie.

When the rude wintry win'
  Idly raves round our dwelling,
And the roar of the linn
  On the night breeze is swelling,
So merrily we'll sing,
  As the storm rattles o'er us,
Till the dear shieling ring
  Wi' the light lilting chorus.

Now the summer's in prime
  Wi' the flowers richly blooming,
And the wild mountain thyme
  A' the moorlands perfuming;
To our dear native scenes
  Let us journey together,
Where glad innocence reigns
  'Mang the braes o' Balquhither.

THE MIDGES DANCE ABOON THE BURN

The midges dance aboon the burn;
  The dews begin to fa';

The paitricks down the rushy holm
  Set up their e'ening ca'.
Now loud and clear the blackbird's sang
  Rings through the briery shaw,
While flitting gay the swallows play
  Around the castle wa'.

Beneath the golden gloamin' sky
  The mavis mends her lay;
The redbreast pours his sweetest strains,
  To charm the ling'ring day;
While weary yaldrins seem to wail
  Their little nestlings torn,
The merry wren, frae den to den,
  Gaes jinking through the thorn.

The roses fauld their silken leaves,
  The foxglove shuts its bell;
The honeysuckle and the birk
  Spread fragrance through the dell.
Let others crowd the giddy court
  Of mirth and revelry,
The simple joys that Nature yields
  Are dearer far to me.

RICHARD GALL (1776-1801)

FAREWELL TO AYRSHIRE

Scenes of woe and scenes of pleasure,
    Scenes that former thoughts renew;
Scenes of woe and scenes of pleasure,
    Now a sad and last adieu!
Bonny Doon, sae sweet at gloaming,
    Fare-thee-weel before I gang—
Bonny Doon, where, early roaming,
    First I weaved the rustic sang!

Bowers, adieu! where love decoying,
    First enthrall'd this heart o' mine;
There the saftest sweets enjoying,
    Sweets that memory ne'er shall tine!
Friends so dear my bosom ever,
    Ye hae rendered moments dear;
But, alas! when forced to sever,
    Then the stroke, oh, how severe!

Friends, that parting tear reserve it,
    Though 'tis doubly dear to me;
Could I think I did deserve it,
    How much happier would I be!
Scenes of woe and scenes of pleasure,
    Scenes that former thoughts renew;
Scenes of woe and scenes of pleasure,
    Now a sad and last adieu!

MY ONLY JO AND DEARIE O

Thy cheek is o' the rose's hue,
    My only jo and dearie O;
Thy neck is like the siller-dew
    Upon the banks sae briery O;
Thy teeth are o' the ivory,
Oh, sweet's the twinkle o' thine ee!
Nae joy, nae pleasure, blinks on me,
    My only jo and dearie O.

The birdie sings upon the thorn
    Its sang o' joy, fu' cheerie O,

342

Rejoicing in the summer morn,
  Nae care to mak it eerie O;
But little kens the sangster sweet
Aught o' the cares I hae to meet,
That gar my restless bosom beat,
  My only jo and dearie O.

When we were bairnies on yon brae,
  And youth was blinking bonny O,
Aft we wad daff the lee-lang day,
  Our joys fu' sweet and mony O;
Aft I wa'd chase thee o'er the lea,
And round about the thorny tree,
Or pu' the wild-flowers a' for thee,
  My only jo and dearie O.

I hae a wish I canna tine,
  'Mang a' the cares that grieve me O;
I wish thou wert for ever mine,
  And never mair to leave me O;
Then I wad daut thee night and day,
Nor ither warldly care wad hae,
Till life's warm stream forgot to play,
  My only jo and dearie O.

BENJAMIN THOMPSON (1776?-1816)

A SONG

from "The Stranger"

To welcome mirth and harmless glee,
We rambling minstrels, blythe and free,
With song the laughing hours beguile,
And wear a never-fading smile:
    Where'er we roam
    We find a home,
And greeting, to reward our toil.

No anxious griefs disturb our rest,
Nor busy cares annoy our breast;
Fearless we sink in soft repose,
While night her sable mantle throws.
    With grateful lay
    Hail rising day,
That rosy health and peace bestows.

JAMES KENNEY (1780-1849)

A SONG

from "Matrimony"

Can an Irishman practise such guile
   With a lady so sweet to dissemble,
And when he would make the rogue smile,
   To think but of making her tremble?
Indeed, Mister Grimgruffinhoff,
   If these are the rigs you must run,
You may think yourself mighty well off,
   That you're only a gaoler for fun.

To be sure 'tis a comical plan,
   When two married folks disagree,
To pop them as soon as you can,
   Both under a huge lock and key.
Should we blab of this project of ours,
   To cure matrimonial pother,
One half of the world, by the powers!
   Would very soon lock up the other.

Oh Liberty! jolly old girl!
   In dear little Ireland, you know,
You taught me to love you so well,
   They never shall make me your foe!
My practice will nothing avail,
   And this little frolic once o'er,
Never give me the key of a gaol,
   Except it's to open the door.

HENRY KIRKE WHITE (1785-1806)

TO AN EARLY PRIMROSE

Mild offspring of a dark and sullen sire!
Whose modest form, so delicately fine,
    Was nursed in whirling storms,
    And cradled in the winds.

Thee, when young Spring first questioned Winter's way,
And dared the sturdy blusterer to the fight,
    Thee on this bank he threw
    To mark his victory.

In this low vale, the promise of the year,
Serene, thou openest to the nipping gale,
    Unnoticed and alone,
    Thy tender elegance.

So Virtue blooms, brought forth amid the storms
Of chill adversity; in some lone walk
    Of life she rears her head,
    Obscure and unobserved;

While every bleaching breeze that on her blows,
Chastens her spotless purity of breast,
    And hardens her to bear
    Serene the ills of life.

GLOSSARY

a'	all
adamantine	unbreakably hard
aff	off
ain	own
aith	oath
alake	alack
alane	alone
amang	among
amry	storehouse; compartment
ane	one
anes	once
auld	old
ava	of all; at all
aw	all
awa	away
ay	any; ever; always
bailie	alderman
bairn	child
baith	both
barley-mow	heap of barley
bauk	ridge left between two furrows in ploughing
bawsint	having white spots on a black or bay background; said of animals
bays	the wreaths of bay leaves bestowed on poets
bedeen	anon; at once; in a little while; all together
beinly	comfortably
bencher	magistrate; judge; alderman
beseem	to be suitable
bigonet	bonnet
birdlime	a sticky substance spread upon twigs of trees with which birds are caught and held
birk	birch
blaw	to blow
bleez	to declaim
bob	a wig
bohea	black tea
boot	to profit; to benefit

borrows-town	royal borough
bowsy	drunk
brace	a pair; two
brae	bank or hillside
braw	fine
brawest	most excellently attired
brawner	a boar
brither	brother
bug-bear	causing needless fear or anxiety
bught	sheep-fold
bumper	glass of liquid filled to the brim
burn	a stream
busk	to dress
byre	cow-barn
caitiff	evil; mean; despicable
cale	cold
cam	came
caulder	colder
cauler	fresh; cool
celness	coldness
cess	assessment; tax
cestus	a girdle which belonged to Venus, which gave the wearer the power to excite love
chaunter	chanter
chiel	child
chymist	alchemist; chemist
cit	citizen
clarty	sticky; dirty; nasty; vicious
compleat	complete
corse	corpse
crook	a shepherd's staff
cryne	hair
cud	could
cullender	colander
curricle	a type of horse-drawn carriage
currish	bad-tempered
daffing	merry-making
daft	crazy; silly; foolish
daut	to pet; fondle; caress
deeght	to adorn
deil	devil
dight	to adorn
dochter	daughter
dog-days	the hot days of July and August
doggrel	verse of vastly inferior quality

348

dome	house; mansion
dool	grief
dorty	bad-tempered
dowf	dull
dowie	gloomy; somber; dismal
draff	refuse; dregs
dringing	drumming
drouth	drought
dule	grief
dwaam, dwam	a swoom; to swoon
een	eyes
eglantine	a type of wild rose
eke	also
emmet	an ant
eneugh	enough
entail	the settlement of the succession of a landed estate, so that it cannot be bequeathed at pleasure by any one possessor.
ermine	in heraldry, a white field with black spots.
fa'	to obtain
fair	beauty; female sex
fane	shrine
feace	face
feck	plenty
feg	fig
fleech	to beseech
flude	flood; waters
fock	folk
forgie	to forgive
forsooth	in truth; indeed
frae	from
fraise	fuss
fuddling	boozing; intoxicating
gae	to go
gang	to go
gar	to do; make; cause
geane	gone
gear	possessions; property
geck	to scoff
gie	to give
gin	if; whether
girlond	garland
glebe	the land
glewy	gluey
glistering	glittering

gowan	the English daisy
gowany	covered with gowan
gowd	gold
gowk	a fool
graith	dress
grannum	grandmother; old woman
gree	prize
green	to yearn
greet	to weep
grot	a grotto
gudeman	goodman; husband; master
guid	good
gules	red
hae	to have
haffits	cheeks
halcyon	the kingfisher
hame	home
hap	wrap
haud	to hold
haycock	pile of hay set in a field to dry
heame	home
heart-scad	disgust; aversion
heese	to lift
heie	they
hie	to hasten
hogan	any strong drink
houff	a haunt; resort; to raise; to lift
hymeneal	pertaining to a marriage
ilk, ilka	each; same; every
jillet	giddy young woman
jimp	slender; delicate
keekin'-glasses	looking-glasses
keen	fervid; full of life
ken	to know; knowledge; sight
kent	known
kirk-yard	churchyard
kittle	troublesome
kye	cows
laird	lord; landowner
landskip	landscape
lang	long
lappet	loose flap of a garment
lassitude	weariness

350

Lawland	lowland
leel	loyal; faithful; true
leglin	a milk-pail
leyfe	life
leyke	like
linsey-woolsey	a coarse type of cloth
lue	to love
luver	lover
lyart	grizzled
mair	more
maist	most
mak	to make
marl	ground; earth; soil
marrow	a mate
matin	morning-song
maun	must
mawkish	sickening
mawn	mown
meade	made
meast	most
meed	a reward
meikle	much
mergh	bone marrow
mien	bearing and manner
mither	mother
mony	many
muckle	much
na	no
nae	no
nane	none
nascent	born
nim	to steal or take
nin	none; nine
no	not
nobbet	only; nothing but; unless; if only
noddle	head
nog	a kind of strong beer
nostrum	remedy; medicine; punishment
ombre	a card game originally from Spain
ony	any
osier	willow
ouphante	elfin
out-owre	over; across; beyond
paitrick	partridge

pat	to put
pensy	peevish; fretful; troublesome
pickle	little
pie	magpie
pied	covered with spots of different colors
plack	apron; petticoat; small coin
pleace	place
pleugh	plough
poortith	poverty
pother	commotion
pow	head
puissant	mighty; powerful
quire	choir
reynynge	running
rin	to run or flow
rino	money
rode	complexion
sae	so
sair	sore
sang	song
sark	shirt
sel	self
seuing	sewing
shaw	to show
shoon	shoes
sic	such
siller	silver
sith	since
skair	share; portion; to share
skaith	pains
skittles	the game of nine-pins
slaes	fruit of the blackthorn
sleight	trick; deception
sna	snow
snaw	snow
souple	supple
spak	spoke
speckets	spectacles
spulzie	to plunder; a plundering
stingo	an extremely sharp beer or ale
stirk	heifer
stirrah	young man
sumph	simpleton; sullen person; heavy; lumpish
surtout	a men's long overcoat
swack	abundant and good

syne	since; ago
tawdry	gaudy
telt	told
thegither	together
thole	to suffer
thout	thought
thrang	crowded
timbrel	an ancient tambourine
tint	lost
tochered	dowry'd
tod	a fox
toofall	oncoming
toper	drunkard
trews	trousers
trice	an instant
trigly	trimly
troth	truth
trow	to think; believe
tuik	took
tulzie	to quarrel; a quarrel
twa	two
twin'd	separated; parted with
tyne	to forfeit; to lose
van	summit
venal	mercenary
visto	vista; scene
wad	would
waeful	woeful
waesuck	alas!
wame	belly
wark	work
wede	weeded
weel	well
ween	to think; to suppose
weids	weeds; dress
weird	fate; destiny
weyfe	wife
wha	who
wherry	light boat or barge
wheyles	while
whilk	which
whilom	at one time
whyterre	whiter
wight	a person
wilding	an apple; any wild plant

353

wit	to know
wot	I know
yaldrin	yellow-hammer
yaud	an old, worn-out mare
yen	one

THE POETS LAUREATE OF BRITAIN

John Dryden	1670-1689
Thomas Shadwell	1689-1692
Nahum Tate	1692-1715
Nicholas Rowe	1715-1718
Laurence Eusden	1718-1730
Colley Cibber	1730-1757
William Whitehead	1757-1785
Thomas Warton	1785-1790
Henry James Pye	1790-1813
Robert Southey	1813-1843
William Wordsworth	1843-1850
Alfred Tennyson	1850-1892
Alfred Austin	1896-1913
Robert Seymour Bridges	1913-1930
John Masefield	1930-1967
Cecil Day Lewis	1968-1972
John Betjeman	1972-

INDEX OF FIRST LINES

Gad-a mercy! devil's in me   297
George came to the crown without striking a blow   35
Gi'e me a lass with a lump of land   71
Go, patter to lubbers and swabs, do you see   285
Go, tuneful bird, that glad'st the skies   152
God bless the king!——I mean the Faith's Defender   83
Great god of sleep, since it must be   18

Hail, beauteous stranger of the grove!   302
Hail, beauteous stranger of the wood   290
Hail sacred stream, whose waters roll   165
Hang my lyre upon the willow   223
Happy insect! ever blest   131
Have my friends in the town, in the gay busy town   97
Have ye seen the morning sky   33
He that Love hath never try'd   245
Hear me, ye nymphs, and every swain   87
Here, a sheer hulk, lies poor Tom Bowling   285
Here lies Sam Johnson:——Reader, have a care   106
His angle-rod made of a sturdy oak   7
Ho! why dost thou shiver and shake   288
How are deluded human kind   98
How many saucy airs we meet   66
How pleas'd within my native bowers   152
How sleep the brave, who sink to rest   204
How steep yon mountains rise around   251

I am Content, I do not care   82
I hate all their nonsense   179
I hate that drum's discordant sound   250
I heard two neighbours talk, the other night   84
I love to rise ere gleams the tardy light   301
I never bark'd when out of season   199
I sent for Radcliffe; was so ill   11
If, dumb too long, the drooping Muse hath stay'd   73
If gentle love's immortal fire   319
If this pale Rose offend your Sight   37
If we, O Dorset, quit the city-throng   31
In a fair summer's radiant morn   182
In a plain pleasant cottage, conveniently neat   241
In Cottages and homely cells   36
In such a Night, when every louder Wind   3
In the dead of the night, when with labour opprest   322
In the downhill of life, when I find I'm declining   254
In times of selfishness and faction sour'd   107
It puzzles much the sages' brains   120
It was a friar of orders gray   234
I've heard them lilting, at the ewe milking   226

Oh! would the night my blushes hide   213
Olivia's lewd, but looks devout   59
On Leven's banks, while free to rove   194
On the eastern hill's steep side   250
On these white cliffs, that calm above the flood   332
On this fair ground, with ravish'd eyes   98
On this my pensive pillow, gentle Sleep!   228
Once of forbidden fruit the mortal taste   170
Once on a time, a Monarch, tir'd with whooping   275
Once was I fam'd, an awful sage   168
One night a fellow wandering without fear   8

Palemon, in the hawthorn bower   239
Poets and painters, who from Nature draw   178
Poets invoke, when they rehearse   45
Polly, from me, tho' now a love-sick youth   91
Poor melancholy bird, that all night long   305
Pray, young man, your suit give over   330
Prethee Cloe, not so fast   22
Prithee tease me no longer, dear troublesome friend   161
Pursuing Beauty, Men descry   2

Queen of every moving measure   206
Queen of Fragrance, lovely Rose   79

Rock of ages, cleft for me   279
Rude was the pile, and massy proof   230

Sandy, the gay, the blooming swain   196
Say, Myra, why is gentle love   128
Say, sire of insects, mighty Sol   12
Says a gosling, almost frighten'd out of her wits   170
Says my Uncle, I pray you discover   62
Says Pontius in rage, contradicting his wife   13
Says Tom to Jack, " 'Tis very odd   317
Scenes of woe and scenes of pleasure   342
See! Flavia, see! that flutt'ring thing   133
See, Sir, here's the grand approach   50
See, Sylvia, see, this new-blown rose   60
See what a conquest Love has made!   1
Shelter'd from the blight, ambition   240
Short and precarious is the life of man   190
Should Jove descend in floods of liquid ore   136
Silent and clear, through yonder peaceful vale   163
Silent Nymph, with curious eye!   94
Sillia, with uncontested sway   78
Since I have long lov'd you in vain   24
Since we can die but once, what matters it   315

Sirs, it may happen, by the grace of God 278
Sly Merry Andrew, the last Southwark fair 11
So fairy elves their morning-table spread 131
So rude and tuneless are thy lays 151
So smooth and clear the fountain was 59
Still hovering round the fair at sixty-four 114
Survey, my fair! that lucid stream 155
Sweet are the Charms of her I love 56
Sweet bird, that cheer'st the heavy hours 328
Sweet daughter of a rough and stormy sire 280
Sweet object of the zephyr's kiss 246

Take a knuckle of veal 64
Tell me, my Caelia, why so coy 122
Tell me, ye sons of Phoebus, what is this 128
Tell not me of the roses and lillies 178
That Macro's looks are good, let no man doubt 17
The beauty which the gods bestow 255
The bride cam out o' the byre 92
The dews of summer nighte did falle 258
The folks of old were not so nice 180
The garlands fade that Spring so lately wove 305
The golden Sun, emerging from the main 189
The heavy hours are almost past 129
The hinds how blest, who ne'er beguil'd 228
The Lawland lads think they are fine 70
The midges dance aboon the burn 340
The moon had climbed the highest hill 308
The nymph that I lov'd was as cheerful as day 216
The poker lost, poor Susan storm'd 209
The reigning fair on polish'd crystal shine 35
The sable bird melodious from the bough 335
The silver Moon's enamour'd beam 240
The smiling Morn, the breathing Spring 113
The western sky was purpled o'er 156
The wind is up, the field is bare 271
Thee, Flora's first and favourite child 291
There is no ill on earth which mortals fly 124
There was an auld wife had a wee pickle tow 93
There was ance a May, and she lo'ed na men 14
These spotless leaves, this neat array 172
This day, which saw my Delia's beauty rise 137
This dismal morn, when east winds blow 36
Those who in quarrels interpose 65
Thou fairest sweetest Daughter of the Skies 26
Thou noblest monument of Albion's isle! 232
Though since my date of woe long years have roll'd 282
Three hours from noon the passing shadow shows 248

Thus, thus I steer my bark, and sail   89
Thy braes were bonny, Yarrow stream!   302
Thy cheek is o' the rose's hue   342
Thy splendid halls, thy palaces forgot   320
'Tis the voice of the Sluggard; I hear him complain   29
To all you ladies now at Bath   81
To Craven's health, and social joy   170
To know the mistress' humour right   142
To welcome mirth and harmless glee   344
'Twas at the silent, solemn hour   114
'Twas in a land of learning   149
'Twixt Death and Schomberg, t'other day   135
Two foot companions once in deep discourse   84

Untaught o'er strings to draw the rosin'd bow   247

Vain were the task to give the soul to glow   184

Wanton Zephyr, come away!   46
We kings, who are in our senses   160
What ails my heart when thou art nigh?   327
What beauties does Flora disclose!   87
What woes must such unequal union bring   80
When Bright Roxana treads the green   153
When clouds that angel face deform   292
When Delia on the plain appears   129
When father Adie first pat spade in   309
When first I slipp'd my leading strings, to please her little Poll
  287
When fraught with all that grateful Minds can move   25
When I behold thee, blameless Williamson   100
When I was at home, I was merry and frisky   334
When in the crimson cloud of even   265
When, my dear Cloe, you resign   39
When nature joins a beauteous face   169
When Phoebus shoots his radiant beams   292
When Sappho struck the quiv'ring wire   193
When silent time, wi' lightly foot   294
When sons of fortune ride on high   117
When that the fields put on their gay attire   324
When the rough North forgets to howl   194
When thy beauty appears   51
When to my pretty Poll I went   336
When Tom to Cambridge first was sent   153
When William at eve meets me down at the stile   224
When yielding first to Damon's flame   10
When you meet a tender creature   268
Where Hitch's gentle current glides   219

363

INDEX OF AUTHORS